Cities of Vesuvius

POMPEII AND HERCULANEUM

PAMELA BRADLEY

CAMBRIDGE
UNIVERSITY PRESS

CAMBRIDGE UNIVERSITY PRESS
Cambridge, New York, Melbourne, Madrid, Cape Town, Singapore, São Paulo

Cambridge University Press
477 Williamstown Road, Port Melbourne, Vic 3207, Australia

www.cambridge.edu.au
Information on this title: www.cambridge.edu.au/0521608953

© Pamela Bradley 2005

First published 2005
Reprinted 2005, 2006, 2009

Designed by Mary Mason
Typeset by Post Pre-press Group
Printed in Australia by Ligare Pty Ltd

National Library of Australia Cataloguing in Publication data
    Bradley, Pamela.
    Cities of Vesuvius : Pompeii and Herculaneum
    Bibliography
    Includes index
    For NSW year 12 students.
    ISBN-13 978-0-521-60895-4 paperback
    ISBN-10 0-521-60895-3 paperback
    1. Pompeii (Extinct city). 2. Herculaneum (Extinct city).
    I. Title.
937.7

ISBN-13 978-0-521-60895-4 paperback
ISBN-10 0-521-60895-3 paperback

Contents

Acknowledgements

Cover image: Pierre Henri de Valenciennes *The Eruption of Vesuvius*. Musée des Augustins, Toulouse. Photo: Daniel Martin.

Figure 2.2: Jakob Phillip Hackert *View of Pompeii*. © National Trust Photo Library/John Hammond; **2.3, 12.26**: From Francois Mazois *Les Ruines de Pompéi* (1812). Bibliothéque Nationale de France; **2.4**: Théodore Chasseriau (1819-1856), *Le Tepidarium*. Musée d'Orsay, Paris. © Photo RMN – Gérard Blot; **2.5**: Edouard Alexandre de Sain (1830-1910), *Fouilles à Pompéi*. Musée d'Orsay, Paris. © Photo RMN – Jean-Pierre Lagiewski; **4.15, 4.18, 4.22, 7.25, 7.30, 9.3, 10.3**: © CORBIS/Australian Picture Library; **4.23, 5.9, 12.20**: © CORBIS/APL; **4.27** Wallace-Hadrill, Andrew, *Houses and Society in Pompeii and Herculaneum* © 1994 Princeton University Press. Reproduced by permission of Princeton University Press; **5.6**: © Werner Forman Archive; **6.17**: © Heritage Image Partnership/Australian Picture Library; **7.12**: © Milton Fitzsimmons; **8.17**: © The Trustees of the British Museum; **9.2**: © APL/SIME srl; **10.2**: © APL/Corbis/David Lees.

Author's images reproduced with permission of the Soprintendenza Archeologica di Pompei.

Introduction

Within the Roman Empire of the 1st century AD, the provincial Campanian towns of Pompeii and Herculaneum did nothing to influence or change the world. According to Robert Etienne, Pompeii was 'an average city inhabited by average people' and should 'have achieved a comfortable mediocrity and Both towns disappeared from the face of the earth over an 18-hour period between the early afternoon of 24 August and the morning of 25 August AD 79, as the neighbouring volcano of Vesuvius erupted. Everyday life was stopped in its tracks as a towering column of ash and pumice rose over 28 kilometres into the air, followed by a series of glowing avalanches of superheated gases, ash and rock. Both towns were so completely buried that eventually their existence was obliterated from people's memories. The site of Pompeii became known simply as 'civitas' or 'settlement'.

From the early 18th century, when both sites were discovered and a frenzy of treasure hunting began, they became part of the Grand Tour taken by aristocratic young men from Britain and Europe. Artists and writers, influenced by the neo-classical and 'romantic' movement of the time, left their impressions in travel diaries, paintings, engravings, watercolours, novels and poetry. All were fascinated, although some saw the ruins as melancholy, grisly, or even as the vengeance of God wreaked upon a pagan people. Others included fantasy elements in their depictions. Most visitors interpreted the sites from the perspective of their own day. This applied not only to the lay visitor, but to the archaeologists working on the sites.

From the mid-19th to the mid-20th century, when archaeologists such as Giuseppe Fiorelli, Vittorio Spinazzola and Amedeo Maiuri adopted more systematic methods, two 'living' communities were brought to life: time capsules with their myriad messages through which 'the ancient world speaks to us directly' and 'touches us through thousands of events of an apparently normal, everyday world'.[2] However, along the way, much valuable evidence has been lost due to failure to document carefully—if at all.

Until late in the 20th century, Pompeii tended to be a one-layer site, with archaeological interest focused on the 79 AD level. Now archaeologists are probing deeper at previously excavated spots to reveal surprising information about pre-AD 79 Pompeii, and, more particularly, about the pre-Roman period of the town. Earlier interpretations are being challenged and, as more scientific disciplines are being employed along with advanced computer technology, the story of the site is being retold.

However, nothing seems to be able to prevent the 'second death' facing the cities of Vesuvius. This is not a violent and instantaneous death like the first, but a slow and continuous one due to the effects of exposure to light, the elements, and human intervention, particularly the massive impact of modern tourism. The irony of the situation is that while tourism is essential for the survival of the sites, it is one of the chief causes of destruction, especially as more areas are closed to the public, forcing the increasing numbers into ever decreasing spaces.

Dealing with the problems facing the sites is not just an Italian responsibility, but a worldwide concern. International organisations are throwing their human and financial resources behind preservation and conservation efforts so that a unique cultural legacy can be handed down to the future. However, as more 'voices' need to be taken into consideration in attempting to save these invaluable sites, archaeology has entered the world of politics, and questions are constantly being raised about who owns the past and how it must be treated in the future.

There are now serious ethical choices to be made.

AUTHOR'S NOTE

It is impossible to really 'know' the past, even when there is an abundance of evidence. In writing this book I have attempted to follow the consensus among scholars today based on the most recent investigations. Of course other interpretations may be proposed in the future in the light of new discoveries at the sites or by virtue of scientific advancements.

Although archaeologists and others working at the sites use Giuseppe Fiorelli's numbering system in referring to regions, insulae and houses, I have used the modern house and street names found in most books about the sites. These are based on some distinguishing feature or on the name of the owner if identified.

PART 1

Background Information for a Study of Pompeii and Herculaneum

IN PART 1 STUDENTS LEARN TO:

- identify the historical factors that contributed to change in Pompeii and Herculaneum from 8th century BC to AD 79 and to present them in sequence form
- understand the lack of archaeological evidence for pre-Roman occupation of Pompeii and Herculaneum
- assess the impact of particular individuals on the archaeological sites in the 17th, 18th and early 19th centuries
- describe the various written and visual representations of Pompeii and Herculaneum.

IMPORTANT TERMS

antiquities

artefacts

civitas

Hellenic

Hellenistic

imaginative interpretation

neo-classical

occupation

patronage

'Romantic' movement

socii

systematic excavation

veteran colony

Brief historical overview

1

THINGS TO CONSIDER

- The scanty evidence, both archaeological and literary, of occupation of Pompeii and Herculaneum from the 6th to the 3rd centuries BC

- The adoption of Hellenistic culture during the 2nd century BC
- The changing urban fabric of Pompeii under the Romans in the 1st century BC
- Significant events during the imperial age of the 1st century AD

Contradictions in the evidence

Until recently, most of the theories about the occupation of Pompeii and Herculaneum by different groups, were based on literary sources, not archaeological evidence. Now, new information is coming to light as archaeologists continue to probe beneath the AD 79 level at Pompeii. However, there is still not a lot known about the town's pre-Roman history. The 'picture of archaic Pompeii remains a tantalising series of contradictory glimpses into a settlement whose appearance changes almost every time archaeologists start to dig down.'[1]

What follows is an account of the general history of the Vesuvian area based on some archaeological discoveries, but predominantly on the literary sources.

OSCAN, GREEK AND ETRUSCAN PRESENCE IN POMPEII AND HERCULANEUM

Possible Oscan origins

The origins of the towns of Pompeii and Herculaneum are not really known. It has been suggested by Strabo the geographer, writing in the 1st century AD, that the Oscans, a local Italic group living in scattered settlements in Campania, and whom the Romans referred to as the 'ancients', were the founders of Pompeii. The origin of Herculaneum is lost in legends associated with Heracles, the town's patron deity, and its toponym (place name)—

2

Heracleum—is clearly Greek, but Strabo believed the Oscans were also its original founders. Figure 1.1 shows the location within Italy of the groups who had an influence on these towns.

In the early 8th century BC, the Greeks established colonies at Pithecusae on the island of Ischia, and at the northern end of the Bay of Naples at Cyme (Cumae) and at Neapolis (Naples). During the 7th century, they extended their influence to other places around the coast and in Campania as a whole. At this time, the native cultures of the Sarno valley adopted some Hellenised (Greek) characteristics. As the Greeks were a seafaring people, they may have seen the strategic location of the primitive Oscan settlement of Pompeii, located at the mouth of the Sarno River. However, it would only have been used as a trading outpost for the hinterland, not as a permanent Greek settlement.

✖
Influence of Greek colonies on the coast of Campania

Sometime about 650 BC the Etruscans, from north of Rome, penetrated Campania and established Capua which became the leading city in the plain. It has been suggested by some scholars that the growth of Pompeii was associated with Etruscan civilisation in southern Campania, for these people were essentially urban and often settled on fortified plateaus with access to the sea. However, the material that has come to light in Pompeii from this period belongs to all three cultures—Oscan, Greek and Etruscan—which reveals a complex mingling of trade and exchange. Objects bearing Etruscan inscriptions, including Etruscan black pottery (*bucchero*), were found alongside Greek black-figure vases. Recent scholarship tends towards the view that neither Greeks nor Etruscans controlled Pompeii politically. There appears to have been a major restructuring in Pompeii during this time, which indicates that the local Oscan inhabitants wanted greater security for themselves as well as facilities for visiting traders.

Figure 1.1 Greeks, Etruscans, Samnites and Romans

✖
Etruscan contacts and influence

SAMNITE POMPEII AND HERCULANEUM (C. 423–80 BC)

Etruscan power in Campania collapsed after their defeat by a coalition of Greek cities at the Second Battle of Cumae in 474 BC. The Greek cities extended their sphere of influence along the coast but were not particularly interested in settling permanently inland, and the vacuum left by the Etruscans was filled by the Samnites, a warlike Italic people from the harsh mountains of central Italy. These tough hillmen, who coveted Campania's fertile lowlands, swept down from their Apennine fortresses, captured Capua, then Cumae and later the whole Campanian plain. Its towns, including Pompeii and Herculaneum, eventually became part of a Samnite League.

During this period, Pompeii expanded and its layout was defined, although there is no clear evidence of sequence. The city took on a recognisable urban configuration as it became part of a wider communications network. The area north of the original settlement was laid out on a geometric grid based on the principles of the Milesian architect Hippodamos, who had designed the port of Athens. Wealthy Samnites built large handsome houses in traditional Italic style surrounded by high walls, and new fortifications were constructed: two parallel walls of solid black lava faced with limestone, buttressed by an earth mound.

In the 4th century, the Romans came into conflict with the Samnites in a series of wars (the Samnite Wars). About 343 BC, the Romans entered Campania and by 302 had landed at the mouth of the Sarno River. Livy, in his *History of Rome* (9.38, 2–3) mentions Pompeii in his account of the Second Samnite War. He describes how a Roman fleet dropped anchor off Pompeii, but apparently its fortifications dissuaded the Romans from attacking. Instead, they sacked the countryside around neighbouring Nuceria.

By 300 BC, the Samnite towns of Campania, including Pompeii and Herculaneum, had become part of a Roman confederation, each community bound to Rome by a separate treaty (*foedus*). The inhabitants were granted the status of Italian allies (*socii Italici*), which entailed full rights of local self-government, but with foreign policy controlled from Rome and an obligation to provide troops when necessary. Despite Rome's expansion into the area, the culture of Pompeii and Herculaneum remained strongly Samnite until 80 BC.

In the second half of the 3rd century, Rome and Carthage—a powerful city in north Africa—were at war (known as the Punic Wars) for control of the western Mediterranean. Campania felt the impact. The Bay of Naples became the centre of ship-building for the infant Roman navy, and it is likely that Pompeii and Herculaneum benefited from the increase in business generated in the area. From 218 until 201, the presence in Campania of the brilliant Carthaginian general Hannibal had an effect on the Sarno Plain. Many towns

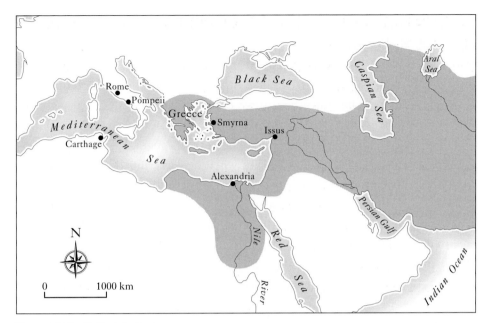

Figure 1.2 The Hellenistic East

opened their gates to the invader, but Pompeii and Herculaneum remained loyal to the Romans.

In the later stages of the 2nd century, when Rome had won control of both the western and eastern Mediterranean, Pompeii benefited from the expansion of maritime trade. There was a demand for Campanian wine and oil, while luxury goods and metals poured into the region, and slavery substantially increased local agricultural productivity. Pompeian traders accumulated great wealth which they spent on magnificent houses. Even the lower classes enjoyed an economic upturn.

🕸
Benefits to Campania as Rome expands

As at Rome, the adoption of Hellenistic culture (a mix of Greek and eastern culture) was seen in both domestic and public architecture. Some houses, in size and decoration, were reminiscent of Hellenistic 'palaces' (see Chapter 7). Public buildings also reflected the influence of the Hellenistic world, and the cults of Isis and Dionysus were imported from the East.

🕸
Hellenistic influences

CHANGE IN THE STATUS OF POMPEII AND HERCULANEUM (91 BC–20 BC)

Between 125 and 95 BC, trouble was brewing among the Italian allies of Rome, including Pompeii and Herculaneum. Most had remained loyal during the Hannibalic War and many had contributed troops during Rome's expansion in the eastern Mediterranean. They had been promised Roman citizenship, or at least the right of appeal against Roman magistrates, but all efforts during this time were thwarted by the senate in Rome. When a

🕸
Italian allies take up arms against Rome

Roman reformer who was working towards granting them citizenship was murdered, 'the long smouldering hostility of Rome's Italian allies' broke out into open war in 91 BC. The Social War (named after the *socii* or allies) 'was on a great scale, had various changes of fortune, did enormous damage to Rome, and brought her into the utmost danger'.[2]

Pompeii, believing that its former loyalty to Rome was unappreciated, joined the war, taking a leading role. The Roman general Aulus Postumius Albinus laid siege to Pompeii in 89, but when he was hanged by his mutinous troops, Lucius Cornelius Sulla took charge of operations. Marks made by the Roman siege engines can still be seen on the walls of Pompeii and lead 'missiles' were found outside one of its gates. Both Pompeii and Herculaneum eventually capitulated, but although all Italian allies were granted Roman citizenship, Pompeii paid dearly for its involvement in the war.

In 80 BC it became part of Sulla's policy of placing colonies of his demobilised troops 'to hold Italy under garrisons, sequestrating their lands and houses and dividing them among his soldiers'.[3] Two thousand of Sulla's veterans were assigned the lands and villas of many of the disenfranchised Oscan-Samnite families who had taken an anti-Roman position during the Social War.

Pompeii was renamed *Colonia Cornelia Veneria Pompeianorum* ('the colony of Pompeians under the auspices of Cornelius Sulla and the goddess Venus'). The new municipal administration was composed mostly of new settlers and Latin, rather than Oscan, was imposed as the official language. Cicero says there was considerable ill will towards the new colonists, but 30 years later, Pompeii's old families were reintegrated into the political life of the city.

As new wealth poured into Pompeii, it was embellished with lavish houses and the layout of the city was changed to cater for more public buildings required by the new inhabitants. The change in status of Pompeii was marked by the transformation of the Temple of Jupiter into the Temple of the Capitoline Triad (Jupiter Optimus Maximus, Juno and Minerva) and restructured on the model of the Capitolium in Rome. It became the real symbol of Rome's power in Pompeii (see Chapter 9). The Odeon, or covered theatre, was built for the performance of plays in Latin and a 20,000-seat amphitheatre was built at the personal expense of two of Sulla's commanders (see Chapter 8).

Pompeii's walls were no longer needed for defensive purposes, and building extended outside the walls with new villas appearing on the seaward side. Herculaneum became one of the most fashionable centres for wealthy Romans on the Bay of Naples, rivalling Cumae and Baiae.

THE IMPERIAL AGE

After Julius Caesar's assassination in 44 BC, civil war raged across the Roman Empire between the armies of Mark Antony and Octavius (the future

Augustus), but by 27 BC, the success of Octavius and the peace he established brought many benefits to the cities and ports of Campania as they shared in the revitalised trade between the provinces.

❄
Economic and
social impact of
Julio-Claudians

Pompeii flourished, its luxury industries expanded, agricultural output from the surrounding lands increased and people flocked to the region to build villas in the country-side and by the sea, and to take the cure at the thermal springs. There was an increase in social mobility under Augustus. Freedmen (former slaves) began to accumulate wealth and participate in public affairs, often assuming high administrative positions. Many of their offspring intermarried with the more estab-lished families in Pompeii, creating a new dynamic and wealthy middle class. As in Rome, which was trans-formed from a city of brick to one of marble, architecture in Pompeii

Figure 1.3 Travertine columns in the Pompeian Forum

became a form of propaganda to promote the new 'Golden Age' of Augustus (27 BC–AD 14) and the cult of the emperor. Richer inhabitants of Pompeii and Herculaneum dedicated public buildings to Augustus and his successors, the Julio-Claudians. The forum's older columns and flagged pavements of tufa were replaced with marble and travertine (white limestone), and the Temples of Venus and Apollo, to whom Augustus was particularly devoted, were restored. Augustus commissioned an aqueduct to bring fresh water from the mountains to the fleet headquarters at Misenum with extensions to Pompeii and Herculaneum, which changed the face of the towns by provid-ing running water to public fountains as well as to private homes.

A RIOT IN POMPEII'S AMPHITHEATRE

Although the government in Rome rarely interfered in the affairs of Pompeii, it was forced to do so in AD 59 when rioting broke out in the amphitheatre between the Pompeians and a group of visiting Nucerians. Tacitus describes the riot as having originated in 'a trifling incident at a gladiatorial show'. There was an exchange of abuse 'characteristic of these disorderly country towns', followed by stone throwing and 'then swords were drawn'. Local militia had to subdue the combatants but many people were wounded or killed. The Nucerians appealed to Rome for justice and Nero 'instructed the senate to investigate the affair'.⁴ Pompeii was debarred from holding any similar gathering for 10 years.

❄
Roman interference
in Pompeii

Figure 1.4 Riot in the Pompeian amphitheatre in AD 59—fresco (Naples National Archaeological Museum)

THE EARTHQUAKE OF **AD 62**

✤
Seneca on
earthquakes

According to Tacitus, AD 62 was the year in which an earthquake 'largely demolished the populous Campanian town of Pompeii'[5] (see Chapter 5). Seneca, philosopher as well as tutor and minister to the Emperor Nero, who wrote a contemporary account of the earthquake, confirmed that 'Pompeii, the famous city in Campania had been laid low by an earthquake . . . on the Nones [fifth] of February, in the consulship of Regulus and Verginius', a time of the year that 'our ancestors used to claim was free from such disaster'.[6] Pompeii was probably the epicentre of the upheaval, but other areas were affected including Herculaneum and Nuceria. Naples suffered only minimal damage. According to Seneca, wide clefts in the ground swallowed up a flock of six hundred sheep in an instant and entire orchards disappeared into the gaping chasms.

✤
Impact on
Pompeii

In the towns, houses, public buildings and statues swayed and collapsed and roads opened up. There is evidence that in Pompeii the situation was chaotic as people hurled themselves headlong outside, abandoned their household possessions and trusted to their luck outdoors, 'so shocked that they wandered about as if deprived of their wits'.[7] Pompeii's town reservoir was damaged and its water pipes broke, flooding the streets; the forum was in ruins; many homes were uninhabitable. A banker named L. Caecilius Jucundus was an eye witness as the Temple of the Capitoline Triad collapsed, and many people tried to make their escape by chariot to the open countryside as aftershocks continued throughout the day. Rubble blocked their way, horses took fright and chariots overturned. Jucundus had these events sculpted on a shrine which he dedicated to his household gods.

Eventually, the people of Pompeii and Herculaneum began a massive demolition and rebuilding program. Obviously, town services such as water supply and the repair of public buildings took priority, as engineers drew up a master plan. Some wealthy inhabitants thought it their duty to contribute to the rebuilding of the city's temples.

THE ERUPTION OF VESUVIUS IN AD 79

Seventeen years later, at about 1 pm on 24 August AD 79, while the inhabitants of Pompeii and Herculaneum were sitting down for lunch, slaking their thirsts in one of the many taverns, relaxing in their shady gardens or cooling off in one of the public bath complexes, Vesuvius split apart with a thundering roar. Within 18 hours, both cities had disappeared from the face of the earth (see Figure 5.2). In a 'sinister coincidence' 24 August was 'the yearly occasion of an obscure rite deigned to give free egress to the inhabitants of the underworld'.[8]

❋ Catastrophe

When the sun finally reappeared, not only was the countryside unrecognisable, but so too the mountain; all that was left was a gaping crater and a remnant of its north flank. Dio Cassius described how Roman residents could see and smell the acrid clouds of ash emanating from the smouldering epicentre to the south in Campania. The extent of the catastrophe reverberated around the Roman world.

❋ Reverberations around the Roman world

The emperor Titus, who had come to the throne only months before the eruption, attempted to restore some semblance of order in Campania by first appointing *curatores* to protect the ruins from looters. Teams of salvagers were sent south to retrieve, wherever possible, statues and marble veneer and remove them to Rome. Fortunately, in Pompeii many statues undergoing restoration had been stored in warehouses since the earthquake of AD 62 and were easily located, but the salvage operation became too risky and expensive and the government teams left. Tunnels dug through the ash suggested that some Pompeians returned to their city some time in the immediate aftermath of the destruction, looking for valuables, but modern scholars doubt this, as the returning inhabitants would have had to excavate not only through the rubble of the collapsed buildings, but through at least four metres of volcanic deposits.

❋ Salvage operations

Eventually, the winter rains hardened the ash and pumice covering Pompeii, which made any further excavation ineffective, and with time the site disappeared totally under a layer of soil and grass. The vanished city of Pompeii became known simply as *civitas* or 'settlement'.

❋ Civitas

Chapter review

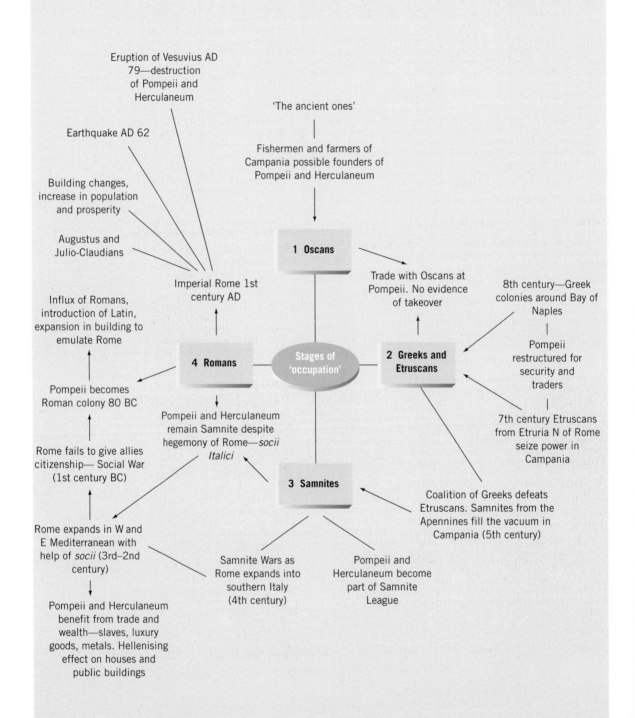

Eruption of Vesuvius AD 79—destruction of Pompeii and Herculaneum

Earthquake AD 62

Building changes, increase in population and prosperity

Augustus and Julio-Claudians

Imperial Rome 1st century AD

Influx of Romans, introduction of Latin, expansion in building to emulate Rome

4 Romans

Pompeii becomes Roman colony 80 BC

Rome fails to give allies citizenship— Social War (1st century BC)

Rome expands in W and E Mediterranean with help of *socii* (3rd–2nd century)

Pompeii and Herculaneum benefit from trade and wealth—slaves, luxury goods, metals. Hellenising effect on houses and public buildings

'The ancient ones'

Fishermen and farmers of Campania possible founders of Pompeii and Herculaneum

1 Oscans

Trade with Oscans at Pompeii. No evidence of takeover

Stages of 'occupation'

2 Greeks and Etruscans

8th century—Greek colonies around Bay of Naples

Pompeii restructured for security and traders

7th century Etruscans from Etruria N of Rome seize power in Campania

Coalition of Greeks defeats Etruscans. Samnites from the Apennines fill the vacuum in Campania (5th century)

Pompeii and Herculaneum remain Samnite despite hegemony of Rome—*socii Italici*

3 Samnites

Samnite Wars as Rome expands into southern Italy (4th century)

Pompeii and Herculaneum become part of Samnite League

Activities

1   Draw up a time line showing the significant events that are believed to have affected the fortunes of Pompeii and Herculaneum between the 8th century BC and AD 79.

2   What does Figure 1.5 reveal about the events and influences that affected Pompeii and Herculaneum in the 2nd century BC?

3   Identify the author, event and date to which each quote is referring. Write one sentence describing the effect the event had on Pompeii and Herculaneum.

a

'THE WAR WAS ON A GREAT SCALE, HAD VARIOUS CHANGES OF FORTUNE, DID ENORMOUS DAMAGE TO ROME AND BROUGHT HER INTO THE UTMOST DANGER.'

b

'THE THREAD OF MY PROPOSED WORK, AND THE CONCURRENCE OF THE DISASTER AT THIS TIME, REQUIRES THAT WE DISCUSS THE CAUSES OF THESE EARTHQUAKES.'

Figure 1.5 Animal life on the Nile River—mosaic from the House of the Faun, Pompeii (Naples Archaeological Museum)

Early history of the excavations and representations of the sites over time

2

THINGS TO CONSIDER

- The careless destruction and looting that occurred at Pompeii and Herculaneum in the early years
- The use of archaeology to glorify a political regime
- The gradual adoption of more systematic archaeological techniques in the 18th and 19th centuries
- The variety of written and visual representations, particularly the 'Romantic' images of the 18th and early 19th centuries

In the aftermath of the eruption, a local Latin poet, Statius, posed the question:

> IN A FUTURE GENERATION, WHEN CROPS SPRING UP AGAIN, WHEN THIS WASTELAND REGAINS ITS GREEN, WILL MEN BELIEVE THAT CITIES AND PEOPLE LIE BENEATH? THAT IN DAYS OF OLD THEIR LANDS LAY CLOSER TO THE SEA?[1]

EARLY DISCOVERIES AND LOOTING

Finds at 'civitas'

It was not until the end of the 16th century that the mound known simply as 'civitas' slowly began to give up its secrets. In 1592 Domenico Fontana, the court architect for the Austrian Hapsburgs, who controlled Naples, discovered slabs of marble and frescoed walls as he directed a civil engineering project to divert the waters of a tributary of the Sarno River. Even when he later discovered inscriptions in vernacular Latin, he did not realise what lay beneath him.

In 1689, another court architect, Francesco Pichetti, came across a stone inscribed with 'Decurio Pompeiis'. He believed it referred to Pompey the Great, but in a book called *De Vesuvio*, published in 1699, Giuseppe Macrini declared that what Pichetti had in fact found was Pompeii.

Herculaneum was discovered 10 years later in 1709. An Austrian general,

Count D'Elbeuf, was searching for antiquities and a cheap source of marble with which to decorate a villa he was building nearby. When his workmen sunk a shaft, reaching the level of the stage of the ancient theatre, the 'rapacious looting of the only intact theatre remaining from Roman antiquity' began, and 'for years they literally mined the theatre of its marble facing and statuary.'[2] Numerous shafts and tunnels were dug—at times gunpowder was used—and the site was plundered with little care for the destruction that occurred. Eventually the shaft entrances were sealed up.

❃ Hapsburg looting at Herculaneum

HISTORY OF THE EXCAVATIONS UNDER THE BOURBONS (1734–1860)

In 1734, Charles of Bourbon won a decisive battle against the Austrian Hapsburgs and acceded to the throne of the Kingdom of the Two Sicilies as Charles VII. The new kingdom, which was ruled from Naples, did not initially receive universal recognition and during this period Charles did his utmost to turn it into an international cultural showpiece. He built a spring palace in the area and initiated a program of feverish exploration and excavation. It is against this background that the excavations of Herculaneum and Pompeii should be viewed. 'The aim of the excavations was not primarily to gain knowledge about the past, but to gain prestige for the present, and it is this that overwhelmingly influenced the progress of the excavations throughout the rest of the 18th century.'[3]

❃ Bourbon need to gain prestige

THE APPOINTMENT OF ROQUE JOACHIM DE ALCUBIERRE

Charles VII appointed a Spanish military engineer, Roque Joachim de Alcubierre, to supervise the work. He began with an assault on Herculaneum where he directed an engineering corps to hack 20 metres into the hardened pyroclastic material and dig more tunnels out from the ancient theatre discovered nearly 30 years before. They worked in the faint light provided by oil lamps and smoky torches 'which were constantly being extinguished, plunging the men into claustrophobic blackness or threatening them with suffocation.'[4] They carelessly broke through frescoed walls and tunnelled through houses, destroying many precious artefacts in the process. Only those objects considered suitable for a private royal collection were removed and transported to Naples. Other more common artefacts, as well as damaged frescoes, were destroyed and discarded, and once a site had been cleared of all the finest objects, it was usually back-filled. Years later, the art historian, Johann Winckelmann, in his *A Critical Account of the Situation and Destruction of Herculaneum, Pompeii and Stabiae*, wrote that de Alcubierre 'knew as much of antiquities as the moon does of lobsters'.[5]

❃ De Alcubierre's destruction of Herculaneum

By 1748, the flow of treasure from Herculaneum was beginning to dry up

✷
Problems at
Pompeii

and the king gave de Alcubierre permission to dig into the *civitas* mound (Pompeii) which he carried out with a small crew of 24 slave labourers. But Pompeii had its problems which caused endless delays: pockets of foul-smelling, and sometimes lethal, *mofeta,* a combination of carbon monoxide, hydrogen sulphide and decayed organic matter trapped in some of the strata. De Alcubierre, motivated by the search for 'treasure' and not with discovery of a past civilisation, became impatient with the constant hold-ups and disappointment at the quality of the finds at Pompeii. He returned to Herculaneum, leaving only a small number of workers at Pompeii.

KARL WEBER

✷
A more organised
approach

It was fortunate for both Pompeii and Herculaneum that in 1750 the king appointed a Swiss engineer named Karl Weber to join the excavation team. According to the art historian Johann Winckelmann, 'it is to his [Weber's] good sense, that we are indebted for all the good steps since taken, to bring to light this treasure of antiquities.'[6] Unlike de Alcubierre, under whose supervision he worked, Weber believed it was important to 'uncover the site systematically section by section' rather than 'carrying out selective and

✷
Attempts to
document sites

uncoordinated digs',[7] and to document the excavation. He began drawing up plans and maps, and recording artefacts and paintings wherever he could. 'The first thing he did was to make an exact map of all the subterranean galleries [at Herculaneum], and the buildings they led to. The map he rendered still more intelligible, by a minute historical account of the whole discovery.'[8] De Alcubierre thought Weber's methods were ridiculous and often deliberately put obstacles in his way, even preferring to destroy a find rather than allow Weber to record it. Despite de Alcubierre's destructive methods, Weber's more systematic approach led to the discovery of the Villa of the Papyri at Herculaneum in 1751, and the Villa of Julia Felix in Pompeii in 1755.

✷
Pompeii identified

The king exploited the new discoveries 'as an instrument of political influence',[9] deciding to open the excavation sites and his antiquities collection at the palace at Portici to foreign dignitaries with royal permission, and in 1755 the Herculaneum Academy was founded to record some of the more important finds. Finally in 1763, an inscription— 'respublica Pompeianorium' or commonwealth of Pompeii—was discovered in the Street of the Tombs, positively identifying the site of Pompeii.

FRANCESCO LA VEGA

✷
Built on and
improved the
methods of Weber

A year later, Weber died and was replaced with another Spanish engineer called Francesco La Vega. Although still responsible to de Alcubierre, La Vega was given the post of Director of Pompeii, where he built on the work done by Weber. He adopted a much more systematic approach which included uncovering each building in its entirety, making a complete search for artefacts, documenting all notable interiors and writing detailed dairies of all work carried out. He unearthed the Odeon, or small theatre, and the Temple of Isis. La Vega surveyed the temple and employed a notable draughtsman to copy its wall paintings, but because of the fear of looting, they were removed. Three years later the Gladiator's Barracks were excavated, and in 1771 the Villa of Diomedes was discovered outside Pompeii containing the bodies of 18 people. In 1780 de Alcubierre died, removing 'one of the greatest hindrances to the development and execution of proper archaeological practice at Pompeii'.[10] In the same year, the excavations at Herculaneum were suspended.

In the next few decades, architects, painters, engravers and writers flocked to the Campanian sites as the excavations were given new impetus from a new regime in Naples.

❀ La Vega's discoveries

A SHORT INTERLUDE UNDER NAPOLEONIC PATRONAGE (1801–1814)

In the aftermath of the French Revolution (1799), the Bourbons were forced to flee Naples. When Joseph, the brother of Napoleon, was given the throne in 1801, he felt that work at Pompeii must be expanded and accelerated. He commissioned Michele Arditi to draw up a plan of action which included increasing the workforce to 1500 and acquiring all land on the perimeter of Pompeii so that the system of wall, gates and major roads could be identified, and the dream of La Vega—of one united archaeological site—could be fulfilled.

❀ A new plan of action

In 1808, Joseph was sent by Napoleon to become the king of Spain, and Caroline his sister, and her husband Joachim Murat, became the rulers of Naples. Caroline contributed to the excavations out of her private income. An itinerary was drawn up to accommodate the visits of scholars, and the artist/architect Francois Mazois was encouraged to devote himself to drawing individual artefacts as well as views, sections and plans of the various buildings of Pompeii, including the ancient forum which was unearthed in 1812.

❀ Tourists, scholars and artists

RESTORATION AND FINAL EXPULSION OF THE BOURBONS (1815–1860)

With the end of Napoleon's empire in 1814 and the restoration of the Kingdom of Naples to the Bourbon monarchy, the excavations and collections were used, as they had been in the 18th century, as a glorification of the royal court, but the director of the site, Carlo Bonucci, was corrupt and incompetent, with no concern for the preservation of finds. Administrative irregularities and even theft were rife in both the museum and excavations. Pompeii was faced with financial difficulties and a cutback in the labour force. As well, political unrest in Naples during the 1840s and 1850s did not help the situation in Pompeii.

❀ Corruption and incompetence

Despite these problem, many important finds were unearthed between 1824 and 1860 including the Forum Baths, the Temple of Fortuna Augusta, the House of the Tragic Poet, the House of the Faun, whole city blocks and the Stabian Baths.

The movement for the liberation and reunification of Italy gained momentum under Garibaldi, and the Bourbon monarchs were finally expelled from Naples in 1860. When Giuseppe Fiorelli was appointed as superintendent of excavations and head of the Naples Museum by the new king, Victor Emmanuel, in 1863, Pompeii entered a new phase. 'Under Fiorelli's aegis, the site increasingly came to be viewed as a town with a history rather than simply as a treasure trove of artistic objects.'[11] Fiorelli and his successors in the second half of the 19th and first half of the 20th century introduced more systematic and scientific methods to the excavations. Their contribution to archaeology and conservation are discussed in detail in Chapter 11.

Unification of Italy and appointment of Fiorelli

Figure 2.1 Development at the sites between 1863 and 2002

1863	Giuseppe Fiorelli, a numismatist, Director of Excavations e.g. plaster casts
1875	Michele Ruggerio, architect, Director e.g. the House of the Centenary and Central Baths
1882	August Mau, art historian, developed a sequential classification of wall paintings
1893	Giulio de Petra, epigraphist, Director e.g. House of the Vettii
1901	Ettore Pais, historian, Director e.g. remains of Vesuvian Gate and water tower
1905	Antonia Sogliano, Director e.g. focused on conservation
1910	Vittorio Spinazzopla, Director, e.g. investigated the length of the main commercial street
1924	Amedeo Maiuri, Director until 1961, e.g. House of Menander and Villa of Mysteries
1927	Excavations resumed at Herculaneum
1943	Excavations suspended during WWII, Pompeii suffered severe damage
1947	Excavations resumed, e.g. Villa Imperiale found under the damaged Antiquarium (museum)
1951	Feverish activity for next decade, e.g. over ten blocks totally cleared
1957	Karl Schefold carried out an inventory of all existing wall decorations at Pompeii
1961	Amedeo Maiuri retired, e.g. 26 hectares of Pompeii still not unearthed
1970s	Call for the end of all major excavations in favour of conservation and beginning of
1980s	'Houses in Pompeii' project. 1980–85 a series of earthquakes rocked Campania
1994	Pier Guzzo, Director and joint Anglo-American project began to restudy Insula VI.I
1996	Pompeii added to the World Monuments Watch List of the 100 most endangered sites
1997	Pompeii and Herculaneum listed as a UNESCO World Heritage Site
2002	Pompeii Trust, part of the Anglo-American Pompeii Project specifically focused on conservation and education

REPRESENTATIONS AND IMPRESSIONS OF POMPEII AND HERCULANEUM (1740–2004)

Variety of written and artistic impressions

In museums, art galleries and private houses around the world, particularly in Europe, are reminders of the impact the discovery of Pompeii and Herculaneum had on the upper classes, antiquarians, historians, architects, writers and artists of the 18th and 19th centuries. They recorded their impressions of the emerging ancient towns and their own particular feelings about the sites, in travelogues, letters, diaries, engravings, water colours, oil paintings and architectural cross-sections.

Even though the court of Naples kept strict control of the excavations throughout the 18th century, two Englishmen, Horace Walpole and the poet Thomas Gray, were able to visit Herculaneum as early as 1740. Gray, in a letter to his mother, informed her of his astonishment at the excavations.

❈
A poet at
Herculaneum

TODAY WE HAVE SEEN SOMETHING OF WHICH I AM CERTAIN YOU HAVE NEVER HEARD TELL. HAVE YOU EVER HEARD OF A SUBTERRANEAN CITY, OF AN ENTIRE ROMAN CITY, COMPLETE WITH ITS BUILDINGS, THAT HAS REMAINED BENEATH THE EARTH'S SURFACE? IN THE WHOLE WORLD THERE IS NOTHING LIKE HERCULANEUM.[12]

The discovery of the inscription identifying Pompeii created great interest in Europe, and the Grand Tour of Europe, undertaken by young aristocrats, soon included Naples on its itinerary. No longer did the tourists turn around at Rome but travelled south to see the excavations at Herculaneum and Pompeii which acquired the status 'as an instant museum.'[13]

❈
The Grand
Tour

The Neopolitan court encouraged artists to record the glory of all aspects of the Bourbon kingdom, and with the publication of nine books produced by the Herculaneum Academy from 1757 onwards, and the discoveries of La Vega, particularly an intact Roman temple complete with frescoes, the 'lure of Italy was irresistible.'[14] The engravings of the antiquities at Pompeii by the Italian engraver Giovanni Battista Piranesi stimulated the neo-classical movement in Europe and had a great influence on the work of architects such as Robert Adam. The interior design and decoration of many of the homes of the well-to-do featured Pompeian motifs. However, many intellectuals and artists, rather than debating in the salons of France and England, preferred to made the journey to Italy to see for themselves.

❈
The lure of
Italy and
neo-classicism

The writer Johann Goethe recorded in his 'An Italian Journey, 1786–8': 'Pompeii surprises everyone by its compactness and smallness of scale.'[15] The neo-classicists of the 18th century had a mental image of Roman grandeur and so those who visited the sites were not necessarily impressed with the houses so far excavated. It was to be some time before the great houses (House of the Vettii, House of Menander and the Villa of Mysteries) were to be restored to the light of day. Goethe wrote 'The streets are narrow, though straight and provided with pavements, the houses small and windowless . . . and even the public buildings, the bench tomb at the town gate, the temple and villa nearby look more like architectural models or dolls' houses than real buildings.'[16] Even though he wrote that 'the mummified city left us with a

❈
Goethe's impressions

His impressions

curious, rather disagreeable impression,'[17] he was fascinated by the way the people had lived and with their unique paintings.

Jakob Phillip Hackert became the official painter for the court at Naples, and one of the first to record his impression of the state of the excavations in 1799. In his *View of Pompeii* he combined an image of the ruins with that of a pastoral idyll: a peaceful, fertile landscape with flocks, orchards, vineyards and peasants.

Figure 2.2 Painting by Jakob Phillip Hackert of the theatre district of Pompeii (National Trust, UK)

Francois Mazois and the poetry of the ruins

Like the engravings of Piranesi reproduced in *Antiquities of Pompeii* in 1804, which were an imaginative interpretation of the past, the 454 drawings of Francois Mazois in *The Ruins of Pompeii* (1812), seemed to bring out 'the poetry of the ruins'[18] even while attempting to document what he saw. In a letter to a friend, Mazois continued his poetic feel for the site:

> I WAS IN POMPEII, PERCHED ON A NARROW, RUINED WALL, WHEN SUDDENLY IT SHIFTED AND THEN COLLAPSED, THROWING ME STRAIGHT DOWN, HEAD FIRST ONTO THE ANTIQUE MARBLE FLOOR BENEATH. I MUST CONFESS, I CAN THINK OF NO BETTER WAY TO DIE, NOR OF ANY BETTER PLACE TO BE BURIED.[19]

The Romantics' view of the sites based on 'feelings'

This was the period of the Romantic writers and painters. 'A school of poets who revelled in the melancholy engendered by the aspect of ruins'[20] had already developed in France and England. These visitors to Pompeii recorded

Figure 2.3 A Pompeian house from Francois Mazois' *Les Ruines de Pompeii*, 1812 (Bibliothéque Nationale de France)

what they felt on the site rather than what they saw. They presented an interpretation based on their own moods and memories, and added characteristic touches of their own. In the strange novel *Corinne, ou L'Italie*, published in 1807, the Frenchwoman Germaine de Stael wrote of the 'most curious ruins of antiquity', 'the sad eternal silence', 'ruin upon ruin, tomb upon tomb' and life cruelly snuffed out.

Some visitors wanted to experience the ruins in a romantic fashion, such as under moonlight, while for others it was the mysterious and macabre that was fascinating. Grisly scenes, complete with skeletal remains, were often staged for visitors, as the 'prepared' discovery drawn by Francois Mazois shows (see Chapter 12). The painter Paul Alfred de Curzon imbued the ruins with a number of fantasy elements—inaccurate, but appealing to their audiences—like his *Dream Amid the Ruins of Pompeii*.

The new finds discovered in the first quarter of the 19th century continued to inspire writers such as Stendhal (*Rome, Naples and Florence*, 1817), engravers such as Sir William Gell whose engravings and comments were published in *Pompeii: the Topography, Edifices and Ornaments of Pompeii*, 1817–32, and artists such as Samuel Palmer (*The Street of the Tombs*, 1837)

The English poet Percy Shelley had settled in Italy in 1818 and his 'Ode to Naples' with its superb natural imagery might have been inspired by Pompeii.

🞕
The appeal of
the grisly and
mysterious

🞕
Engravers, artists
and writers continue
to be inspired

🞕
Shelley's imagery

I STOOD WITHIN THE CITY DISINTERRED
AND HEARD THE AUTUMNAL LEAVES LIKE LIGHT FOOTFALLS
OF SPIRITS PASSING THROUGH THE STREETS; AND HEARD
THE MOUNTAIN'S SLUMBEROUS VOICE AT INTERVALS
THRILL THROUGH THOSE ROOFLESS WALLS

❈
Fascination with the 'last day'

However, some painters and writers now chose to give their impressions of the horror of the last days of Pompeii, the eruption of Vesuvius and the devastation and death it wreaked upon Campania. The Frenchman P.H. Valenciennes painted the *The Death of Pliny*, and Bruelow Karl Pawlowitch painted *Doomsday in Pompeii*, as though god was taking vengeance on a pagan people. Giovanni Pacini wrote an opera, 'The Last Day of Pompeii', complete with erupting Vesuvius, which was an immediate hit at La Scala, and the popular novel of the same name written several years later by Edward George Bulwer-Lytton—an imaginative reconstruction of the human and social tragedy—became a best seller.

❈
The strange and melancholy

Writers like Charles Dickens, the English author, spent extended periods in Italy, 'fascinated by Pompeii's mixture of the macabre and beautiful' and 'the thought of sudden death.'[21] In 1845 he wrote in 'Pictures from Italy' that at Pompeii 'one loses all sense of time and heed of other things in the strange and melancholy sensation of seeing the Destroyed and the Destroyer making this quiet picture in the sun.'[22] He then lists all the familiar things of everyday life to be seen at the site, 'all rendering the solitude and deadly lonesomeness of the place, ten thousand times more solemn than if the volcano in its fury, had swept the city from the earth, and sunk it in the bottom of the sea.'[23]

❈
Languid sensuality

Some years later, an Italian poet, Giacomo Leopardi, presented an apocalyptical view 'of life lived in the shadow of death'[24] but in contrast, many painters such as Theodore Chasseriau in his *Women in the Tepidarium* (baths), chose to evoke the type of 'languid sensuality popular at the time'[25] in Europe.

❈
Earliest photos

As Pompeii was made more accessible to the public from the time of Giuseppe Fiorelli, visitors left their impressions in water colours, letters and travel diaries. Black and white photography came into its own in the second half of the 19th century and the camera captured the feverish activity on the excavations from approximately 1863. Some of the earliest photographs taken by A.F. Normand were creative compositions, using interesting architectural fragments and ancient artefacts removed from their context to express 'the romantic and rather melancholy visions of the antiquary'.[26]

❈
A New World perspective of the ruins

Pompeii's fame spread to North America, and in 1875 the author Mark Twain visited the sites and recorded his impressions in *Innocents Abroad*. However, his representation of Pompeii was, according to Wolfgang Leppman, 'typical of the transatlantic visitors of the time'.[27] His view was not

Figure 2.4 Theodore Chasseriau's *Women in the Tepidarium* (Musée d'Orsay)

that of the European with thousands of years of history, nor of a poet, philosopher or art historian, but of 'a representative of a young and democratic nation'.[28] He found it 'a quaint and curious pastime, wandering through this old silent city of the dead—lounging through utterly deserted streets' which he thought 'were wonderfully suggestive of "the burnt district" in one of our cities'. He alluded to the cleanliness of the streets, 'as cleaner, a hundred times cleaner than ever Pompeian saw them in her prime'[29] and referred several times to biblical history.

Throughout the 19th and 20th century, artists painted watercolours of what they saw and others drew and painted reconstructions of life in Pompeii and Herculaneum as they believed it to have been. Today, modern photographic records, television documentaries and the internet make it possible to enjoy both towns without ever making the trip to the sites. Even more impressive are the images and representations being produced thanks to the computer technology of virtual reality.

✠
20th-century images

✠
Technology and virtual reality

Chapter review

Century	History of the excavation	Representations
18th	• Bourbon monarchy uses excavations for political prestige. • De Alcubierre—in charge of royal looting, careless destruction at Herculaneum • Excavations begin at Pompeii—Karl Weber, under de Alcubierre, introduces a more systematic approach but with difficulty • Pompeii positively identified • Francesco La Vega—builds on the work of Weber and improves methods at Pompeii	Representations and impressions of the sites by engravers, poets, antiquarians, writers and artists Examples: • Thomas Gray's letters—amazement Joachim Winckelmann—criticism of the excavations • Jakob Phillip Hackert—image of ruins and pastoral idyll • Johann Goethe—travel writing observations of a neo-classicist
19th	• Brief patronage under Napoleonic regime • Attempts to draw up a plan of action for a united archaeological approach • Restoration of the Bourbons—corruption, theft, lack of preservation and political unrest, affect the excavations • Expulsion of Bourbons and reunification of Italy • Appointment of Fiorelli—great influence on archaeology and the excavations—the beginning of scientific archaeology • The sites made more accessible to the public • Fiorelli's 19th-century successors follow his example	Romantic movement in art and writing reflected in representations of Pompeii and Herculaneum Examples: • G.B. Piranesi—engravings reveal imaginative interpretation of the past. • Francois Mazois—architectural and wash drawings—reflect the poetry of the ruins • Sir William Gell engraver; Samuel Palmer, artist; Germaine de Stael, writer; Percy Shelley, poet; continue the romantic view • Disaster and doomsday images in art, novel and opera • The change in observations of writers such as Charles Dickens and Mark Twain • The beginning of photographic representations of the excavations
20th	• Spinazzola introduces changes • Amedeo Maiuri—the predominant excavator of the century. Excavations suspended during WWII. After his retirement in 1961, decision taken to concentrate more on conservation than excavation. • 1970s, 80s and 90s projects (international) to conserve, re-look at earlier digs and to educate • Sites placed on UNESCO World Heritage List in 1997	• Artistic reconstructions, black and white photography • Colour television documentaries • Internet representations • Virtual reality representations

Activities

1   What do the two sources below reveal about the aim of the earliest excavators and the methods they employed?

a

THE WORKMEN, HAVING DISCOVERED A LARGE PUBLIC INSCRIPTION . . . IN LETTERS OF BRASS TWO PALMS HIGH; HE ORDERED THESE LETTERS TO BE TORN FROM THE WALL, WITHOUT FIRST TAKING A COPY OF THEM, AND THROWN PELL MELL INTO A BASKET; AND THEN PRESENTED THEM, IN THAT CONDITION TO THE KING.

Joachim Winckelmann,
A Critical Account of the Situation and Destruction of Herculaneum, Pompeii and Stabiae, *1771*

b

AS ROOMS OR BUILDINGS WERE UNCOVERED, OBJECTS AND STATUES WERE SET ASIDE. LIGHT DOCUMENTATION WOULD TAKE PLACE FOR TAX PURPOSES AND CAMILLO PADERNI, CURATOR OF THE KING'S MUSEUM AT PORTICI, WOULD ARRIVE AND THE SELECTION PROCESS WOULD BEGIN. CHARGED WITH THE TASK OF CHOOSING ONLY THE FINEST OBJECTS FOR THE KING'S COLLECTION, AND SINCE THERE WAS NO REPOSITORY FOR MORE COMMON OBJECTS, THE REST WERE DESTROYED BY HAMMER AND DISCARDED.

C. Amery & B. Curran,
The Lost World of Pompeii, *2002, p. 35*

2   Using the two 19th-century sources below, and information in the chapter, describe the types of reactions visitors had to the excavations. How differently might a modern day visitor experience the sites?

BY FLICKERING TORCH FLAME
THE VISITORS DESCEND
TO VIEW THE BODIES AGONISED BUT OF ETERNAL FAME
PALACES, SCENES OF TEMPLES AND COLONNADES STILL DENIED THE LIGHT OF DAY.

Giacomo Leopardi, c.1860

Figure 2.5 A romanticised version of archaeology—*The Excavations at Pompeii* by Edouard Alexandre de Sain (Musée d'Orsay)

Geographical Context

IN PART 2 STUDENTS LEARN TO:

- describe the physical features of Campania and the particular site features of Pompeii and Herculaneum
- identify significant places and features on a map
- explain the importance of the region's fertility for the inhabitants of Pompeii and Herculaneum
- use plans and photos to understand the urban landscape of Pompeii.

IMPORTANT TERMS

Campania felix

cardini

decumani

dormant phase

estuary

grid system

hinterland

insulae

seismic activity

volcanic processes

The physical environment and urban landscape

3

THE PHYSICAL ENVIRONMENT OF CAMPANIA

Ancient Pompeii and Herculaneum were located in the fertile region known as Campania in Southern Italy: a crescent-shaped volcanic plain of approximately 13,595 square kilometres at the foot of the Apennine escarpment, extending from the Volturno River in the north to the mountains of the Sorrentine Peninsula in the south. It was, and still is in part, an area 'incredibly favoured by nature'.[1] The Romans referred to it as Campania Felix (productive Campania).

Pliny the Elder, a well-known naturalist who lived in the 1st century AD, described it in his *Natural History* as 'one of the loveliest places on earth'.[2] In the following passage he explains why.

⊗
Size and location of Campania

HOW AM I TO DESCRIBE THE COAST OF CAMPANIA, A FERTILE REGION SO BLESSED WITH PLEASANT SCENERY THAT IT WAS MANIFESTLY THE WORK OF NATURE IN A HAPPY MOOD? THEN INDEED THERE IS THAT WONDERFUL AND LIFE-SUSTAINING AND HEALTHY ATMOSPHERE THAT LASTS ALL THE YEAR THROUGH, EMBRACING A CLIMATE SO MILD, PLAINS SO FERTILE, HILLS SO SUNNY, WOODLANDS SO SECURE AND GROVES SO SHADY. CAMPANIA HAS A WEALTH OF DIFFERENT KINDS OF FOREST, BREEZES FROM MANY MOUNTAINS, AN ABUNDANCE OF CORN, VINES AND OLIVES, SPLENDID FLEECES PRODUCED BY ITS SHEEP, FINE-NECKED BULLS, NUMEROUS LAKES, RICH SOURCES OF RIVERS AND SPRINGS THAT FLOW OVER THE WHOLE REGION. ITS MANY SEAS AND HARBOURS AND

⊗
Favoured by nature

25

THE BOSOM OF ITS LANDS ARE OPEN TO COMMERCE, WHILE EVEN THE
LAND EAGERLY RUNS OUT INTO THE SEA AS IF TO ASSIST MANKIND.[3]

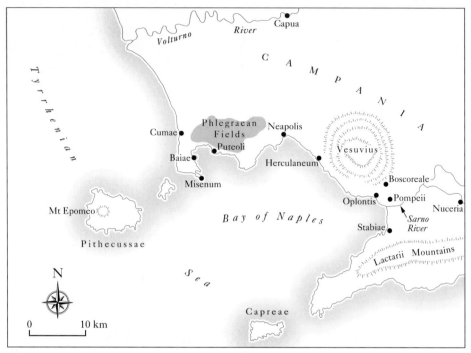

Figure 3.1 The Bay of Naples and the immediate environs of Vesuvius

CLIMATE

❈
Mild and
pleasant

The year is divided into two main seasons: hot dry summers with brilliant
sunshine from May to September, and mild wet winters from October to
April with an annual rainfall about 845 mm on the coast. Sometimes the winters are overcast, sometimes clear and cold with a strong wind blowing from
the north-east.

❈
Sea and
mountain
breezes

The following extract, written by a visitor to the area in the early 20th
century, describes the breezes that cooled Pompeii during a summer's day.

ABOUT TEN O'CLOCK IN THE MORNING A SEA BREEZE SWEEPS OVER THE
CITY, STRONG COOL AND INVIGORATING. THE WIND BLOWS TILL JUST
BEFORE SUNSET. THE EARLY HOURS OF THE EVENING ARE STILL; THE
PAVEMENTS AND WALLS OF THE HOUSES GIVE OUT THE HEAT WHICH THEY
HAVE ABSORBED DURING THE DAY. BUT SOON — PERHAPS BY 9 O'CLOCK —
THE TREE TOPS AGAIN BEGIN TO MURMUR, AND ALL NIGHT LONG, FROM
THE MOUNTAINS OF THE INTERIOR, A GENTLE, REFRESHING STREAM OF AIR
FLOWS DOWN THROUGH THE GARDENS, THE ROOMY ATRIUMS AND
COLONNADES OF THE HOUSES, THE SILENT STREETS, AND THE BUILDINGS
ABOUT THE FORUM WITH AN EFFECT INDESCRIBABLY SOOTHING.[4]

Mount Vesuvius and its effects on the landscape

Mount Vesuvius, which sits on an intersection of two fissures in the earth's crust, is the only active volcano on the European mainland, and since its devastating explosion in AD 79, has erupted over 30 times, the most violent occurring in 1631 when Campania was shaken by seismic activity for six months before the eruption, and lava engulfed 3000 people. The most recent eruption occurred during World War II, in 1944.

The outline of the mountain today—actually two mountains—is very different from its appearance in AD 79. Mount Vesuvius, at a height of approximately 1277 metres and with a crater 11 kilometres in circumference, is partly encircled by the 1110-metre ridge of Mount Somma, which alone existed up to AD 79.

The Greek historian Diodorus, writing in the 1st century BC, provides evidence that the early Greek settlers in the area knew of its active nature. He had seen signs of the ancient conflagration himself, as had the Greek geographer Strabo. In his *Geography* (AD 19), Strabo described Vesuvius as 'a mountain covered with fertile soil, which seems to have had its top cut off horizontally, forming an almost level plain which is completely sterile and ash-coloured' with 'caverns full of cracks made of blackened rock, as if subjected to fire.' He surmised that 'there used to be a volcano here, which died out once it had consumed all the inflammable material that fed it.'[5] Strabo's account remains the first accurate description of the volcano in a dormant phase. Other Greek and Roman writers of the time, such as Virgil, Martial and Suetonius, were more interested in the mythological associations of the mountain than in any scientific description, identifying it with the realm of Vulcan, the Roman god of fire and the giants in its gloomy caverns.

The volcano dominates the Plain of Campania and divides it into two regions: the larger one to the north-west drained by the Volturno River, and the smaller one—a distinct geographical entity—in the south-west traversed by the Sarno River. The Sarno rises in two springs below Monte Torrenone, meanders through the wide fertile plain of Nola, and flows into the Tyrrhenian Sea in a low-lying area of the coastline between the Sorrento peninsula and the southernmost slopes of Vesuvius.

✵ Activity

Figure 3.2 Vesuvius from Pompeii

✵ Early sources on Vesuvius

✵ Divides Campania into two plains

The whole landscape of Campania is a result of volcanic processes and, just as in ancient times, the area today is still subjected to earth tremors. Its volcanic nature can be seen in the Phlegraean Fields, behind Puteoli, a 15-kilometre-wide series of craters, pools filled with boiling mud, and vents through which sulphur and steam escape. The area, formed by a massive eruption 86,000 years ago, was believed by some of the ancients to be the entrance to the Underworld. In the 1st century AD, visitors came there to experience the hot spa baths.

✾
Herculaneum and
Pompeii built on
a volcanic spurs

The Sarno plain was dotted with mounds and spurs formed by an ancient lava flow. From earliest times, Pompeii occupied the largest volcanic spur— 70 hectares in area and between 25 and 40 metres above sea level—giving it a commanding position overlooking the mouth of the Sarno River and the sea. On its volcanic spur, Pompeii caught the breezes from both the sea and the mountains. Herculaneum, on the coast, was built on a steeply sloping spur of land that projected from the lower slope of Vesuvius and ended in a cliff-face where the headland fell away sharply to the sea. The promontory was bounded on both sides by deep ravines. Despite the limitations of its land form, Herculaneum's position on the coast of the Bay of Naples meant that the views from the houses built on terraces that descended to the edge of the cliffs, and the moderating influence of the sea, made it an ideal resort town. Strabo was enchanted by the view and commented that nowhere could a period of residence and *otium* (leisure) be more agreeable.

The material that spewed from the volcano weathered into extremely fertile soil: grey-black and rust-brown, and rich in phosphorus and potash. The type of natural vegetation that flourished in the region before the eruption of AD 79 has been identified as poplars, willows and alder trees along the rivers, and a variety of species of oak and beech on the lower slopes of Vesuvius. Today in the mountain sector are holm oak and pine woods, and further down, where the weathered lava is interspersed with ash and lapillus, are bay laurel, rosemary and other herbaceous plants.

The soil's spongy nature retained enough of the winter rains to produce an impressive variety of crops in ancient times, even during the hot rainless days of summers (see Chapter 6). The slopes of Vesuvius in the mid-1st century AD were covered with vines, their superior grapes producing the famous Vesuviana favoured by Pliny, showing, he said, the superiority of Bacchus (god of wine) over Ceres (the god of grain). Today those same slopes of Vesuvius are famous for the wine called Lachryma Christi. Virgil also mentions the vineyards in his 'Georgics' and a famous fresco from the household shrine in the Pompeian House of the Centenary verifies their importance. Pliny recorded that in Campania the vines 'never stop growing'. They were staked against poplar trees, climbing 'with unruly arms in a knotted course among their branches,'[6] rising level with their tops.

Olives of extremely high quality provided not only cooking oil but the basic ingredient of the perfume industry, together with flowers such as roses. The area supported a wide variety of fruit: peaches, apricots, lemons, cherries, plums, pears and figs. Cato, in his treatise on agriculture, revered the figs of Herculaneum, while Lucius Junius Columella, in his work *De re rustica*, spoke of the importance of cabbages and onions in the area, which also produced three or four cereal crops a year, plus hay for fodder. At the southern end of the Bay of Naples herds of sheep roamed the lush fields, providing Pompeii with wool for textile production. Many of the Pompeian wall paintings and mosaics feature the abundant produce of the area.

✼
Importance of
grapes and olives

✼
Fruit, vegetables,
cereals and sheep

Apart from the fertile soil, the volcano provided for the inhabitants of the plain in other ways: pumice stone was exported and lava was used in stone millstones for grinding grain and pressing olives (see Chapter 6). Cato noted that the top olive presses made of volcanic stone were to be found in Pompeii and admits that he bought one there for his own villa despite the great cost of transportation. Various types of volcanic material were also used for building and paving the roads.

✼
Uses of volcanic rock

Figure 3.3 Vesuvius and Bacchus (Naples National Archaeological Museum)

Figure 3.4 Mosaic of fruit (Naples National Archaeological Museum)

Figure 3.5 A grain mill made of lava stone

THE COASTLINE

The Campanian coastline faces the Tyrrhenian Sea with the wide sweep of the Bay of Naples partially enclosed by peninsulas on its northern and southern extremities, and the offshore islands of Capri and Pithecussai. The bay provided a number of safe anchorages, particularly at Misenum on the western extremity of the Gulf of Puteoli. There, a double-shaped basin made a perfect natural harbour which was reinforced during Augustus's reign and became the main naval station of the Roman fleet. Pliny the Elder, admiral of the fleet, was stationed there at the time of the eruption. The Greek port settlements along its northern shore—Naples, Cumae and Puteoli—had trading and cultural connections with the Greek East which contributed to the prosperity of the other settlements in Campania.

✼
Safe anchorages

✼
A naval station
and trade

❦
Fish and salt

Salt pans developed where the waters of the bay washed into a depression close to the coast on the road to Herculaneum, and the produce from these, together with the oily fish (tuna, mackerel, anchovies and moray eels) caught in the bay by the various fishing fleets, provided the raw materials for the famous fish sauces (garum) for which the region was known.

❦
The estuarine port
of Pompeii

Further to the south, the Sarno River widened into a lagoon-like estuary as it entered the sea; Columella in his *De re rustica* talks about the delightful estuarine marshes of Pompeii. According to Seneca, 'where the Stabian and Sorrentine coast meets that of Herculaneum' is 'a soft and sinuous bay'[7] which provided an ideal harbour and port for inland settlements, as the river was navigable to seagoing cargo ships at the time. The port of Pompeii, which Strabo says 'accommodates a traffic in both imports and exports'[8] was at the crossroads of the coastal route from Cumae to the Sorrentine peninsula and the inland route to Nuceria, Acerrae and Nola.

Figure 3.6 Produce from the sea—mosaic (Naples National Archaeological Museum)

Figure 3.7 Fresco of a villa by the sea (Naples National Archaeological Museum)

THE URBAN LANDSCAPE

❦
Villas

It is not surprising that Campania, with its temperate sea breezes, mountainous background, magnificent panoramas, thermal pools, fertile soil and brilliant colours, attracted many famous and infamous Romans who made it their playground. Cicero, the noted Roman orator and politician, thought it a most delightful and desirable place to reside. Senators, wealthy businessmen, and even members of the imperial family in the 1st century AD built imposing villas in and around Cumae, Misenum, Neapolis, Herculaneum, Oplontis, Stabiae and Pompeii, and transformed farmsteads into luxurious villa rusticae. 'The handiwork of man blended into a landscape of the grand style.'[9]

The Sarno Plain and adjacent coastline were dotted with bustling towns like Pompeii, Nuceria, Boscoreale, Stabiae and Herculaneum, as well as tranquil villages and farms engaged in an intensive form of agriculture.

❦
Size of Pompeii and
Herculaneum Walls

Unlike Naples, Pompeii and Herculaneum were relatively small and compact, the former covering an area of approximately 66 hectares, although only two-thirds of the ancient town has been excavated. The area of Herculaneum

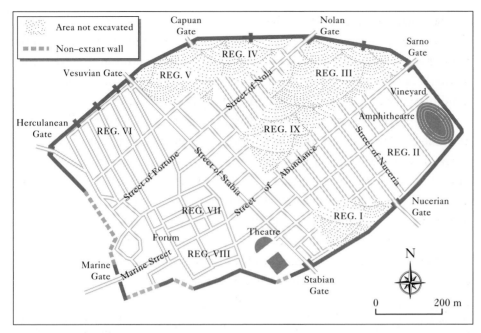

Figure 3.8 Plan of Pompeii

is much harder to estimate, since only about four blocks have been completely unearthed, the rest still hidden under the modern town of Resina. Some scholars have suggested it was a third of the size of Pompeii, others say it would have been no more than 12 hectares. Both towns had walls. Although Herculaneum's was modest, according to the historian Sisenna, Pompeii was enclosed by a 3.2-kilometre wall which tended to follow the most defensive line of the natural landscape.

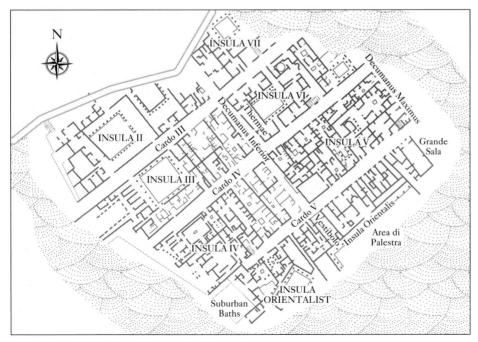

Figure 3.9 Plan of Herculaneum

❀
Pompeian gates

Pompeii was accessed by seven gates, five of them focused on roads to other towns in the Campanian region. The oldest seems to be the Stabian Gate to the south comprising a narrow, single-arched passage flanked by ramparts descending to an outer moat. The Nola Gate in the north was the most formidable, but as military defence became less important, gates became more complex. During the 1st century AD, large stretches of wall were knocked down altogether to facilitate the construction of houses. Streets were laid out on a grid system, the main axial roads (*decumani*) crossed by minor roads (*cardini*) creating blocks (*insulae*) about 35 metres by ninety metres. At its full dimensions, Pompeii's main road, was 8.5 metres wide. Others varied between 3.5 and 4.5 metres wide, but many were not wide enough for two-way traffic.

❀
Grid system
of roads

❀
The Forum

Public buildings associated with administration, religion and commerce were clustered around or near the Forum which was the chief meeting and trading place in the town. In Pompeii the Forum was located where the main roads from Naples, Nola and Stabiae met (see Chapter 6). Analyses of the urban structure of Pompeii have revealed 'a confused jumble of shops, workshops, crafts, residential and horticultural plots and houses across the whole city, with no real attempt at commercial segregation or concentration beyond the tendency of shops to line the main roads and horticulture to cluster on the margins'.[10]

Figure 3.10
The Marine Gate
at Pompeii

Figure 3.11 Streetscape in Pompeii

❀
Land use within
Pompeii

Land use within Pompeii was not exclusively urban. It included cultivated areas and open spaces. Polyculture was practised, with fruit trees, vines and vegetables grown together. Evidence of several commercial vineyards and a large orchard has been found.

Chapter review

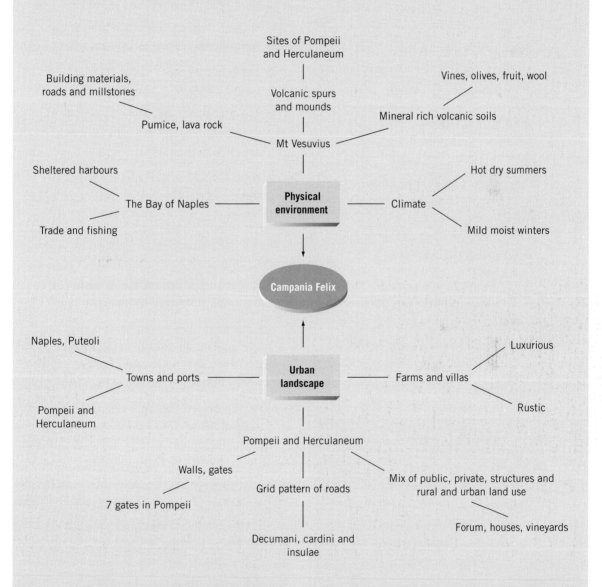

Sites of Pompeii and Herculaneum

Building materials, roads and millstones

Vines, olives, fruit, wool

Volcanic spurs and mounds

Pumice, lava rock

Mineral rich volcanic soils

Mt Vesuvius

Sheltered harbours

Hot dry summers

The Bay of Naples

Physical environment

Climate

Trade and fishing

Mild moist winters

Campania Felix

Naples, Puteoli

Luxurious

Towns and ports

Urban landscape

Farms and villas

Pompeii and Herculaneum

Rustic

Pompeii and Herculaneum

Walls, gates

Mix of public, private, structures and rural and urban land use

Grid pattern of roads

7 gates in Pompeii

Forum, houses, vineyards

Decumani, cardini and insulae

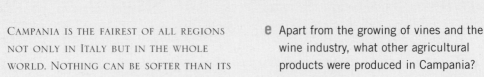

Activities

1   CAMPANIA IS THE FAIREST OF ALL REGIONS
    NOT ONLY IN ITALY BUT IN THE WHOLE
    WORLD. NOTHING CAN BE SOFTER THAN ITS
    CLIMATE; INDEED IT FLOWERS TWICE A YEAR.
    NOWHERE IS THE SOIL MORE FERTILE; FOR
    WHICH REASON IT IS SAID TO HAVE BEEN
    AN OBJECT OF CONTENTION BETWEEN LIBER
    AND CERES . . . HERE ARE THE VINE-CLAD
    MOUNTAINS . . . VESUVIUS THE FAIREST OF
    THEM ALL . . . TOWARD THE SEA-COAST LIE
    THE CITIES OF NAPLES, HERCULANEUM AND
    POMPEII.

    Florus, Epitome of Roman History, *I. II. 3–6*

    a   Describe the location of Campania within
        Italy.

    b   What does Florus mean by a 'soft
        climate'?

    c   To what is he referring when he says 'it
        flowers twice a year'?

    d   Why is Campania's soil so fertile?

    e   Apart from the growing of vines and the
        wine industry, what other agricultural
        products were produced in Campania?

    f   Suggest a reason for Florus's opinion that
        Vesuvius was the 'fairest of them all'.

    g   List four facts about Mount Vesuvius,
        pre-AD 79.

    h   How was the topography of Pompeii and
        Herculaneum associated with the former
        activities of Vesuvius?

    i   Write a short description of the physical
        features of the coastline of the Bay of
        Naples.

    j   What part did cities like Naples and
        Misenum play in the Campanian region?

    k   How important was the Bay of Naples to
        the towns of Pompeii and Herculaneum?

2   Use the information in Chapter 3 to draw a
    simple diagram illustrating the advantages
    that location and site provided for the
    people of Pompeii.

3   What evidence do Figures 3.12 and 3.13
    provide for the resources of the Vesuvian
    area?

Figure 3.12

Figure 3.13

Activities

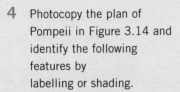

4 Photocopy the plan of Pompeii in Figure 3.14 and identify the following features by labelling or shading.

a Label the:
   – walls and towers
   – Marine Gate
   – Herculanean Gate
   – Nolan Gate
   – Stabian Gate
   – Forum

b Use different forms of shading or colouring to show:
   – the unexcavated parts of the town
   – the two main roads that traversed Pompeii from west to east
   – the main north-south road
   – an area that illustrates the rectangular grid pattern of streets
   – an insula or block
   – an example of a cultivated area

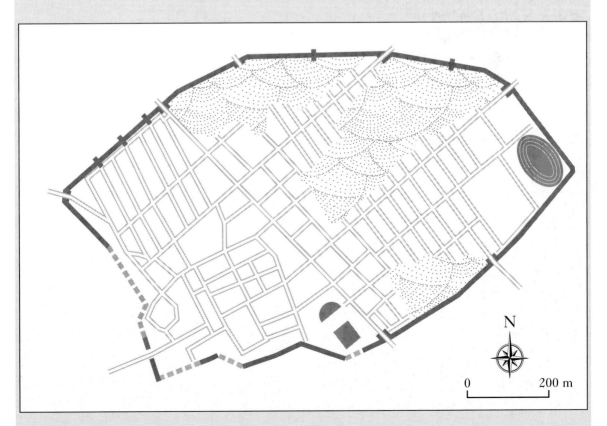

Figure 3.14

PART 3

The Nature of Sources and Evidence

IN PART 3 STUDENTS LEARN TO:

- comprehend the nature of the sources available for a study of Pompeii and Herculaneum
- identify limitations in the sources (gaps, bias) and evaluate the implications for understanding life in Pompeii and Herculaneum in the 1st century AD
- analyse both ancient and modern sources on the eruption of Vesuvius and the manner of death of the inhabitants of the Vesuvian towns
- build up a body of evidence from a wide range of ancient sources to reconstruct the social, economic, political and religious life of Pompeii and Herculaneum in AD 79
- communicate findings in a variety of written, diagrammatic and oral forms.

IMPORTANT TERMS

amphorae
basilica
clients
dolia
duoviri
economic interdependence
edicta munerum
Epicureanism
epigraphy
epitaph
eulogy
farces
forum
freedmen
frescoes
garum
genius
graffiti
lares
manumission
megalography
mosaics
paterfamilias
Pompeian 'styles'
popular painting
thermae
velarium

The range of sources and their reliability

4

THINGS TO CONSIDER

- The extent to which archaeological evidence has been ignored, neglected, destroyed, left unreported and unpublished
- The subjective nature of some of the earlier interpretations of the architecture
- The difference of evidence provided by Hellenistic style and popular painting

- The value of the ordinary—graffiti and everyday objects—in understanding Pompeii and Herculaneum
- The insights provided by a scientific study of the human and plant remains
- The fragmented nature of many of the literary sources
- The value of Pliny the Younger's 'Letters to Tacitus' as a historic and scientific text

There are three broad categories of sources which throw light on the fate of the cities of Vesuvius, as well as on the architecture, social structure, politics, religion and aspects of everyday life. There is an abundance of archaeological and epigraphic source material, but the literary sources, except for Pliny the Younger's eye-witness account of the eruption of Vesuvius, are relatively few and fragmented.

⬚ Archaeological and literary sources

ARCHAEOLOGICAL SOURCES

From beneath the pyroclastic deposits, archaeologists have unearthed remarkably intact public and private structures, inscriptions and wall writings (slogans and graffiti), papyri rolls and wax tablets, wall paintings, mosaics and other decorative arts, objects of everyday life, and human, animal and plant remains. These provide visitors to the sites, and to the Naples Museum, with a sense of immediacy, of being in touch with the lives of ordinary people and with their tragic deaths.

⬚ The immediacy of archaeology

However, according to Andrew Wallace-Hadrill, while Pompeii is probably the most studied of the world's archaeological sites, it is perhaps the least understood, as a result of past neglect, damage and a failure to document carefully, if at all. Although the average visitor would not be aware of it, 'much of the "Life of Pompeii" literature and the oral tradition' offered to them is too

⬚ Unreliability of many records

'unreliable to be of use'.[1]

Fortunately there are teams now challenging the story of the sites by:
- questioning widely-held concepts about Roman life
- asking different questions about the material finds: 'There appears to be virtually no limit to the number of questions that could be asked of our archaeological evidence.'[2]
- shifting 'away from the old certainties of "fact" and "truth" towards multiple and varied interpretations'[3]
- recognising the ways in which the views of the past were affected by the politics and ideologies of the present
- accepting that while they try to make sense of the past, it is never possible to 'know the past'.[4]

THE PAST IS SHAPED AND RE-SHAPED IN THE PRESENT, JUST AS MUSICIANS INTERPRET AND RE-INTERPRET MUSICAL SCORES, AND ACTORS ENDLESSLY REINTERPRET SHAKESPEARE'S PLAYS, DIFFERENT INTERPRETATIONS BRINGING OUT DIFFERENT MEANINGS.[5]

ARCHITECTURE

There is a wide variety of architectural structures and spaces in Pompeii and Herculaneum. Some of these are listed in Figure 4.1, with reference to the chapters where more information can be found.

Figure 4.1 References to public and private structures in the text

Types of architectural structures and spaces			
Public		Private	
Walls, gates and streets	Ch. 6	Town houses from the palatial to the humble	Ch. 7
Aqueducts, water towers, fountains and sewerage systems	Ch. 7	Suburban and country villas—*rusticae* (farming villa) and *otium* (for leisure)	Ch. 7
The Forum—temples, law courts, markets	Ch. 6	Shops e.g. bakeries, hot food bars	Ch. 6
Public lavatories	Ch. 6	Taverns and inns	Ch. 6
Public baths	Ch. 8	Workshops e.g. fulleries	Ch. 6
Theatres	Ch. 8	Brothels	Ch. 8
Amphitheatre	Ch. 8	Tombs	Ch. 9
Exercise ground (palaestra)	Ch. 8		
Other temples	Ch. 9		

Although architecture can provide an image of the society—both the big picture and its constituent parts—it must be understood that much of the architectural evidence has disappeared forever, and the 800 excavated houses and 600 shops and workshops have not been the subject of serious study. For some, 'reporting has been patchy',[6] for others there are no excavation reports or maps, and some are totally unpublished. A great deal of the information produced about the buildings was based on 'subjective impression and uncontrolled conjecture.'[7]

New studies, based on more advanced techniques, are now being carried out in particular houses, *insulae* (blocks), public spaces and buildings. Some of these projects are discussed in detail in Chapter 11. Figure 4.5 summarises some of the information to be gained from the architecture of Pompeii and Herculaneum.

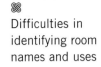
Difficulties in identifying room names and uses

Figure 4.2 Garden and peristyle of a Pompeian house

Figure 4.3 Facade of the Pompeian amphitheatre

Other information, such as ownership, functions of rooms, standards of living and status of the people who used the buildings, is harder to deduce from the architecture without some knowledge of associated artefacts, decorations, epigraphy and literary sources. Unfortunately, many of the artefacts and paintings were looted or removed to the safety of the Naples Archaeological Museum, without any record of their context, and sometimes literary evidence is not available, or does not tally with the architecture.

For example, without really knowing how a room was furnished, it is difficult to know what activities were carried out in that space, and archaeologists really do not know what the Pompeians called the various rooms. Although they use the names most commonly mentioned in the written texts, there is often no consistency. When a room in Pompeii is labelled a *cubiculum* or bedroom it can be misleading, because the literary sources describe a cubiculum as having a variety of functions and 'there is no evidence that the concept of bedrooms as we know them today even existed for Pompeians.'[8] When a German scholar in the 19th century tried to use the textual evidence of Vitruvius to draw the plan of a Roman house, it turned out to be quite different from any of the houses being excavated in Pompeii and Herculaneum. As Wallace-Hadrill says, 'the world of the metropolitan Roman elite to whom we owe our literary sources might be ill-matched with that of a second-rate Italian town of local landowners and traders. Indeed, it is quite normal for the

Figure 4.4 The Temple of Isis in Pompeii

❋
How to read private structures

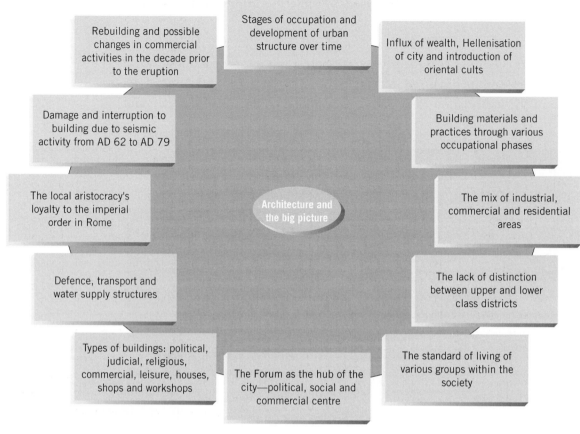

Figure 4.5 Evidence provided by architecture

basic structures of Pompeian houses . . . to date back to the period conventionally termed "Samnite" when Pompeii was an independent town, not "Roman".[9]

The architecture of private structures (houses, shops and workshops) should be read with the understanding that Romans:

❈
Mix of residential
and commercial

- did not see home and work as separate
- lived in close proximity with their dependants, slaves, freedmen, clients and tenants who were the source of their social and economic power
- had a different idea of the meaning of house and family
- unlike the Greeks, did not segregate women within the house and did not create special space for children
- were chiefly concerned with using architectural and decorative features to distinguish between the private and public areas of the house, between the grand and the humble, and as a social orientation or guide for the different groups of people who frequented their houses
- used their houses to enhance their social status.

Unlike our modern boundaries between home and work, there was no obvious distinction between residential and commercial units in Pompeii and

Herculaneum. Not only did they sit side by side in the streets, but in many houses, both large and small, shops and workshops were incorporated into the house's structure.

Figure 4.6 shows the types of premises in two urban blocks, one in Pompeii (published by Maiuri 1933 and Elia 1934) and one in Herculaneum (published by Maiuri 1958).

Figure 4.6 Types of premises in two urban blocks

Pompeii Regio 1, Insula 10	Herculaneum Insula 4
Taberna (workshop dwelling, c.90 sq. m. Stairs to upper floor, backyard with kitchen, 3 rooms.	House of the Mosaic Atrium, c. 1150 sq. m. Peristyle with 4-sided colonnades, stairs from atrium and peristyle, 14 rooms. View over the bay.
Caupona (eating place) c.80 sq. m. Bar with a back room linked to dwelling, Circulation area with stairs, 3 rooms.	House of the Alcove, c.460 sq. m. stairs from street to rooms above front. Densely packed with 18 rooms.
House of Menander, c.1700 sq. m. Entrance to main reception area, atrium, peristyle with 4-sided colonnade, stairs at front of atrium, 12 rooms, 4 storage spaces, bath site and 3 bathrooms; garden and kitchen area plus 2 rooms and cellars behind baths. Secondary entrance to service area with separate atrium and backyard, 9 rooms on ground floor, more above. Shop entrance gives access to service area. Access also to stable yard with 4 rooms.	Fullonica (laundry) c.230 sq. m. Shops on either side. Circulation space leads to atrium at back, fuller's basin installed in impluvium.
	House of the Papirio Dipinto, c.110 sq. m. stairs up from street. Long passageway leads to a small light well and 6 rooms.
Officina, c.40 sq. m. Workshop with treading stalls for fullery plus a back room. External stairs lead to rooms above, supposedly a brothel (dubious evidence).	Shop and dwelling, c.110 sq. m. Shop with jars (*dolia*). Back room linked to dwelling, 3 rooms.
House of Fabbro (cabinet maker), c.310 sq. m. Atrium, peristyle with single colonnade and wooden outdoor triclinium, stairs at back, 6 rooms.	Taberna and dwelling, c.215 sq. m. Shop and marbel veneer counter; food and drink served in back room. Private entrance via corridor, stairs up, to atrium at back, 6 rooms.
House of Minucius, c.270 sq. m. Atrium, secondary court with stairs, back garden, 7 rooms.	Taberna and dwelling, c.240 sq. m. Shop with counter, back room linked to dwelling. Main entrance down a corridor to columned courtyard surrounded by 10 rooms. Stairs up by door and at back. Possible guest house (*hospitium*).
Taberna, single room, c.10 sq. m.	
House of the Amanti, c.470 sq. m. Workshop linked to dwelling. Entrance to atrium, peristyle with 4-sided colonnade on 2 levels, stairs up at front of atrium and back of peristyle, 13 rooms plus storage spaces.	House of the Stofa, c.145 sq. m. Stairs from street. Shop/workshop area, passage to a small court. 5 rooms.
Officina, single room with stairs, c.25 sq. m. Thermopolium (take away) single room with stairs, c.25 sq. m.	House of the Cervi, c.1190 sq. m. Side entrance to atrium without impluvium, with stairs. Atrium leads directly into a suite of reception rooms fronting on the peristyle with 3-sided colonnade, suite of rooms on fourth side with stairs to upper suites. Kitchen and service areas in back extension. Views over the bay.
House of Aufidius Primus, c.120 sq. m. Atrium, stairs back yard, 5 rooms.	

Observation of this mixture of residential and commercial units led Amadeo Maiuri, the predominant excavator of the 20th century, to conclude that Pompeii had become a city of nouveaux riche with a decline in the patrician class, prior to the eruption. Although this view is still presented in many of the guides and popular books on Pompeii, it has been challenged by scholars such as Andrew Wallace-Hadrill in *Houses and Society in Pompeii and Herculaneum* (1994), who suggests that Maiuri's view is not based on archaeological or statistical evidence, but rather on inaccurate assumptions.

INSCRIPTIONS AND WALL WRITINGS

❈
Pompeii, an epigraphic archive

Pompeii 'may be likened to one vast archive'.[10] Apart from the formal inscriptions on stone, marble and bronze, most of the epigraphy 'is of a spontaneous character'[11] painted or scratched on the outer walls of both private and public structures. Those examples that have survived reveal very intimate and human moments, as well as events, great and small of city life: 'The vibrating humanity of the city still echoes with a thousand voices in every corner that is disinterred.'[12]

Inscriptions on stone, marble and bronze

❈
Types of formal inscriptions

These inscriptions, which were meant to be permanent, included:
- civic charters and regulations on bronze plates fixed to walls of public buildings
- dedications by wealthy citizens who saw it as their social duty to provide buildings and festivals, and to support the imperial cult. Their commemorative plaques can be found at prominent positions within the city, on public buildings, temples and pedestals for statues.
- funerary inscriptions found on the tombs lining both sides of the road outside the Herculaneum Gate in Pompeii.

❈
Evidence

From these inscriptions, historians can learn who the prominent families were in various periods; the structure of government; the main political players; when buildings were constructed or renovated; and the economic, political and social transformations that occurred in society, especially in the 1st century AD.

❈
Early and late glimpses of Pompeii

The earliest surviving dedicatory inscription is dated to the Samnite period just before Pompeii became a Roman colony in 80 BC. According to the inscription, a magistrate named Vibius Popidius dedicated a portico in the Forum. One of the last glimpses of Pompeii, revealed by an official inscription, is from the post-earthquake period. This inscription indicates that there were serious political and administrative problems in Pompeii and that the Emperor Vespasian was forced to send a tribune, Titus Suaedius Clemens, to reclaim public land appropriated by private citizens. Other examples include:
- an inscription placed at the entrance of the Stabian Baths which records

how the magistrates (*duoviri*), Gaius Uulius and Publius Aninusce, renovated the porticoes and the gymnasium and added a room for steam baths and another for physical exercises

- two epigraphs on the facade of the Building of Eumachia in the Forum which tell how a rich widow Eumachia, priestess of Venus, dedicated the building to the Julio-Claudian dynasty. One was a eulogy of Romulus, the mythical founder of Rome, the other a eulogy of Aeneas, the legendary forefather of the family of Augustus 'Eumachia, daughter of Lucius, public priestess, built the hall, the covered gallery and the portico in her name and that of her son M. Numistrius Fronto at her own expense: she herself dedicated it to Concordia and to Pietas Augusta.'[13]

❊ Dedications

- epitaphs on the tombs in the necropolis which reveal some of the names of prominent citizens such as: Mamia, priestess of Venus; Umbricius Scaurus a well-known producer of garum, the famous fish sauce; the Augustale Caio Calventio Quieto, and M. Portius who had the Odeon (theatre) and amphitheatre of Pompeii built.

❊ Epitaphs

Figure 4.7 A commemorative plaque proclaiming the beneficence of G. Quinctius Valgus and Marcus Porcius who paid for the building of the amphitheatre

Figure 4.8 Inscription on a pedestal of a statue of Quintius Sallustius, in the Forum

Wall writings—public notices

Most of the wall writings refer to activities and events in the years immediately preceding the eruption of AD 79. These texts have been published in Volume IV of the 'Corpus Inscriptionum Latinarum' (CIL) and its supplements.

Public notices were written with a brush in red or black on freshly whitewashed walls. Most of these notices were painted by professional scribes (*scriptores*) on the outer walls of houses or other buildings at the person's disposal. The walls were whitewashed with lime by a whitewasher (*dealbator*) and then at night, the electoral manifesto was written by the light of an oil lamp held by a *lanternarius*. However, sometimes an individual did not employ professionals, but did the job himself, like Mustius, a laundry worker who, after urging people to vote for Marcus Rufus as chief magistrate, added 'Mustius the laundry worker . . . wrote this alone,

❊ Professional scribes

without other companions'.[14] Aemilis Celer boasted that he painted his notice without any help, by moonlight. 'Scripsit Aemilis celer singulus ad lunam'.[15]

Electoral manifestos or slogans (*programmata*), which urged citizens to vote for a particular candidate, figure most in Pompeii's epigraphy. They were not signed by the candidate himself but by family, friends, clients or guilds: 'Vesonius Primus urges the election of Gnaeus Helvius as aedile, a man worthy of public office'[16] and 'The aurifices (goldsmiths) support the candidature of Caius Cuspicius Pansa for aedileship'.[17] Of the 30 per cent that were signed, 52 were by women, even though they could not vote. For example, a woman named Asellina, who ran a tavern, had a manifesto painted on its walls urging her customers to vote for 'Caio Lolio Fusco for duovir'.[18] Other women signed the *programmata* with her.

The *edicta munerum*—programs that announced to the public the shows coming to the amphitheatre—were as important as electoral posters. The *editores munerum* were local magistrates, responsible for paying all or part of the expenses of the gladiatorial shows or spectacles. These programs included the magistrate's name, political and religious positions, the occasion and type of spectacle. From several of these, historians learn that a certain A. Clodius Flaccus, who was a member of the local aristocracy and the owner of vineyards in the vicinity of Vesuvius, was an editore three times. In his first term as chief magistrate c.20 BC, during the feast of Apollo, he organised a solemn procession (*pompa*) of all the games participants through the Forum. He presented bulls and toreros, boxers and three pairs of *pontarii* (type of gladiator who fought on a platform) and staged theatrical productions with clowns and mimes. In his second term in office, he held a *pompa* in the Forum with bulls and toreros and boxers. There was a day of contests between 30 pairs of wrestlers and 40 pairs of gladiators in the amphitheatre, as well as bullfights and a hunt with wild boars and bears.

Notices for property sales and rentals were also painted on the city walls. For example, Julia Felix, one of Pompeii's chief property owners in the years before the eruption, advertised: 'In the property of Julia Felix, daughter of Spurius, elegant thermal baths for refined people, shop with lodgings above and apartments on the first floor to let for five years from 1st August until 1st August of the sixth year. The contract may be renewed by mutual agreement after five years have passed.'[19]

Wall writings—graffiti

Graffiti (inscriptions or drawings) were scratched into the surface of any available wall 'with stylus, iron nail, wooden splinter or tooth pick'.[20] Any man, woman or child who wanted to share his or her feelings, thoughts or jokes; spread gossip; show their admiration or love for someone; keep a record of gambling debts; add up shop accounts; remember important dates;

advertise their services and fees; sing the praises of a gladiatorial champion; express contempt for a politician or frequenter of a brothel; or threaten an enemy, would not hesitate to express themselves on the face of a wall.

Many people, including children, quoted and misquoted the great poets of the day, and some even tried to write their own verses. An amateur poet named Tiburtinis wrote several lyric verses on the wall of the Odeon (small theatre): 'What happened? After drawing me helplessly into the fire, O my eyes, now your cheeks run with tears. But the tears cannot put out the flames. They spread across your face and darkness comes into the spirit.'[21]

✇ Amateur poetry

But other attempts at verse were rather crude. A guest in a tavern left the following on a bedroom wall: 'My host, I've wet the bed. My sins I bare, But why? you ask. No pot was anywhere.'[22] And another: 'While I was alive I drank with glee; Drink, all you who alive still be.'[23]

✇ Crude verse

The Basilica in Pompeii, where justice was administered, trials were held and business transactions carried out, featured—as might be expected—some of the angrier graffiti: 'Samius to Cornelius: Go hang yourself'[24] and 'Chius, I hope your piles are chafed once more, that they may burn worse than they've burnt before.'[25]

✇ Angry outbursts

Comments concerned with gambling and drinking were common in taverns: 'I won 855 sesterces at dice—no cheating'[26] and 'Suavis demands full wine-jars, please, and his thirst is enormous.'[27]

✇ Tavern scrawlings

Lovers throughout Pompeii had no hesitation in expressing their deepest feelings on the city's walls.

✇ Amorous messages

IF YOU CAN BUT WONT, WHY DO YOU PUT OFF THE PLEASURES OF OUR MEETING. WHY DO YOU BUILD UP MY HOPES AND THEN TELL ME TO RETURN TOMORROW? IN THIS WAY YOU FORCE DEATH UPON ME, BECAUSE YOU FORCE ME TO LIVE WITHOUT YOU. CERTAINLY IT WILL BE A KIND ACTION THAT PUTS AN END TO MY SUFFERING.[28]

The most explicit messages were found on walls near and inside brothels and lavatories: 'May I always and everywhere be as potent as I was here.'[29] In the lavatory of the House of the Gem in Herculaneum was the graffito 'Apollinaris, the physician of the Emperor, Titus, had a good shit here.'[30]

✇ Erotic and explicit

Writing on walls was so widespread that the following comment in various forms circulated in Pompeii: 'I wonder, Wall, that you do not go smash, Who have to bear the weight of all this trash.'[31] It may have seemed trash or nonsense at the time, but today, the ancient graffiti is an invaluable source of information about the inhabitants of Roman towns.

WAX TABLETS AND ROLLS OF PAPYRI

Two bundles of wooden tablets coated with wax have been excavated from Pompeii and reveal the business activities of the banker Caecilius Jucundus and

✇ Business and legal documents

two merchants, Sulpicius Cinnamus and Sulpicius Faustus. Three more dossiers, referred to as the 'Herculaneum Tablets', cover the period from AD 60 until AD 75, and throw light on the legal status of a manumitted slave, relationships between neighbours, family structure, quarrels over slaves and between land-owners. They reveal the nature of a tight-knit business community.

❈
Philosophical
treatises

Considering the search for pleasure obvious in the Vesuvian cities around the Bay of Naples, it is not surprising that a library of Epicurean writings on papyri should have come to light in the remains of a villa in Herculaneum. The Epicurean school of philosophy taught that one's duty was to attain personal happiness and peace of heart by overcoming irrational desires and fears. It is believed that the writer of most of the papyri was the Greek Philodemus, who was a great friend of Lucius Calpurnius Piso, the father-in-law of Julius Caesar and owner of the so-called Villa of the Papyri. Philodemus was probably the leader of Epicurianism in the Vesuvian area. His full enjoyment of life was also revealed in a group of racy verses which, although deplored by Cicero, throw some light on the love-life of Herculaneum and areas round about.

DECORATIVE ARTS

❈
Wide
variety

These include:
- frescoes derived from the great Hellenistic pictorial schools, categorised by the chronological system known the 'Four Pompeian Styles'
- paintings, referred to as 'popular' which were little affected by the Greek artistic tradition and featured aspects of real Italian life
- mosaics: pictures and designs on walls, floors, grottoes and fountains, done in thousands—in some cases millions—of *tesserae* (tiny chips of coloured glass, stone, pottery and seashells)
- geometric patterned floors and pavements usually composed in a variety of stones such as coloured marbles, limestone and travertine
- decorative sculpture in bronze and marble, featured in the atria, peristyles and gardens of Pompeian and Herculaneum homes. 'Garden paths were lined with columns and pedestals displaying herms, masks, statues of Bacchus, Venus, Hercules, Eros and various woodland deities.'[32]
- a magnificent array of household furnishings: precious silver, fine ceramic tableware, personal ornaments, glass vases, and table settings.

Frescoes—Hellenistic pictorial style painting

Throughout the Roman world there was a fashion for covering the walls of both public and private buildings with paintings. This fashion spread right across all levels of society, from the elaborate and colourful motifs of specialised workshops in the great reception rooms of the wealthy to the simple thin lines of colour or geometric patterns in the homes of the less dignified. Only those areas isolated from view, such as kitchens and the slaves' quarters, were usually devoid of wall paintings.

Because very few inhabitants of Pompeii and Herculaneum, like the elite in Rome, could afford to decorate their houses in original Greek art, they had to be satisfied with imitations on their walls of sacred Greek landscapes, Greek panel painting and Greek mythology. Even the walls of their garden porticos became 'veritable outdoor art galleries'.[33]

❀
Imitation of Greek art

The quantity and quality of the frescoes in the homes of prominent families in the area around Vesuvius have:

- provided archaeologists and historians with valuable documentation of lost Greek and Hellenistic painting
- allowed them to trace the development of Roman pictorial art over an uninterrupted period of three centuries

❀
Evidence of development and process of painting

- given them an appreciation of the process of fresco painting and helped them to gain some understanding of the various workshops from which the private patrons commissioned their work, although usually not the names of the particular artists. However, Pliny the Elder does leave some clues as to the original Greek artists and their works, which the Romans copied (see page 61).

Frescoes also revealed changes in society. For example, during the Republican period, nobles and those in high political and religious positions were surrounded by hordes of clients and colleagues and much business was carried out in the public reception rooms of their homes. The decoration of these rooms, which imitated and alluded to the public places in the city, shows something of the owner's social aspirations and resources, as well as the volume of social activity focused on their homes. According to Wallace-Hadrill, the 'decoration allowed the visitor a social orientation. It helped steer them within the house guiding them round the internal hierarchies of

❀
Painting as evidence of social aspirations

Figure 4.9 Garden wall painting (Naples National Archaeological Museum)

Figure 4.10 Mythological wall painting, *The Sacrifice of Iphigenia*, from the House of the Tragic Poet in Pompeii (Naples National Archaeological Museum)

social space'.[34] Clients had no need of large elegantly decorated rooms, but those just below the elite on the social ladder often copied the decoration of the grander houses. As Cicero says, 'generally speaking, one tries to imitate the ways of the illustrious people'.[35] From the Augustan Age there was a more upwardly mobile group in society—wealthy freedmen—and by the time of Nero these members of 'the bustling, ostentatious society'[36] of Pompeii and Herculaneum were anxious to reveal their changed social status, by the decoration of their homes.

✖ **Reflections of imperial periods**

Paintings from the stable Augustan Age reflected not only the emperor's taste for order and moderation, but the subtle reinterpretation of Greek myths by Augustus's court poets, playwrights and writers. During the time of Nero, 'who indulged in every voluptuous excess'[37] and adopted a lifestyle in which the extremes became the daily reality, the decoration of walls and floors in Pompeii revealed variety and originality.

✖ **The four 'styles'**

These wall paintings have been classified into four 'styles'. In 1882, August Mau devised a sequential classification based on comments by the Roman architect Vitruvius' in his 'De architectura'.

✖ **'Structural'**

The first style (3rd century–c.80 BC) is often referred to as the 'structural' or 'encrustation' style because the wall decoration is not in the form of frescoes but rather painted stucco to represent the stone or marble masonry of sacred Greek architecture.

✖ **'Architectual'**

The second style (c.80 BC–c.20 BC) is referred to as the 'architectural' style because the paintings concealed the wall surfaces with Hellenistic architectural elements such as columns, porticoes and niches, creating an illusion of extended space with landscape vistas through arches and painted windows. Figures, objects and animals were integrated into the architectural compositions. Within this style, there developed a pictorial genre called megalography featuring monumental figures within architectural spaces such as windows, doors, arcades and garden terraces. The paintings in the

✖ **Megalography e.g. of the Villa of Mysteries**

Villa of Mysteries are the most famous of this genre. A series of larger-than-life figures extends over all the walls of a salon. Since their discovery from the early 20th century to the present day, these paintings have provoked much debate. The scenes have been variously identified as a reference to the god Dionysus/Bacchus himself; as the initiation of a bride into the Dionysiac mysteries; as the initiation rituals of pain and suffering (physical and sexual) necessary to enter the divine realm; as a representation of the professed faith of the owners of the Villa; or as a theatrical representation. The debate continues.

Vitruvius was an admirer of the early second style, but he ruthlessly criticised the new developments that occurred towards the end of the 1st century BC, moving from architectural reality to purely decorative forms.

The third style (c.20 BC–c.AD 50) is referred to as the 'ornamental' style. The illusionary element was replaced with pictorial reality and the wall was divided into three horizontal zones and two pairs of narrow vertical panels, creating a central area usually occupied by a mythological painting (stories of the gods, heroes and famous lovers). In the smaller panels were still lifes, theatre masks, fantastic figures, imaginary gardens and features of the natural world. After Augustus's conquest of Egypt, Egyptian motifs were also favoured: Nile landscapes, exotic animals, and deities. The upper zone was painted with architectural perspective.

🕸
'Ornamental'

Figure 4.11 First Pompeian 'style' (Naples National Archaeological Museum)

Figure 4.12 Second Pompeian 'style'—a reproduction of the original in the Metropolitan Museum of Art (Naples National Archaeological Museum)

Figure 4.13 Third Pompeian 'style' (Naples National Archaeological Museum)

Figure 4.14 Fourth Pompeian 'style'

❧
'Fantastic'

❧
Megalography

The fourth style (c.AD 50–AD 79) is referred to as the 'fantastic' style and most of the surviving domestic paintings in Pompeii and Herculaneum are of this type. Bright shimmering colours created a theatrical fantasy, architectural perspective returns to the middle section and there is a greater range and flexibility in colour, motifs and framework. The House of the Vettii in Pompeii contained the best collection of the paintings in this style.

In the last 20 years, the study of painting has begun to expand beyond artistry and chronology.

> QUESTIONS OF ROOM FUNCTION, CO-ORDINATION WITH FURNITURE AND OTHER MOVEABLE GOODS, ARTIST WORKSHOPS, REGIONAL STYLES, AND REVIVAL OF PREVIOUS STYLES IN LATER PERIODS ARE NOW BEING RAISED. THE 'PICTURE' IS NO LONGER SO SIMPLISTIC: THE IMPLICATIONS OF HOW AND WHY THE POMPEIANS DECORATED THEIR BUILDINGS AS THEY DID ARE MORE COMPLEX AND INTERESTING . . . [38]

Popular art

❧
Reveals a range of
human activities

What is referred to as popular painting, most of which is found on exterior walls or trade signs, is simple and easy to translate and covers the whole range of human activities whether scenes of different phases in the production of wool from the walls of Pompeii's largest textile workshop, a carpenter at work, a baker handing out loaves of bread, tavern life, religious processions or the bustle of the Forum (see Chapter 6). They are invaluable sources of everyday life for the historian.

Figure 4.15 An example of popular painting found on a shop sign

❧
Materials, 'emblems
and figurative elements

Mosaics

A range of geometric and figurative mosaics were found on walls, floors, columns and nymphaeum, and even the vaulted roofs of baths.

The earliest floors of the buildings of Pompeii and Herculaneum were composed of mortar mixed with crushed tiles or volcanic stone, with occasional chips (*tesserae*) of coloured limestone inserted in a geometric design. Geometric patterns in back and white became more widespread and incorporated a central polychrome picture (*emblema*) often featuring a mythological scene or a copy of a famous Hellenistic composition, such as the incredible mosaic in the exedra of the House of the Faun—Alexander the Great fighting Darius at the Battle of Issus (see Chapter 10). The floor mosaics of this house had more in common with Hellenistic 'palaces' than most other local upper-class houses. With time, the central *emblema* tended to disappear, to be

Figure 4.17 A mosaic floor

Figure 4.16 A colourful mosaic wall decoration in a summer dining room

replaced with a wider variety of geometric designs and figurative elements in some rooms, such as the chained dog in the entrance of the House of the Tragic Poet (see Chapter 7). During the Augustan and Julio-Claudian period, marble from Carrara was more commonly used for floors in the better homes, but little of this has survived due to looting after the eruption.

Decorative garden and household furnishings

Sculptures placed as ornaments in the homes and gardens were copied from Classical and Hellenistic age prototypes. A gold oil-lamp-holder statue found in the Pompeian House of the Citharist is said to have been inspired by an 'Apollo' by the Greek master Phidias. The simple household items of ancient times were substituted by refined and precious silver table services which the nobles loved to flaunt at their feasts and banquets as a sign of their social and economic status.

Antique pieces were particularly sought after, such as the cups depicting bucolic scenes among the treasures of the House of Menander. The treasure comprised 118 pieces of silverware, several of which were quite ancient and

✂
Greek influences

✂
Treasure from the House of Menander

Figure 4.18 Decorative silverware from the treasure found in the House of Menander (Naples National Archaeological Museum)

Figure 4.19 Animal bronzes from the Villa of the Papyri in Herculaneum (Naples National Archaeological Museum)

evidently restored. They were found, covered by pieces of cloth and wool, at the bottom of a wooden chest in the cellar of the house. Among the silverware were several valuable cups embossed with scenes of Greek myths and traditional Hellenistic landscapes. The upper part of the case contained a gold pendant that hung from the neck to identify a freeborn child, earrings, gold bracelets and rings set with precious stones, a silver purse and mirror, and a hoard of gold and silver coins amounting to 1432 sestertii. (See Chapter 11 for an interpretation of the silver hoard.)

Figure 4.20 illustrates some aspects of life in Pompeii and Herculaneum revealed by the decorative arts.

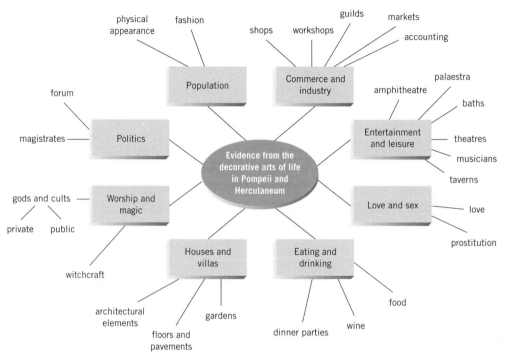

Figure 4.20 Evidence of everyday life gained from a study of the decorative arts

OBJECTS OF EVERYDAY LIFE

The importance of the ordinary

The very ordinariness of most of the objects found in Pompeii and Herculaneum are what make them so valuable to historians in building up a picture of daily life in the 1st century AD: pots on a kitchen stove, carbonised wooden furniture such a cradle and a clothes press, household shrines, matting and ropes, a fisherman's net, even scorched cloth and papyrus. Figure 4.21 provides other examples of these everyday objects.

Figure 4.21 Examples of everyday objects excavated at Pompeii and Herculaneum

Category	Object	Original location
Household	Wooden cradle	House of the Carbonised furniture (H)
	Tripod	House of Julia Felix (P)
	Bronze kitchen utensils	House of Vettii (P)
	Bronze heaters	Pompeii and Herculaneum
	Terracotta and bronze lamps	Pompeii and Herculaneum
	A brazier	Herculaneum
	A day couch	House of Menander (P)
	A three-legged table	House of Paquius Proculus
	A bell for calling servants	House of the Stags (H)
	Bronze handles for doors and chests	Herculaneum
Food	81 carbonised loaves of bread	Bakery of Modestus (P)
	Eggs and fish on a table	Temple of Isis (P)
	Carbonised eggs in a kitchen cupboard	House of the Relief of Telephus (H)
	Bread, salad, cakes and fruit, on a dining table	House of the Relief of Telephus (H)
	Beans and grains on a shop counter	Shop of the green grocer, Aulus Fuferus (H)
	A full jar of nuts under a counter	Shop of the Drinking Priapus (H)
Commerce	Wine and olive presses	Villa of Mysteries (P)
	Amphorae	Shop in the House of the Neptune Mosaic (H)
	A cart packed with wine jars	Street (P)
	Lava millstones	Bakery of Popidius Priscus (P)
	Dolia	Thermopolia (P and H)
	Bronze scales	Pompeii
	Glass jars	House of The Wooden Partition (H)
Transport	A gig for the transportation of people	House of Menander (P)
	A boat	On the beach at Herculaneum
	Woven cord 'sandals' for horse hooves	House of the Wooden Partition (H)
Entertainment	A gladiator's helmet	Gladiators' barracks (P)
	A pair of dice	House of the Stags (H)
	Black and white 'backgammon' pieces	House of the Wooden Partition (H)
Medicine	Surgical instruments such as needles, probes, gynaecological forceps, catheters, pincers, scalpels and scissors	House of the Surgeon (P)

HUMAN, ANIMAL AND PLANT REMAINS

It is not known exactly how many people died during 24 and 25 August AD 79, but the human skeletal remains excavated so far from Herculaneum, as well as the disarticulated bones, plaster and resin casts from Pompeii, are a valuable source of information about the victims. They reveal such things as:

* sex and age
* appearance
* average height of men and women
* general health

- specific medical problems and evidence of surgery
- population affinities
- probable occupations and social status
- cause of death and mental state at the time.

The skeletons of Herculaneum

✦
Changing view of the
fate of Herculaneum

In 1982, three skeletons were discovered on the beach of the small ancient harbour of Herculaneum. Up until that time, very few human remains had been found in the town compared with the approximately five hundred corpses in Pompeii. As more skeletons emerged throughout that year in a row of chambers built into the retaining wall of the harbour, it was obvious that the previous hypothesis that there had been time for a mass exodus of Herculaneum's population became less likely. In time, as the beach area is excavated further, it is expected that more bodies will be found.

✦
State of the
skeletal remains

The skeletons of Herculaneum have been preserved in good condition because of the 20-metre thick layer of moist volcanic material which accumulated over the town. As the bodies of the inhabitants decayed, the material compressed about the bones, preventing oxygen from causing further deterioration and eventually solidified to the consistency of rock.

Figure 4.22 Carbonised olives

Figure 4.23 A skeleton found at Herculaneum

✦
Dr Bisel's process

Dr Sara Bisel, classical archaeologist and anthropologist, explained that 'with exposure came quick deterioration,'[39] and she had to work quickly to prevent it. She washed each bone separately and allowed it to dry for several days, before dipping it in an acrylic–plaster mixture and leaving it to harden before reconstructing the skeleton. Her study of the skeletons followed two anthropological methods—measurement and observation of the bones and a biochemical analysis.

✦
Physical analysis

She examined:
- the long bones of the legs to ascertain height
- the state of the pelvis of the women to tell their ages and if they had had children
- facial bones for appearance
- the upper shafts of the humeri and thoracic vertebrae to tell if the person worked harder than usual

- the state of all bones for level of nourishment
- teeth for an indication of the age of children and whether there was sugar in the diet as well as general nourishment.

She carried out a chemical analysis to find evidence of lead poisoning and the presence of calcium, phosphorous, magnesium, zinc and strontium. Bones with high levels of zinc indicate the consumption of animal protein, while those high in strontium indicate the consumption of vegetable protein and seafood.

Chemical analysis

In all, Bisel studied 139 Herculaneans—51 males, 49 females and 39 children. She found evidence to support the idea of low birth rate: a mean of 1.69 children per woman. She believes that practices of abortion and contraception, mentioned frequently in the literary sources, were responsible for this, although high levels of lead in the body can cause sterility.

Number studied

There was a great variety in the skulls studied which pointed to 'a widely diverse genetic inheritance of this population . . . the town, if not the region was a great melting pot of people, enjoying the energy and health that result from genetic diversity.'[40]

Genetic diversity

From dental studies she found that samples with 'horizontal hypoplastic lines [grooves] in their tooth enamel'[41] indicated that childhood malnourishment prevented the assimilation of calcium, while pits in the bone along the gum line indicated gum disease. She discovered that the mean number of tooth loss and decay in both sexes was low and was probably due to the heavy consumption of seafood, containing fluorides, and the fact that sugar was not in use, while honey, used as a sweetener, was expensive.

Dental disease, food and nourishment

Bisel discovered that quite a few of the skeletons she examined had high lead levels while five adults and two children had levels high enough to cause poisoning and even brain damage. There seemed to be no difference in lead levels between rich and poor. She suggests that these levels were due to the use of lead in drinking cups, plates and cooking pots, lead water pipes, and from red pigment of paint, as well as the use of lead to whiten a woman's skin, treat bleeding and promote healing of ulcers and superficial wounds, and even as a remedy for headache and arthritis. However, the most common use of lead was as a sweetening agent for sour wine.

Presence of lead and possible causes

Since Dr Bisel's studies, much work has been done on DNA which could be used for identifying genetic disorders as well as diseases which leave no mark on the bone. Figure 4.24 summarises her conclusions about a number of the skeletons studied. However, it is believed that she based her analysis on the assumption that girls normally married between 12 and 14, whereas B.D. Shaw in 'The Age of Roman Girls at Marriage' thinks it more likely to have been in late teens.[42]

Figure 4.24 Examples of Sara Bisel's findings from a study of the skeletons from Herculaneum

Skeleton sample	Approx. age	Height (cm)	Socio-economic class and occupation	Notable features
Erc 86	46	174.2	Upper class	Sign of good nutrition, well-developed muscles but not due to overwork, possibly from sports such as hurling the javelin or discus—time to work out at the palaestra.
Erc 65	46	157.2	Wealthy matron—gold jewellery on and beside body	Heavy robust bones indicating good nourishment. Probably gave birth to 2–3 babies. Had a bad overbite which would have marred her beauty. Dental problems would have led to infections and abcesses.
Erc 132	8	average	Upper class—a gild ring set with stone, plus glass beads	Considerable tooth decay perhaps indicating that she was given a lot of honey-laden desserts.
Erc 10	14	155.9	Female slave looking after mistress's baby	Pretty, but did a lot of running up and down stairs or hills. Teeth reveal that at a young age she did not receive the right nourishment or that she was seriously ill.
Erc 11	10 mths		Baby wore jewellery	
Erc 25	24	151	Upper class—pregnant with 7-month-old foetus	First pregnancy—rather late. Bones indicate that she did not have to work hard and her teeth are perfect—healthy, well-nourished and free of infections.
Erc 110	16	152.3	Lower class than Erc 25 with 7-month-old foetus	Some evidence of minor periods of childhood illness. Infantile pelvis suggests that she would have died in childbirth.
Erc 28	16	173	Fisherman	Healthy, well-developed musculature of the upper body, perhaps indicating that he did a lot of rowing. The wear pattern on his teeth show some industrial use of teeth such as holding a bobbin cord used to repair nets.
Erc 26	37	174.5	Soldier—found with bronze military belt and sword	Bones show that he was big, tough and well exercised. He appears to have been well nourished. There is evidence of trauma e.g. stab wound in the left leg and teeth missing but not from decay. Evidence from his knees of a career on horseback.
Erc 13	48	155.3	Lower class or slave—possibly a prostitute	Pelvic abnormality also seen in modern prostitutes. Light bones with some degenerative arthritis.
Erc 98	49	162.2	Lower class or slave—possibly a prostitute	Pelvic abnormality and possible birth of 4–5 children. Indication of hard work.
Erc 27	46	163.5	From the lowest socio-economic free class or a slave	Bones showed a life of hard labour, poor nutrition and poverty. He had 7 lost, 4 decayed and 4 abscessed teeth. Fusion of 7 vertebrae indicate Forestier's disease, hyperstosis of the spine, plus arthritis in other bones.
Erc 49	41	170.7	Labourer, possibly a horse handler, carter or construction worker	Evidence shows that he used his hands in heavy work and that he suffered a number of accidents such as a blow to the skull, fracture to his right radius and a crushed right foot. The foot injury occured in late childhood—between 10 and 12.

Bones and casts from Pompeii

Very few intact skeletons have been found in Pompeii because many were destroyed during the early years of excavation. Others were removed, some so carelessly stored in the Pompeian bath houses that the bones became disarticulated and mixed. According to Estelle Lazer, a forensic archaeologist from Sydney University, it is difficult to estimate the number of skeletons from the remaining collection of bones, but she suggests there would be no more than five hundred, approximately equal numbers of men and women, but few children, as small bones were often missed in the excavations. The Pompeii site director, De Caro, in an interview in 1984, said he believed the majority of Pompeii's victims have not been found but were still out there somewhere beyond the gates.

In her detailed study of the Pompeian skeletal remains, Lazer concentrated on the skulls and teeth, and pelvic, leg and arm bones from 300 individuals. From the evidence, she disputes the often-claimed view that most of those who died in Pompeii were women, children, the elderly and infirm. Although obesity and old age might have made it difficult to escape, there is no firm evidence that such people made up the bulk of those who died. She discovered that many skulls showed signs of serious dental problems: caries, gum disease, early tooth loss and thick deposits of calcified plaque. Worn and decayed teeth, however, tell historians nothing about a person's status. According to Suetonius, even the Emperor Augustus had bad teeth, 'small, few and decayed'.[43] Badly worn teeth tell historians more about the people's staple food. Pompeians ate bread, made from flour impregnated with tiny fragments from lava millstones. Estelle Lazer also confirmed that many of the victims had medical problems at the time of death. Ten per cent of the skulls examined revealed a post-menopausal syndrome called hyperostasis frontalis interna which resulted in obesity, benign tumours inside the skull leading to severe headaches, and the growth of facial hair. Other skulls showed signs of past surgery and bone fractures. However, the study confirmed that generally the population of Pompeii was well nourished and in good health.

In Pompeii, unlike in Herculaneum, corpses were covered in a deep layer of fine ash and pumice which did not completely seal the bodies from the deteriorating effect of oxygen. They decayed, leaving cavities in the hardened ash which archaeologists, since the time of Fiorelli (see Chapter 11) have filled with liquid plaster and resin, forming casts of the bodies as they were at the moment of death, including clothes, shoes, facial expressions and desperate gestures. From these casts, historians can deduce, sex, age, possible occupations and status.

THE AVAILABLE CASTS HAVE A GREAT POTENTIAL AS A RESEARCH RESOURCE WHICH HAS NOT YET BEEN EXPLOITED. UNLIKE THE BONES, THE CASTS CONTAIN EVIDENCE OF THE WHOLE PERSON . . . THE ACTUAL BONES STILL EXIST WITHIN THE CASTS. IF THE CASTS COULD BE X-RAYED.

❈ Few intact skeletons

❈ The work of Estelle Lazer

❈ Evidence

Figure 4.25 Plaster cast of a victim from Pompeii

❈ Plaster and resin casts

❈ More research to be done on casts

ENTIRE SKELETONS COULD BE STUDIED WHICH WOULD PROVIDE MUCH
MORE INFORMATION THAN THE ANALYSIS OF INDIVIDUAL BONES. THIS
IMPORTANT WORK STILL REMAINS TO BE DONE.[44]

Animal and plant remains

Although it is believed that many of the horses and mules in Pompeii were
mobilised for escape, some remains have been found: horses still in their stables in the Villa of Pisanella at Boscoreale and seven mules tethered in the
stable in a bakery in Pompeii. Also, dogs have been found still chained near
the entrances to houses and a goat was discovered in a cellar.

✤
Evidence

Dr Wilhelmina Jashemski has carried out extensive studies into soil
contours; root cavities of large ornamental trees, vines and fruit trees; carbonised plant remains (27 plant species were found in the carbonised hay
found at Oplontis), and pollen. By supplementing these with evidence from
paintings, archaeologists have gained a clearer picture of produce and ornamental gardens in Pompeii, as well as many of the timbers used in doors and
furniture. Some of these discoveries, such as the presence of vineyards and
olive trees within Pompeii, have thrown a different light on its economy and
the relationship between town and countryside. Also, archaeologists have
been able to re-create some of the gardens in the finer residences and a large
vineyard near the amphitheatre.

LITERARY SOURCES

✤
The range of
literary sources

Apart from Pliny the Younger's unique eyewitness account of the eruption of
Vesuvius and his own experiences, many of the early and contemporary texts,
while containing useful information, have a particular focus of enquiry. For
example, Strabo's *Geography*, Vitruvius's *Of Architecture*, Seneca's *Natural
Questions* and Pliny the Elder's *Natural History*. Historians have to supple-
ment these with the inscriptions and graffiti from the monuments and walls
of Pompeii and Herculaneum, as well as other literary sources which throw a
general light on the history and life of the late Republic and early Empire.
These include such works as those of Cicero, Livy's *History of Rome*, Tacitus's
Annals, Suetonius's *Twelve Caesars*, Petronius's *Satyricon* and Juvenal's *Satires*.

A VALUABLE HISTORICAL AND SCIENTIFIC DOCUMENT— THE 'LETTERS' OF PLINY THE YOUNGER

✤
Orator and
writer

Pliny the Younger (Gaius Caecilius Plinius Secundus) was a Latin orator and
author born in AD 61. After the death of his father, Caecilius Clio, he was
adopted by his uncle, Pliny the Elder, and later became a friend of the emperor
Trajan and the historian Tacitus. He was a talented writer and left ten books
of letters among which were his famous *Letters to Tacitus,* describing the eruption of Vesuvius, the death of his uncle and his own reactions to the disaster.

The two 'letters' (VI, 16 and 20) written in response to a request from the historian 25 years after the events which Pliny personally experienced as a teenager are unique. According to the noted vulcanologist Haraldur Sigurdsson, 'in the field of science Pliny's letters . . . will remain classics as the first eyewitness report of an explosive volcanic eruption so powerful that it is repeated on our planet only about once in a thousand years.'[45] Pliny's account has been tested and largely reconciled with the geological evidence from the deposits in Pompeii, Herculaneum and at other sites across the Vesuvian plain.

❀
Unique nature of his 'Letters to Tacitus'

Seventeen-year-old Pliny was staying with his mother and uncle, commander of the Roman fleet at Misenum, on the northern edge of the Bay of Naples, when the eruption occurred. Pliny the Elder considered the eruption of the mountain as 'important enough for closer inspection and he ordered a boat to be made ready'.[46] He invited his nephew to accompany him by ship on a fact-finding mission across the bay, but he declined: 'I preferred to go on with my studies.'[47] It was just as well for Pliny the Younger, as well as for modern historians and scientists, that he declined his uncle's offer, because Pliny the Elder took his last breath on the beach of Stabiae. Not only do the *Letters to Tacitus* provide remarkable geological clues used by modern vulcanologists, but are a first-hand account of the reaction of those around Pliny the Younger, including his mother; his own feelings about leaving Misenum during the chaos; and the death of his uncle which was later gleaned from reports of those who accompanied him and survived. (Refer to Chapter 5 for Pliny's description of the eruption.)

❀
Pliny the Younger on his uncle

❀
Geological clues and personal reactions

Although the letters provide two geographical viewpoints of the eruption (from Misenum and Stabiae), unfortunately Pliny says nothing of the overwhelming of Pompeii and Herculaneum. Nor does he record the year as AD 79, and makes no mention of the tremendous detonation that must have preceded the eruption. Dio Cassius describes the 'portentous crash', but since we don't know who his sources were, it may be that he was using his own experiences of the eruption of Vesuvius in AD 202 when he claimed to have heard the detonation as far away as Capua. However, eye-witnesses of other eruptions throughout the centuries describe the terrifying detonations that precede eruptions, so why did Pliny fail to mention it? He was only 30 kilometres from Vesuvius. It is also surprising that someone who experienced such a catastrophe first-hand should not have written more about it.

❀
Omissions

Despite their value as scientific and historical documents, there are several factors which should be considered when gauging the reliability of the letters.

❀
Some questions of reliability

The description of his uncle's experiences, behaviour and death was second-hand: Pliny the Younger was not on the ship with him, nor at the home of Pomponianus nor on the beach at Stabiae. Neither did he see the effects of the eruption from the same vantage point as his uncle. He had to rely on the reports of those who survived—predominantly sailors and

❀
Second-hand account of uncle's death

members of the household of Pomponianus—all of whom would have been seriously traumatised.

There is no evidence that the events were documented until AD 103–107, that is about a quarter of a century after the event, and in the intervening years Pliny must have forgotten much of what he heard and experienced when he was a young man, especially the sequence of events.

It is obvious from the content of the first letter, particularly its introduction, that Pliny and Tacitus were concerned more with celebrating Pliny the Elder's bravery, and in the carefully composed letters both uncle and nephew lose nothing in the telling.

THANK YOU FOR ASKING ME TO SEND YOU A DESCRIPTION OF MY UNCLE'S DEATH SO THAT YOU CAN LEAVE AN ACCOUNT OF IT FOR POSTERITY; I KNOW THAT IMMORTAL FAME AWAITS HIM IF HIS DEATH IS RECORDED BY YOU. IT IS TRUE THAT HE PERISHED IN A CATASTROPHE WHICH DESTROYED THE LOVELIEST REGIONS OF THE EARTH, A FATE SHARED BY WHOLE CITIES AND THEIR PEOPLE, AND ONE SO MEMORABLE THAT IT IS LIKELY TO MAKE HIS NAME LIVE FOR EVER; AND HE HIMSELF WROTE A NUMBER OF BOOKS OF LASTING VALUE; BUT YOU WRITE FOR ALL TIME AND CAN STILL DO MUCH TO PERPETUATE HIS MEMORY. THE FORTUNATE MAN, IN MY OPINION, IS HE TO WHOM THE GODS HAVE GRANTED THE POWER EITHER TO DO SOMETHING WHICH IS WORTH RECORDING OR TO WRITE WHAT IS WORTH READING, AND MOST FORTUNATE OF ALL IS THE MAN WHO CAN DO BOTH. SUCH A MAN WAS MY UNCLE, AS HIS OWN BOOKS AND YOURS WILL PROVE. SO YOU SET ME A TASK I WOULD CHOOSE FOR MYSELF, AND I AM MORE THAN WILLING TO START ON IT.[48]

Was Pliny not only trying to leave a record of his uncle's heroism: 'What he began in a spirit of enquiry he completed as a hero'[49] but also hoping that posterity would remember him [the nephew] as courageous? Or was he simply recording his youthful bravado when he admitted that he sat in the courtyard and 'called for a volume of Titus Livius and began to read', and even continued his notes from it, 'as if nothing were the matter' paying 'enthusiastic attention to it'[50] while the world around him was shaking and exploding?

AN INQUIRING MIND—THE 'NATURAL HISTORY' OF PLINY THE ELDER

Pliny the Elder (Gaius Plinius Secundus), born in AD 23, had already had a military and political career before being appointed as commander of the fleet at Misenum in Campania by the emperor Titus not long before the eruption. He had an inquiring mind and his work *Natural History*, in 37 books, covers such topics as science, art, natural history, human inventions and institutions. According to Jashemski, it was 'a learned and comprehensive work as full of variety as nature itself.'[51]. Pliny was the only ancient author to meticulously cite his sources (over 100) and to include a table of contents. He was not a scientist and wanted his work to be accessible to the general public. He has often been criticised as being 'an uncritical compiler', but although his work is sometimes obscure, uneven and contradictory, 'its value lies in the fact that he records what was believed at the time.'[52]

❀ Reliability

Some of the information in his *Natural History* relevant to an understanding of Pompeii and Herculaneum includes such topics as:

❀ Evidence

- the attributes and produce of the region of Campania. For example, he provides the historian with information on the varieties of grapes in the region, the various wines and their effects on the drinker and details of the olive industry.
- the varieties of fish and medicinal plants
- the processes used by the fullones in the textile industry, one of Pompeii's most important industries
- the various building materials and processes involved in creating mosaic floors
- the gardens of Pompeii and the invention of 'nemora tonsilia', or 'barbered' groves
- the making of pigments for wall paintings
- the names of some of the original Greek and Roman artists and descriptions of their works, from which many of the paintings in Pompeii and Herculaneum were copied. He recalls a Greek artist, Pireikos, from the 4th century BC, who began the painting of still life who was later followed by another Greek, Poxis, living in Rome in the late republican era. According to Pliny, it was from his work that the miniature representations on the walls—both fresco and mosaic—of Pompeian houses were copied.

It was his curiosity in natural phenomena, and determination to help friends stranded around the Bay of Naples, that led him to his death from suffocation on the beach at Stabiae on the morning of 25 August AD 79.

COMMENTS ON BUILDINGS AND PAINTING STYLES BY THE ARCHITECT, VITRUVIUS

Vitruvius, a 1st century architect, wrote *Of Architecture*, a manual on architecture and Roman building methods dedicated to Augustus. Information relevant to a study of Pompeii and Herculaneum includes the appearance of Greek and Roman houses and the activities that took place in the various rooms (although this did not always correspond to the archaeological evidence), comments on the construction of public buildings such as the acoustics of theatres, how a basilica should be constructed, the features and dimensions of Italian fora, the heating of baths, and the process of painting. His descriptions and comments on wall paintings formed the basis of the four chronological 'Pompeian' styles.

❀ The usefulness of Vitruvius

Figure 4.26 summarises other useful literary sources.

Figure 4.26 Useful literary sources

Name	Date	Type of writing and reliability	Examples of information associated with Pompeii and Herculaneum
Cicero Politician, orator, lawyer and man of letters; had a villa in Pompeii	160–43 BC	Various works	• The physical attributes of Campania • Political activities in Pompeii after it become a colony in 80 BC. • Comments on the social and moral effects of the behaviour of the Roman elite
Livy Latin historian	59 BC–AD 17	*History of Rome* in 142 books covering the period 742–9 BC Lacked a critical approach to history; a Roman patriot	• The Samnite Wars • Effects of Hannibal's invasions of Campania • The spread of the cult of Bacchus (Dionysus) in Italy
Strabo Greek geographer from Pontus	c.63 BC–AD 21	*Geography* written in AD 19 based on his own travels and research from the great Alexandrian library	• Description of Vesuvius in its dormant phase • Description of Sarno Valley and the port of Pompeii
Seneca Latin stoic philosopher, studied rhetoric and law; tutor to the future emperor Nero	c.4 BC–AD 65	*Moral Essays*, one of which was *Naturales Quaestiones*	• The geography of Campania • Earthquakes • The earthquake that destroyed Pompeii and Herculaneum in AD 62
Tacutis Historian and intimate of Pliny the Younger	c.AD 55–120	*Historiae*—History of the empire from Galba to Domitian (AD 68–96) much of this lost *Annals* (a year-by-year treatment of the Julio-Claudian emperors from the death of Augustus to Nero) Reliable witness despite his sometimes obvious bias	• It is possible that he included in his *Historiae* information provided to him by Pliny on the eruption, but this work from AD 70 is lost. There is only a brief allusion to the earthquake in his prologue. • The riot between the Pompeians and Nucerians in the Pompeian amphitheatre in AD 59
Statius, Martial Poets	c.AD 61–96 c.AD 40–c.104	Statius's *Silvae* and Martial's *Epigrams*—Poets' viewpoint; Written in a moralising fashion	The fate of Pompeii and Herculaneum
Dio Cassius Roman historian	c.AD 150–235	*History of Rome* in 80 books. A mixture of fact and the supernatural; No knowledge of his sources; Much not credible although some coincides with Pliny's account	• The eruption of Vesuvius and the date of AD 79 • A scheme adopted by Titus in response to the eruption

Chapter review

Human remains—whole skeletons, bones and plaster and resin casts

Reveal sex, age, health, appearance, specific problems, genetic diversity, probable occupations, status and cause of death

Architecture—urban fabric of private and public structures

Many destroyed and unrecorded. Some early interpretations based on inaccurate assumptions

Decorative arts—frescoes, popular art, mosaics. Show the impact of Greek influences, local aspirations and various city activities

Many have disappeared and faded with no record of context

Everyday objects—food, household utensils, objects associated with commerce, transport, entertainment and medicine

Valuable to historians as a picture of daily life

Wax tablets—dossiers that reveal business and legal activities, family structure, relationships with neighbours

Rolls of papyri—reveal something of Epicurean philosophy

Formal inscriptions on bronze, marble and stone—civic charters; regulations; epitaphs; dedications

Evidence of form of government, important families, political elite, changes in society

Wall writings—electoral slogans, gladitorial programs, rentals and sales and a wide range of graffiti

City events, great and small, and very human activities

Archaeological

Epigraphic

The range of sources

Epigraphic

Literary

Pliny, the Younger—*Letters to Tacitus*—an account of the eruption of Vesuvius, and the reactions and fate of various individuals and groups

A unique historical and scientific record

Others—Pliny the Elder, Seneca, Strabo, Vitruvius, Tacitus, Livy, Cicero, Statius, Martial and Dio Cassius

Fragmentary and with a particular focus

Activities

1 **a** Use the information in Figure 4.6 to identify the architectural spaces in the plan shown in Figure 4.27.

b What evidence does this figure and the quote provide for an understanding of the arrangement of private buildings in Pompeii and Herculaneum?

ALTHOUGH THERE ARE CONTRASTS FROM REGION TO REGION, THE OVERWHELMING PATTERN IS OF A MIXED DISTRIBUTION OF THE VARIOUS TYPES OF COMMERCIAL AND ARTISANAL ACTIVITY . . . IN AMONG RESIDENTIAL AREA OF THE CITY.[53]

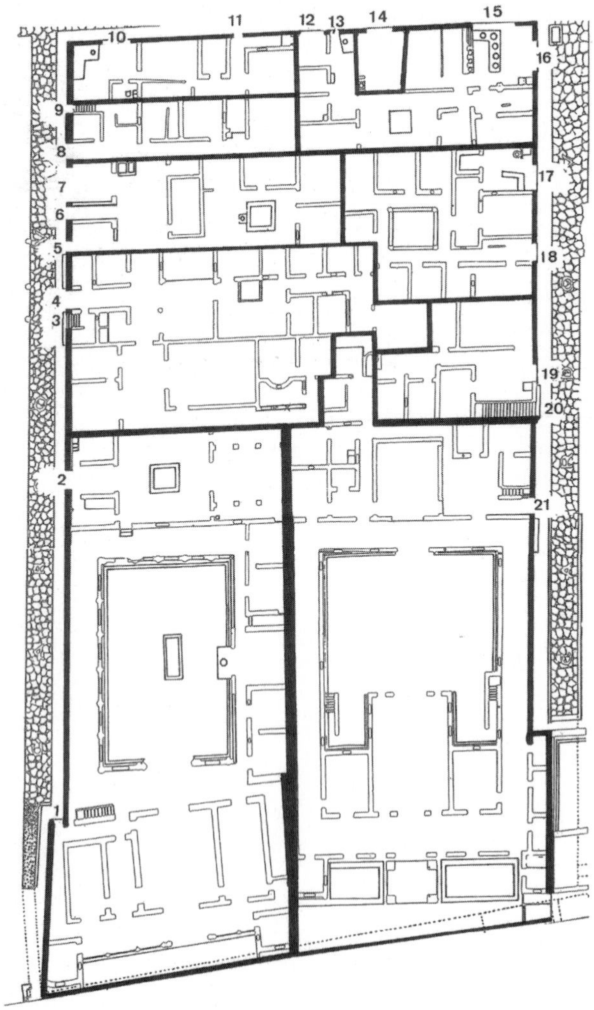

2 **a** What is epigraphy?

b What did Amadeo Maiuri mean when he said the following:
—Pompeii 'may be likened to one vast archive'?
—Most of the epigraphy 'is of a spontaneous nature'?

c How valuable is this spontaneous epigraphy to historians?

3 **a** Identify the types of decorative art depicted below.

Figure 4.28

Figure 4.29

Figure 4.27 Plan of Insula IV in Herculaneum (after Maiuri)

Figure 4.30

Activities

b Where are they likely to have been found?

c What evidence do they provide for Hellenistic influence on the decorative arts of Pompeii?

4 Carefully read this extract from *Herculaneum: Italy's Buried Treasure* by Joseph Jay Deiss (1966, pp. 33–4) and answer the questions that follow.

THE TESTIMONY OF HERCULANEUM HAS SHOWN THAT THE AMOUNT OF WOOD USED IN ANCIENT BUILDING WAS MUCH GREATER THAN FORMERLY SUPPOSED. BEAMS, WINDOW SILL, DOORS, SHUTTERS, AND STAIRS OF WOOD ARE STILL IN THEIR ORIGINAL PLACES. MANY PIECES OF FURNITURE — BEDS, CHAIRS, CUPBOARDS, CABINETS, SHRINES, TABLES — HAVE REMAINED WHOLE. THE QUALITY OF THE CABINET WORK IS OFTEN SUPERB. DOUBLE-LEAVED DOORS STILL SWING ON ORIGINAL HINGES: FOLDING WOODEN GRILLS CAN BE MADE TO FOLD. INTACT ARE A WOODEN WINCH AND AN ENTIRE CLOTH PRESS. EVEN TEMPORARY SCAFFOLDS SUPPORTING A SAGGING ROOF HAVE BEEN PRESERVED.

---

a List the items made from wood that have surprisingly survived in Herculaneum.

b What does this extract show about building and crafts in Herculaneum?

c Name five 'ordinary' items found in Pompeii and give their original location.

d What is the value of 'the ordinary' to the historian?

5 Write a one-page summary of the conclusions made about the population of Pompeii and Herculaneum by Sara Bisel and Estelle Lazer in their studies of skeletal remains.

6 Draw a diagram showing the value of Pliny the Elder's *Natural History* as a source of evidence on Pompeii.

7 Draw up a table headed 'The value of Pliny the Younger's 'Letters to Tacitus' as a source of evidence for Pompeii and Herculaneum'. Then divide it into two columns with the following headings:

1 Value as a source

2 Deficiencies as a source.

Use the information in this chapter to fill in the table in point form.

Activities

8 Carefully read this extract from Vitruvius's *De architectura* (VII, 5.1) and answer the questions below.

THE ANCIENTS WHO INAUGURATED THE USE OF WALL
DECORATIONS AT FIRST IMITATED THE VARIEGATED
APPEARANCE AND ARRANGEMENT OF MARBLED STUCCOES . . .
LATER ON, THEY BEGAN TO IMITATE THE SHAPES OF BUILDINGS,
THE PROTRUDING RELIEFS OF COLUMNS AND PEDIMENTS,
TRAGIC, COMIC AND SATIRICAL SCENIC BACKGROUNDS WERE
PAINTED IN OPEN SPACES SUCH AS EXEDRAE, DUE TO THE
ENORMOUS WALL SPACE . . . THESE FIGURATIVE SUBJECTS
WHICH WERE IMPLIED COPIES OF REAL ELEMENTS, TODAY
DESERVE OUR DISAPPROVAL BECAUSE OF THE DIFFUSION
OF A DEPRAVED STYLE. THE WALLS ARE PAINTED WITH
MONSTROSITIES INSTEAD OF PRECISE DEPICTIONS THAT
CONFORM TO WELL-DEFINED OBJECTS: INSTEAD OF COLUMNS
THERE ARE REEDS: INSTEAD OF PEDIMENTS THERE ARE
ORNAMENTAL DESIGNS WITH CURLED AND SPIRAL LEAVES:
THERE ARE CANDELABRAS BEARING IMAGES OF TEMPLES WITH
DELICATE FLOWERS POKING THROUGH THE PEDIMENTS, AS
WELL AS ROOTS COMING UP THROUGH THE VOLUTES AND THE
CENTRES FOR NO REASON, THERE ARE SEATED FIGURES; SMALL
STEMS BEARING FIGURES DIVIDED INTO TWO HALVES, ONE
WITH A HUMAN HEAD, ONE WITH THE HEAD OF AN ANIMAL.
BUT THESE FIGURES DO NOT EXIST, THEY CANNOT EXIST, THEY
HAVE NEVER EXISTED . . . AND YET, PEOPLE SEE THESE
DECEPTIONS AND, INSTEAD OF CRITICISING THEM, ARE
DELIGHTED WITHOUT REFLECTING IF THEY COULD POSSIBLY
EXIST IN REALITY OR NOT.

---

a Who was Vitruvius?

b When did he live?

c Which of the four Pompeian painting styles can be identified from this extract?

d What evidence is there that he preferred the earlier styles rather than the style emerging at the end of the first century BC?

9 Topic for either an extended response, discussion or oral presentation: 'The problems faced by historians in building up a picture of Pompeii and Herculaneum from the surviving archaeological evidence'.

Eruption and the last agonies of Pompeii and Herculaneum

5

THINGS TO CONSIDER

❈ The power and nature of a pyroclastic eruption

❈ The contribution of modern vulcanologists to our understanding of the last days of Pompeii and Herculaneum

❈ The importance of Pliny the Younger as an eyewitness

❈ The study of human remains and artefacts in determining the fate of the inhabitants of the Vesuvian towns

---

In the last few decades, new research in vulcanology and seismology as well as painstaking efforts by archaeologists (structural damage to buildings, the condition of bodies and their location in the various layers of deposits), have provided more insights into the sequence of events, the nature of the eruption and the deposits that destroyed and sealed Pompeii and Herculaneum. This information is vital 'for an understanding of how the archaeological record was created . . . since the nature of the eruption governed what was left behind for archaeologists to dig up.'[1]

❈ **New research in vulcanology**

Also, over the years there has been a scholarly debate on the actual date of the eruption—August or November—based on a possible corruption in the textual history of Pliny the Younger's *Letters*. Figure 5.1 outlines the evidence used by both sides; however, the general consensus at the present time is for 24 August.

❈ **Debate on date of eruption**

WARNING SIGNS

Vesuvius had apparently been dormant for a very long time. According to vulcanologists there is a strong link between the magnitude of an eruption and the preceding period of dormancy and it has been estimated that the thermal energy released during the AD 79 eruption would have been approximately 100,000 times that of the atomic bomb dropped on Hiroshima in 1945. 'Despite Vesuvius' dormancy for at least seven hundred years'[2] modern experts would have been alerted to the warning signs.

❈ **Power of the AD 79 eruption**

The massive earthquake in AD 62, described by Seneca (see Chapter 1), indicated that the volcano was returning to life. Although Pompeii may have been the epicentre of the upheaval, the earthquake 'also disturbed all the

❈ **AD 62 earthquake**

Figure 5.1 Conflicting views on the date of the eruption

Date of eruption	
24 August AD 79	23 November AD 79
An early codex of Pliny's *Letters* gives the date as Nonum Kal. Septembres, i.e. August 24	Later codices read Nonum Kal. Decembres, i.e. November 23
Empty wine vats found at Pompeii and Boscoreale indicate the eruption occurred before the grape harvest	Discovery of late-ripening fruit which had just been picked
A number of bodies were found dressed in what appear to be woollen clothes	
Maybe worn against the impact of falling pumice	Worn against the chill of a November day

adjacent districts'.[3] Part of Herculaneum was completely destroyed, Nuceria reported severe damage, but Neapolis 'was only mildly grazed'.[4] Seneca maintained that although the area had never really been safe from danger, it had never been damaged before and usually 'got off with a fright'.[5] The earthquake struck with a tremendous roar, the ground heaved, wide clefts opened up in the ground and a tsunami rolled across the Bay of Naples.

Seismologists think it unlikely that there was only one quake in the 17 years prior to the eruption. Although there is no literary record of another quake in Pompeii, structural damage in the town points to the possibility of others. Some of the buildings that had been repaired after the 62 disaster were damaged again before 79. Both Tacitus and Suetonius mention an earthquake that caused a theatre in Naples to collapse in AD 64 where the emperor Nero was performing at the time.

Subsequent quakes and tremors �֎

In mid-August AD 79, a series of small tremors began to rock the area again. This was recorded by Pliny the Younger: 'For several days we had experienced earth shocks, which hardly alarmed us as they are frequent in Campania.'[6] The tremors increased in intensity, probably sounding like thunder to the inhabitants of the area around Vesuvius. It was reported that waves off the coast were larger than normal and that animals were exhibiting agitated behaviour as if sensing something happening. It is quite possible that lethal gases with large quantities of suffocating carbon dioxide began collecting in hollows and valleys. These are commonly emitted before an eruption.

Waves, animals and water supplies �֎

Certain springs ceased to flow and some wells completely dried up. The disappearance of the water indicated an increase in the gases in the underground passages running into the volcano's crater and an 'enormous pressure upon the stratum of material which formed its cap'.[7]

THE ERUPTION

The sequence of events used in this chapter follows what seems to be the consensus at the moment, much of it based on the work of eminent vulcanologist Haraldur Sigurdsson. He reconstructed the phases of the eruption by examining the grain sizes in the strata of volcanic material that covered Pompeii and Herculaneum. According to Sigurdsson, 'grain sizes are the fingerprints of an eruption'.[8] He confirmed his findings by drawing on the experiences of people during the eruption of Mount St Helens in 1980, comparing the eyewitness account of Pliny the Younger with his own, and by studying the position and condition of the human remains at Pompeii and Herculaneum.

Only hours before the eruption, a number of small explosions were supposed to have been heard. Vulcanologists would have recognised these as phreatomagmatic explosions, caused when ground water seeping down through the volcano interacted with the hot magma, showering very fine ash over the sides of Vesuvius. It drifted in an easterly direction, leaving a 5-centimetre deposit of ash spread over 20 kilometres. 'Minor steam explosions are typical opening shots in large volcanic eruptions.'[9]

❈ Evidence for eruption phases

❈ Phreatomagmatic explosions

SEQUENCE OF AN ERUPTION

There were two phases of the eruption, separated by a brief lull in the volcano's activity. Figure 5.2 summarises these phases and their effects on Pompeii and Herculaneum.

Figure 5.2 Phases of the eruption

Time	Phase	Place	Description
Late morning to early afternoon 24 August	'Plinian' phase	Vesuvius	An enormous umbrella-shaped eruptive column resembling a pine tree rose 20–30 kilometres into the air. It contained pumice and ash and was carried downwind by the prevailing wind.
		Pompeii 9 km downwind of Vesuvius	Rain of white frothy pumice (phonolitic magma) discharging at 50,000–80,000 tonnes per second accumulating on roof tops and in streets at an average of approx. 15 centimetres per hour. Day turned to night but the people of Pompeii were not in significant danger at this point.
		Herculaneum upwind of Vesuvius	Received only a light dust of ash.
5–6 pm		Pompeii	Pumice accumulated more quickly in some places, 25–30 centimetres an hour. Buildings begin to collapse under the weight of accumulated pumice: some people tried to flee, others took refuge inside houses. Some struck by larger fragments of volcanic rock others by falls of masonry.

Time	Phase	Place	Description
8 pm			Deeper levels of the magma chamber are tapped and magma composition changes to grey pumice (tephritic phonolite) discharged at 150,000 tonnes per second and carried to heights of perhaps 33 kilometres.
Early hours of 25 August	Relative quiet between two phases		A layer of grey ash and pisolites (small round grains of limestone found between the Plinian and surge layer). During this lull, Pompeians probably ventured into the streets but found their way barred by the metres of pumice. See Pliny page 75.
1–2.15 am 25 August	Pyroclastic phase in the form of six surges and flows	Vesuvius	The volcano's eruptive vent began to widen, decreasing the support of the towering column which started to collapse under its own weight generating lethal avalanches of red-hot volcanic debris and gases or pyroclastic surges and flows.
	S1 and S2 (first and second surge)	Herculaneum 5 km from Vesuvius's crater Oplontis and Boscoreale	Herculaneum, which had only a thin layer of pumice covering the ground, was overwhelmed within minutes by the first surge, composed of billowing volcanic ash and superheated gases (about 100–400 degrees C) travelling at about 200 kilometres an hour. The surge blasted through the town, killing most of the people immediately. See page 77. The denser, ground-hugging flow which followed minutes later was composed of larger fragments of volcanic material made fluid by temperatures as high as 400 degrees C. The flow, which moved at speeds of 65–80 kilometres an hour, followed the natural topography and streets in the town. S2 was hotter and more powerful than S1 and was responsible for widespread destruction of buildings as it carried tiles, columns, statues and portions of walls with it. Pompeii was not exposed to S1 and S2.
2.15–6.30 am			Grey pumice fall and column rises again to c.30 kilometres.
6.30–8 am	S3–S6	Pompeii	S3 swept against the north wall of Pompeii, demolishing parts of it. More grey pumice accumulated before the next surge (the city lay buried under three metres). Pompeii was devastated by three more superheated avalanches, S4–6, in short succession, covering the whole town and bringing death by asphyxiation or thermal shock. S6 was the most severe, covering the city with 90–110 centimetres of material and knocking down the walls of the highest buildings. It moved south as far as Stabiae.
		Herculaneum	The town was sealed completely by the impact of the six surges and flows. It lay under 23 metres of hardened volcanic material.

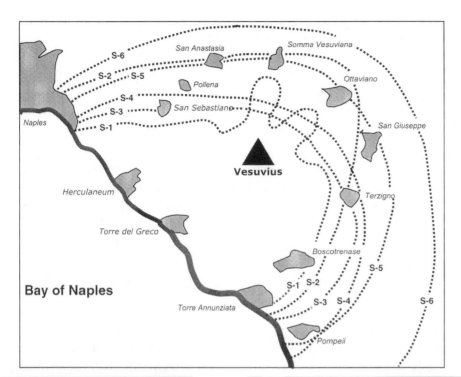

Figure 5.3 Extent of surges 1–6

Figure 5.4 Depth of the pyroclastic flows at Herculaneum. The tree line indicates modern ground level.

Figure 5.5 An umbrella pine tree typical of the Vesuvian area

A PERSONAL ACCOUNT

The first or 'Plinian' phase was described by Pliny the Younger in the following way:

MY UNCLE WAS STATIONED AT MISENUM, IN ACTIVE COMMAND OF THE FLEET. ON AUGUST 24, MY MOTHER DREW HIS ATTENTION TO A CLOUD OF UNUSUAL SIZE AND APPEARANCE . . . ITS GENERAL APPEARANCE CAN BEST BE DESCRIBED AS BEING LIKE AN UMBRELLA PINE, FOR IT ROSE TO A GREAT HEIGHT ON A SORT OF TRUNK AND THEN SPLIT OFF INTO BRANCHES, I IMAGINE BECAUSE IT WAS THRUST UPWARDS BY THE FIRST

⊗
The pine-shaped cloud

BLAST AND THEN LEFT UNSUPPORTED AS THE PRESSURE SUBSIDED, OR
ELSE IT WAS BORN DOWN BY ITS OWN WEIGHT SO THAT IT SPREAD OUT
AND GRADUALLY DISPERSED. SOMETIMES IT LOOKED WHITE, SOMETIMES
BLOTCHED AND DIRTY, ACCORDING TO THE AMOUNT OF SOIL AND ASHES
CARRIED WITH IT.[10]

❈
Impact of eruption
at Stabiae

The remainder of Pliny's first letter to Tacitus was derived from the
accounts of survivors who had been with his uncle. Pliny the Elder had taken
his ship and crossed the bay from Misenum to see at first hand what was happening and to rescue Rectina, possibly at Herculaneum. He was unable to land
and continued on to Stabiae where 'ashes were already falling, hotter and
thicker . . . followed by bits of pumice and blackened stones, charred and
cracked by the flames . . . the shore was blocked by debris from the mountain.'[11] He managed to land, and during the night, from the home of his friend
Pomponianus, he and his party noticed 'broad sheets of fire and leaping
flames'[12] blazing at several points on Mount Vesuvius. The courtyard filled
'with ash and pumice stones' and the buildings shook 'with violent shocks, and
seemed to be swaying to and fro as if they were torn from their foundations'.[13]
Light pumice continued to fall. By morning, although they were still in darkness, they braved the falling pumice and went down to the shore to investigate
the possibility of escape by sea. It was then they saw the flames and smelled
the sulphur which they believed 'gave warning of the approaching fire'.[14]

❈
Impact of eruption
at Misenum

On the other side of the bay at Misenum, Pliny the Younger had experienced
the same quakes during the night. 'That night the shocks were so violent that
everything felt as if it were not only shaken, but overturned.'[15] In the early morning, the sea appeared to have been 'sucked away and apparently forced back by the
earthquake' so that 'quantities of sea creatures were left stranded on dry sand'.[16]
Like those at Stabiae, he saw a 'fearful black cloud . . . rent by forked and quiver-
ing bursts of flame' which, a little while later, 'sank to earth and covered the sea'.[17]
What he was reporting was probably one of the final surges, possibly S6, which
reached as far as Stabiae. However, 'the flames remained some distance off; then
darkness came on once more and ashes began to fall again, this time in heavy
showers'.[18] This final fall may have been that which accompanied the caldera
collapse and the phreatomagmatic activity (volcanic explosion created by heating
of underground water) after S6 at about 8 am on the morning of 25 August.

CONFUSION, TERROR AND DEATH

According to Dio Cassius, in their confusion and terror

PEOPLE FLED: SOME FROM THE HOUSES INTO THE STREETS, OTHERS FROM
OUTSIDE INTO THE HOUSES, SOME FROM THE SEA TO THE LAND AND

SOME FROM THE LAND TO THE SEA; FOR IN THEIR PANIC THEY REGARDED
ANY PLACE WHERE THEY WERE NOT, AS SAFER THAN WHERE WERE.[19]

Pliny's account indicates that many inhabitants sought to escape by sea
during the first phases of the eruption. For example, his uncle received 'a message from Rectina, wife of Cascus, whose house was at the foot of the
mountain [possibly Herculaneum], so that escape was impossible except by
boat. She was terrified of the danger threatening her and implored him to rescue her from her fate.'[20] When he realised the seriousness of the situation, he
decided to help evacuate many more people besides Rectina, for the 'coast was
thickly populated'.[21] However, the sea was already blocked by debris and he
sailed towards Stabiae, the closest port to Pompeii. His friend Pomponianus
was already loading 'his belongings on board ship intending to escape if the
contrary wind fell'.[22] Pomponianus was terrified, but it appears that Pliny the
Elder was quite composed at that time, or at least he appeared so to those
around him and behaved quite normally. He took a bath in Pomponianus's
villa, 'lay down and dined; he was quite cheerful'.[23] At Misenum, on the far
side of the bay, his nephew and sister were not yet aware of the disastrous
nature of the eruption, despite the frequent shocks.

In Pompeii, it seems that many read the early signs and fled, revealed by
the absence of horses or other beasts of burden, apparently all mobilised for
escape. In front of the tradesmen's entrance of the House of Menander, a cart
packed with wine jars was left behind. It appears that at the last moment the
animals had been harnessed and ridden away. Those who left at the first
pumice fall may have had time to cover some kilometres. However, by head-
ing south away from the volcano, they would have been impeded by the
constant fallout downwind, the darkness and earth tremors. Forty-eight bodies were excavated outside the town walls in the direction of the harbour.

Some appear to have ignored the warnings or decided to wait it out. The
following examples of motivation and behaviour are conjectural.

- A family group seems to have decided to visit the cemetery to honour the
  anniversary of the death of one of its members. As they held the custom-
  ary banquet in the beautiful painted chapel of the tomb, ash and pumice
  blocked up the bronze door, sealing them in with the dead.
- Based on the position of the bodies of a group of priests and sacred artefacts found nearby, it has been suggested that when the eruption began, the
  priests from the Temple of Isis were eating a meal of fish and eggs.
  Apparently they did not hurry to escape but thought it more important to
  gather up the objects associated with the worship of the goddess. They
  threw statuettes, plates and vessels into a cloth sack and together made
  their escape. As the priests were crossing the Triangular Forum, a row of
  columns toppled over, crushing a number of them and scattering the holy
  objects. Those who escaped appear to have found shelter in a nearby house,

✖
Attempts to
escape by sea

✖
Pliny the Elder's
composure

✖
Early escape
from Pompeii

✖
Those who
chose to stay

Figure 5.6 Evidence of an attempt to escape from pumice build-up around the House of Menander

✴
Material possessions a priority for some

✴
Some with no choice

✴
The fate of those who fled too late

but were trapped by the steadily rising layer of ash and pumice. One of the priests, in his desperation, perhaps grabbed an axe in the hope of smashing his way out. Unfortunately he was confronted by a solid wall and so died in the act of wielding his hatchet.

- A steward, responsible for his master's buildings and slaves, appears to have ordered the slaves to remain in their rooms until the danger was over. However, when the ash had built up to a considerable height, he seems to have changed his mind, telling them to make their escape from either the upper storey or the roof of the house, but ten of them perished between the stairs and the door, including one with a bronze lantern. Someone tried unsuccessfully to hack a hole in the wall of one of the rooms. The steward locked himself and his small daughter in his room by the entrance to the house still holding the objects of authority entrusted to him by his master—his seal and household purse, containing two gold coins, 90 silver and 13 of brass and copper. He covered himself and his daughter with cushions and there waited stoically for death.

- In a house attached to a tavern, all the occupants went down to the vault and appear to have prepared themselves for a long stay by taking bread, fruit and a goat with them, but they never emerged. In the villa believed to have been owned by Diomedes just outside the walls of Pompeii, 18 people were found dead in a cellar, among them two boys locked in each others' arms.

Some of the wealthy inhabitants of Pompeii appear to have delayed their departure by first collecting, hiding or protecting valuable objects. The mistress of the House of Sallust had apparently instructed her maids to collect her valuables before leaving, but they took too long. She and her three maids died with her jewellery, money and a silver mirror strewn around them. In the House of Pansa, a valuable piece of sculpture was placed for safety in a copper kettle in the garden while in the House of the Ephebe, a statue was removed from the garden and placed in the atrium covered with a cloth.

Not all Pompeians had a choice; some were forced to remain. Of the sixty gladiators who died in the barracks, two of them, manacled by the wrists, were locked up in a prison cell.

Many of those who preferred to take their chances out in the open found it difficult to move through the ever-rising layer of ash and pumice. Members of a whole family were asphyxiated as they opened the window of their home to escape. A mother with a baby clasped to her breast and two small girls hanging on to her robe were struck down as they headed for the city gates; a pregnant woman, unable to move quickly enough, died near several young women who had divested themselves of their clothes so that they could run more easily; a man died as he struggled to drag a goat with a bell attached to its collar, and a well-built servant fell as he struggled to stay upright and help his young mistress through the rain of ashes.

Figure 5.7 Pompeian victims (the Garden of the Fugitives)

Family pets were left behind. One dog, chained in the atrium of the House of Vesonius Primus, climbed as high as his tether would allow as the ash and pumice poured through the central opening in the roof until it died. In the house of the Vestal Virgins a man and his dog perished, but not before the hungry animal gnawed at its master's body.

Of the people of Herculaneum who had not already escaped, many were waiting near the beach as the first surge of toxic superheated gases, saturated with ash, blasted into the town with the force of a hurricane. Terrified family groups

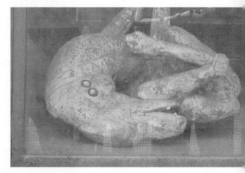

Figure 5.8 Cast of a dog in the throes of death

✻
On the beach at Herculaneum

died as they cowered at the back of boat chambers, huddled together for protection, and several people waiting on the beach were flattened by the force. One of the most graphic examples of the power of the surge was the body of a woman with a smashed skull, crushed pelvis and a thigh bone thrust up to her collar bone, lying on top of a few house tiles. She must have been thrown onto the beach from a great distance. The suddenness of the surge prevented parents rescuing a baby from its cradle and a sickly bed-bound boy from his bed. The charred remains of both were discovered, with the chicken lunch still on a table beside the sick boy's bed. Those who died during the surge were entombed by the flow shortly after. Two skeletons were found 7.5 metres above the level of the ancient street, forced up by the half-liquid mass (see Chapter 4).

✻
Those left behind at Herculaneum

Back at Stabiae, Pliny the Elder slept in the home of his friend Pomponianus, unaware of what had happened in Pompeii and Herculaneum.

✻
Conditions at Stabiae

'Then he went to rest and certainly slept, for he was a stout man, his breathing was rather loud and heavy and could be heard by people coming and going outside his door.'[24] Had he not been awakened by the others who had stayed awake throughout the night 'he never would have got out'.[25] Although it was early morning, 'they were still in darkness, blacker and denser than any ordinary night'.[26] They decided it was safer to stay out of doors and covered their heads with pillows as they made their way, by torch and lamplight, down to the shore. In Misenum, Pliny the Younger had a restless night due to the earth tremors and he and his terrified mother decided to sit in the open courtyard, he reading a book in the 'still faint and uncertain' light,[27] unaware of his uncle's plight.

✠ **The death of Pliny the Elder**

At the sea front at Stabiae, Pliny the Elder ordered a sheet to be placed on the ground so that he could lie down; the bay was far too rough to board ship. He was obviously suffering 'as he called repeatedly for cold water'[28] and found it difficult to stand when it was decided to take flight. He 'struggled to his feet, leaning on two slaves, but immediately collapsed . . . His breathing was impeded by the dense fumes, which blocked his windpipe—for it was constitutionally weak and narrow, and often inflamed.'[29] He died on the beach, 'looking more like a sleeper than a dead man'.[30]

✠ **Panic at Misenum**

At Misenum, Pliny the Younger was urged by a friend of his uncle to leave the town just before the final surge spread out across the bay. As he recounted to Tacitus, 'the panic-stricken crowds followed us, in response to that instinct of fear which causes people to follow where others lead.'[31] Behind them loomed a terrible black cloud, and when it began to descend over the sea, his corpulent mother begged him to escape and leave her behind, but he took her hand and 'hurried her along'.[32]

Figure 5.9 Victims crowded into the entrance of a waterfront chamber in Herculaneum

'LET'S GO INTO THE FIELDS WHILE WE CAN STILL SEE THE WAY,' I TOLD
MY MOTHER—FOR I WAS AFRAID THAT WE MIGHT BE CRUSHED BY THE
MOB ON THE ROAD IN THE MIDST OF THE DARKNESS . . . TO BE HEARD
WERE ONLY THE SHRILL CRIES OF WOMEN, THE WAILING OF CHILDREN,
THE SHOUTING OF MEN. SOME WERE CALLING TO THEIR PARENTS,
OTHERS TO THEIR CHILDREN, OTHERS TO THEIR WIVES—KNOWING ONE
ANOTHER ONLY BY VOICE. SOME WEPT FOR THEMSELVES, OTHERS FOR
THEIR RELATIONS. THERE WERE THOSE, WHO, IN THEIR VERY FEAR OF
DEATH, INVOKED IT. MANY LIFTED UP THEIR HANDS TO THE GODS, BUT A
GREAT NUMBER BELIEVED THERE WERE NO GODS, AND THAT THIS WAS
TO BE THE WORLD'S LAST, ETERNAL NIGHT . . . FINALLY A GENUINE
DAYLIGHT CAME; THE SUN SHONE, BUT PALLIDLY, AS IN AN ECLIPSE. AND
THEN, BEFORE OUR TERROR-STRICKEN GAZE EVERYTHING APPEARED
CHANGED—COVERED BY A THICK LAYER OF ASHES LIKE AN ABUNDANT
SNOWFALL.[33]

Scholars have found it impossible to estimate the number who died
during 24–25 August. Evidence from the pyroclastic eruption of Mount St
Helens in 1980 revealed that most of the victims died of asphyxiation and
thermal shock within a matter of two minutes of the surge. Their upper res-
piratory tracts were 'blocked by a plug of mucous and ash' or else their bodies
'were baked by the intense heat'.[34] It is likely that this was also the cause of
most of the deaths in Pompeii and Herculaneum, but not everyone died this
way. Others were:

❈
Causes of death

- sealed in rooms by the rising level of ash and pumice
- crushed under fallen masonry and struck down by projectiles carried in the
  surge clouds
- trampled to death in the pitch darkness
- drowned in the tumultuous seas.

IT IS A DISTURBING SIGHT, TO ENCOUNTER THESE BODIES TORMENTED
WITH SUFFERING, ANGUISH AND FEAR, AND PETRIFIED BY SUFFOCATION
IN THEIR APPALLING POSTURES, EACH OF WHICH REVEALS THE PANGS OF
AN AGONY INDIVIDUALLY LIVED THROUGH, THE HORROR OF A DEATH
SWIFT OR SLOW AS THE CASE VARIED, BUT INEXORABLE.[35]

Chapter review

The eruption, AD 79

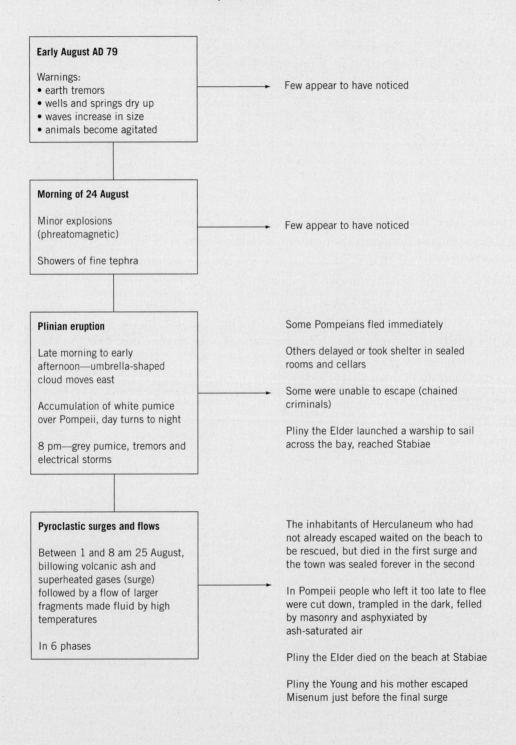

Early August AD 79

Warnings:
- earth tremors
- wells and springs dry up
- waves increase in size
- animals become agitated

→ Few appear to have noticed

Morning of 24 August

Minor explosions (phreatomagnetic)

Showers of fine tephra

→ Few appear to have noticed

Plinian eruption

Late morning to early afternoon—umbrella-shaped cloud moves east

Accumulation of white pumice over Pompeii, day turns to night

8 pm—grey pumice, tremors and electrical storms

Some Pompeians fled immediately

Others delayed or took shelter in sealed rooms and cellars

→ Some were unable to escape (chained criminals)

Pliny the Elder launched a warship to sail across the bay, reached Stabiae

Pyroclastic surges and flows

Between 1 and 8 am 25 August, billowing volcanic ash and superheated gases (surge) followed by a flow of larger fragments made fluid by high temperatures

In 6 phases

The inhabitants of Herculaneum who had not already escaped waited on the beach to be rescued, but died in the first surge and the town was sealed forever in the second

→ In Pompeii people who left it too late to flee were cut down, trampled in the dark, felled by masonry and asphyxiated by ash-saturated air

Pliny the Elder died on the beach at Stabiae

Pliny the Young and his mother escaped Misenum just before the final surge

Activities

1 Read the full text of Pliny the Younger's letters to Tacitus (6.16 and 6. 20) in *Pliny's Letters* (Penguin) and compare his account of the eruption with that of Dio Cassius (below) written over 100 years later. Then answer the following questions.

THIS IS WHAT BEFELL. NUMBERS OF HUGE MEN QUITE SURPASSING ANY HUMAN STATURE — SUCH CREATURES, IN FACT, AS THE GIANTS ARE PICTURED TO HAVE BEEN — APPEARED NOW IN THE MOUNTAIN, NOW IN THE SURROUNDING COUNTRY, AND AGAIN IN THE CITIES, WANDERING OVER THE EARTH DAY AND NIGHT AND ALSO FLITTING THROUGH THE AIR. AFTER THIS, FEARFUL DROUGHTS AND SUDDEN AND VIOLENT EARTHQUAKES OCCURRED, SO THAT THE WHOLE PLAIN ROUND ABOUT SEETHED AND THE SUMMITS LEAPED INTO THE AIR. THERE WERE FREQUENT RUMBLINGS, SOME OF THEM SUBTERRANEAN, THAT RESEMBLED THUNDER, AND SOME ON THE SURFACE, THAT SOUNDED LIKE BELLOWINGS; THE SEA ALSO JOINED IN THE ROAR AND THE SKY RE-ECHOED IT. THEN SUDDENLY A PORTENTOUS CRASH WAS HEARD, AS IF THE MOUNTAINS WERE TUMBLING IN RUINS; AND THE FIRST HUGE STONES WERE HURLED ALOFT, RISING AS HIGH AS THE VERY SUMMITS, THEN CAME A GREAT QUANTITY OF FIRE AND ENDLESS SMOKE, SO THAT THE WHOLE ATMOSPHERE WAS OBSCURED AND THE SUN WAS ENTIRELY HIDDEN, AS IF ECLIPSED. THUS DAY WAS TURNED INTO NIGHT AND LIGHT INTO DARKNESS. SOME THOUGHT THAT THE GIANTS WERE RISING AGAIN IN REVOLT
. . . WHILE OTHERS BELIEVED THAT THE WHOLE UNIVERSE WAS BEING RESOLVED INTO CHAOS AND FIRE. THEREFORE THEY FLED, SOME FROM THE HOUSES INTO THE STREETS, OTHERS FROM OUTSIDE INTO THE HOUSES, NOW FROM THE SEA TO THE LAND AND NOW FROM THE LAND TO THE SEA; FOR IN THEIR EXCITEMENT THEY REGARDED ANY PLACE WHERE THEY WERE NOT AS SAFER THAN WHERE THEY WERE. WHILE THIS WAS GOING ON, AN INCONCEIVABLE QUANTITY OF ASHES WAS BLOWN OUT, WHICH COVERED BOTH SEA AND LAND AND FILLED ALL THE AIR. IT WROUGHT MUCH INJURY OF VARIOUS KINDS, AS CHANCE BEFELL, TO MEN AND FARMS AND CATTLE, AND IN PARTICULAR IT DESTROYED ALL FISH AND BIRDS. FURTHERMORE IT BURIED TWO ENTIRE CITIES, HERCULANEUM AND POMPEII, THE LATTER PLACE WHILE ITS POPULACE WAS SEATED IN THE THEATRE. INDEED THE AMOUNT OF DUST, TAKEN ALL TOGETHER, WAS SO GREAT THAT SOME OF ITS REACHED AFRICA AND SYRIA AND EGYPT, AND IT ALSO REACHED ROME, FILLING THE AIR OVERHEAD AND DARKENING THE SUN. THERE TOO, NO LITTLE FEAR WAS OCCASIONED, THAT LASTED FOR SEVERAL DAYS, SINCE THE PEOPLE DID NOT KNOW AND COULD NOT IMAGINE WHAT HAD HAPPENED, BUT LIKE THOSE CLOSE AT HAND, BELIEVED THAT THE WHOLE WORLD WAS BEING TURNED UPSIDE DOWN, THAT THE SUN WAS DISAPPEARING INTO THE EARTH AND THAT THE EARTH WAS BEING LIFTED TO THE SKY.[36]

a Make a list of the facts that agree with Pliny's account.

b What facts does Dio Cassius provide that Pliny doesn't?

c Write out the sentences that indicate Dio Cassius's penchant for the supernatural and fantastic.

d What fact seems less than credible?

e As Dio Cassius's account was written so long after the event, what would a historian like to know?

2 a What do Figures 5.3 and 5.10 reveal about the methods used by vulcanologists to gain an understanding of the various phases of an eruption?

b What other evidence did vulcanologists use to build up a picture of the AD 79 eruption?

c Use Figure 5.10 to summarise what happened in Stages 1 and 2.

d Why was the initial phase referred to as a Plinian blast?

Activities

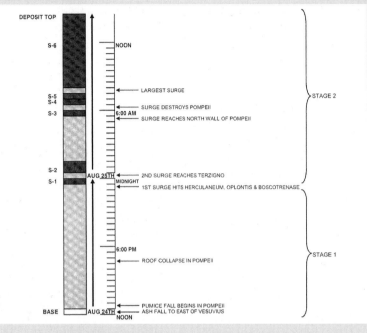

Figure 5.10 Volcanic deposits based on the studies of Carey & Sigurdsson 1987

3 Use the information in Pliny's first letter to Tacitus to complete the following activity.

a Make an enlarged copy of Figure 5.11 and write in the names of the towns marked on the map.

b Beside each place, write a short note using the information provided by Pliny the Younger.

c Draw in the approximate route taken by Pliny across the bay.

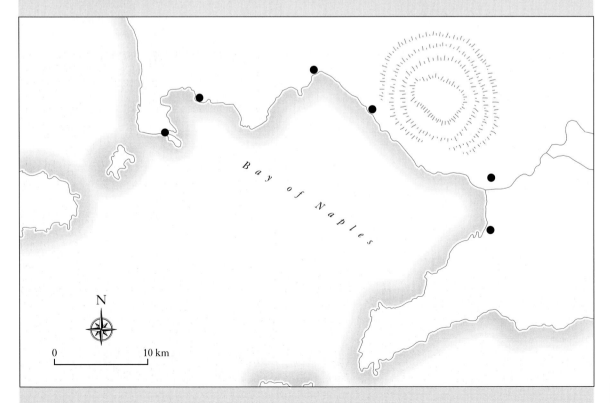

Figure 5.11

Activities

4 **a** What was the significance of the vaulted entrances in the sea wall at Herculaneum to excavators and scientists?

b Explain why the excavated streets of Herculaneum are so much lower than the street level in the modern village of Resina.

c Find two pieces of evidence in the text which illustrate the power of the surges in Herculaneum.

5 Facts derived from recent work on the death of the inhabitants of Pompeii.

* Find spots of bodies: 394 bodies found in the initial pumice layer, and about 650 bodies found in the ash layer resulting from the surges.
* Generally those bodies in the pumice layer were within private buildings.
* Far more of the latter were found in the streets, open spaces or near the town gates.

a What do these reveal about the reaction of many Pompeians in the first 12 hours of the eruption?

b What do these facts and the agony of the man captured forever in plaster reveal about the reaction and deaths of those on the morning of 25 August.

c How did Pliny the Elder die five kilometres away at Stabiae?

6 Use the second letter to Tacitus to write a paragraph each about the reactions to the disaster of:
a Pliny the Younger
b Pliny's mother
c the people of Misenum

7 Internet research:
Try to view the 2003 BBC TV documentary 'Pompeii: The Last Day' or read Robert Harris's 2003 novel *Pompeii*. Even if this is impossible, research the internet for newspaper and scholarly reviews on both productions, write a report on the views and conclusions, including a personal evaluation of their suitability as sources for a study of Pompeii.

Figure 5.12 The ancient seafront of Herculaneum

Figure 5.13 Comparison of ancient and modern ground levels at Herculaneum

Social structure, economy and politics

THINGS TO CONSIDER

- The servile origin of much of Pompeii's population
- The mutual dependence of slave, freed and freeborn
- The degree of social and economic emancipation of women
- The Forum as the heart of the city
- The importance of agricultural production and fishing as the basis of the economy
- The proportion of shops, workshops, bars and hotels to population
- The intensity of political interest and competition for office

POPULATION AND SOCIAL STRUCTURE

Conjecture about population size

Although it is extremely difficult to estimate the population size of ancient towns, some authors insist on giving definitive figures, such as '20,000 of which 8000 were slaves . . . and 4200 were adults'.[1] In the 19th century, the director of the site, Giuseppe Fiorelli, estimated a figure of 12,000 for Pompeii, and since his day the figures have fluctuated, with some modern scholars tending towards a lower estimate of 6400–6700. The figure most often quoted is 8–10,000 and this 'may not be unrealistic' based on the 800 houses so far excavated and the fact that 'at least on average, the Pompeian familia must have been considerably larger than the modern household based on the nuclear family'.[2] It is even harder to estimate the population of Herculaneum as only four blocks of the town have been completely excavated. Five thousand has been suggested, apparently based on the seating capacity of the theatre.

SOCIAL DIVISIONS

Three main groups in society

Servile origin of majority

The population was divided into three broad categories: slaves, those freed from slavery, and freeborn. It appears from the existing documentary evidence from Campanian towns that a large proportion of the population of Pompeii was likely to have been of servile origin, creating an obvious ethnic and genetic diversity in the relatively small total number.

Slavery played a significant role in Roman society. Slaves, through capture and auction, or as the offspring of a slave mother, belonged solely to their master. Large numbers were employed in upper-class households as washers, oven-stokers, servers, cooks, entertainers, nurses, tutors, clerks and secretaries, and on agricultural estates tending vines, picking grapes, plough-ing, harvesting and hay-making. Within the slave population there was an obvious social hierarchy. From the evidence of a prison cell and stocks found in the Villa of Agrippa Postumus at Boscotrecase, and an iron block to which slaves were chained, found in a room in the Villa Regina at Boscoreale, those on estates tended to be treated more harshly. Within the urban household there was a great difference in status between a server or oven-stoker for example, and a *dispensator*, who controlled his master's funds, or the *cellarius* who controlled the food supplies. Male slaves with an education were highly privileged. A female slave was not permitted to marry and if she had any off-spring, they followed—according to Roman law—the condition of their mother and so belonged to her owner.

✸ Household and estate slaves

✸ Hierarchy within slave population

Slaves could be manumitted (granted their freedom) by their masters, or could save up enough money themselves to buy their liberty, although in that case they had to pay a freedom tax equal to 5 per cent of their assessed valu-ation. They were then permitted to assume their master's name (see the case of Petronia Justa on page 85).

✸ Manumission

The numbers of freed slaves (male—*libertus* and female—*liberta*) increased during the 1st century AD, with many becoming wealthy and influ-ential even within the imperial household. In Pompeii, the bulk of freed men and women were associated with crafts, trade and commerce. The small shops, workshops, bars and taverns built into the facades of many dignified residences were often run by the freed dependants of the owner of the house. Wives of freedmen helped their husbands in businesses such as bakeries; others ran their own enterprises such as brothels and inns and became quite wealthy. The number of working women in Pompeii appears to have been reasonably high. Figure 6.1 shows some of the occupations of Pompeian women.

✸ Freedmen and small businesses

The luxury of houses owned by many freedmen, such as the brothers Vettii, rivalled those of the Pompeian elite. According to Wallace-Hadrill, wealthy freedmen 'imitated the cultural language of the nobility in order to establish their membership in that society'.[3] Cicero and Pliny the Elder crit-icised the tendency of the rich, successful freedman 'to ape the aristocracy'[4] but blamed the elite and their excesses for setting the example for the lower orders.

✸ Imitation of elite

A *libertinus* was free in all ways, but tended to remain tied to his or her former master in a relationship of gratitude and loyalty, performing services for their patron. Many of them contributed to public life and their children intermarried with freeborn families.

✸ Ties to former masters

Ingenui, like freedmen, ranged from the most humble (*plebs humilus*),

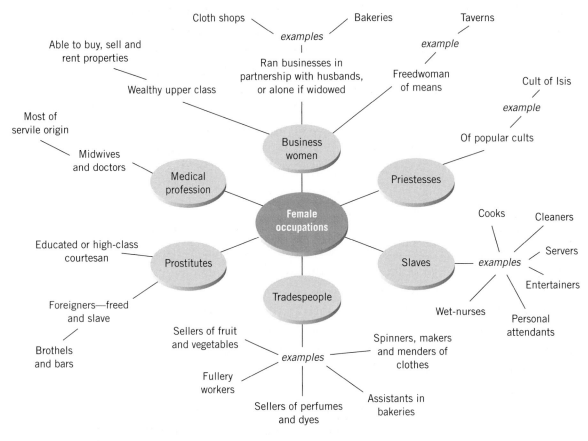

Figure 6.1 Occupations of Pompeian women

✖
Freeborn

✖
Commerce as
a leveller

✖
Patron/client
relationship

✖
Boundaries
between groups
sometimes fluid

through to what Pliny referred to as the *plebs media*, those who were rich, but outside the elite. Like the majority of freedmen, many of these (both men and women) were engaged in some form of commerce. 'Trade served as a leveller' in society.'⁵ Even the elite were concerned with selling the agricultural produce of their country estates and renting parts of their town houses to small businessmen. Women in this group were 'psychologically and socially emancipated over all'⁶ and some were extremely rich. The male members of the upper level of Pompeian and Herculanean society had a network of social ties with friends (*amici*), clients (*clientele*) and dependants, both freeborn and freed, whom they advised, and whose interests they looked after both publicly and privately. As prospective candidates for office, they depended on these groups for political support. The social standing of the members of the elite was enhanced by the number of people who sought them out as patron in their houses during the morning *salutatio*.

The boundaries between slave, manumitted slave and freeborn were often exceedingly fluid. An example of this comes from one of the dossiers that make up the Herculaneum tablets (wax tablets). It concerns a court case centring on the household of Gaius Petronius Stephanus, a member of the *plebs media* who had married a freedwoman named Calactoria Themis. A slave woman within the household, named Vitalis, was manumitted and, as a freedwoman, adopted the name of her former master and was known as Petronia Vitalis. She gave birth to a daughter named Justa, whose father, if known, was not acknowledged. Mother and child remained in the household for over 10 years and the child was brought up like a daughter by the master and his wife. However, when they had children of their own, there was considerable disharmony within the household and Petronia Vitalis decided to leave and set a up a home of her own. Petronius and his wife would not relinquish the girl, as she was intelligent and pretty and so an asset to the household. Her mother, who did very well for herself, eventually brought a suit against her former master and was granted custody of her daughter as long as she reimbursed Petronius Stephanus for the girl's upkeep. This she did, and over the years Petronia Vitalis appears to have amassed a considerable fortune. When she died, followed soon after by Petronius Stephanus, the widow, Calactoria, brought a suit to recover Justa and all the property she had inherited from her mother, on the grounds that Justa was born while her mother was still a slave, prior to her manumission. Because no substantiating documents existed for both sides, the case, which went to Rome several times, was still ongoing when Vesuvius erupted.

✖
Slave or free?

Despite the economic interdependence by which slave and freedman shared in the fortunes of their masters, there were some who were outside the network, such as beggars. The following graffito suggests how some people might have regarded these people: 'I detest beggars.'[7] On the other hand, there are paintings depicting wealthy people offering a beggar, or a handicapped person, a coin or a piece of bread.

✖
Beggars

SOME PROMINENT MEMBERS OF POMPEIAN AND HERCULANEAN SOCIETY

Two well-known businessmen in Pompeii were Marcus Umbricius Scaurus (see page 93) and Marcus Caecilius Jucundus (see page 99). A notable women from a prominent Pompeian family was Poppaea Sabina, who became the town's favourite daughter when she married the emperor Nero. She owned a luxurious villa at nearby Oplontis and members of her family are believed to have owned two magnificent mansions in Pompeii: the House of Menander and the House of the Golden Cupids. Another woman of great standing was the priestess and business woman Eumachia, born into the prominent Eumachii who owned vineyards and brickworks. She played a part in municipal affairs and became the patron of the Fuller's Guild when she dedicated a magnificent building in the Forum. Julia Felix was a business woman of economic independence. She inherited landholdings and a magnificent house in

Figure 6.2 Eumachia, a prominent Pompeian businesswoman/priestess (Naples National Archaeological Museum)

✼

Notable Pompeian
women

✼

A leading citizen
of Herculaneum

Pompeii that took up a whole *insula*. At some late stage, possibly after the earthquake of AD 62, she turned part of her home into public baths, shops and a bar and rented them out.

Two of Herculaneum's leading citizens were Marcus Calatorius, whose bronze statue stood in the theatre among those of emperors and empresses, and Marcus Nonius Balbus, in whose honour at least ten statues were erected at important sites around the town. Balbus was Proconsul of Crete and Cyrenaica (a Roman possession in North Africa) and his family appear to have been the richest and most influential in Herculaneum. He and his son, Marcus junior, were depicted in magnificent marble equestrian statues that flanked the entrance to the Herculaneum basilica, and the portrait statues of the rest of his family—mother Viciria, wife Volasennia, and two daughters probably named Nonia the Elder and Nonia the Younger—stood inside. From the evidence it is believed that the family owned the large house on the seaward side of the town, the House of the Relief of Telephus, which was connected by a staircase and two ramps to the magnificent Suburban Baths. Also a statue placed in a sacred area adjacent to the baths indicates that Balbus was the donor of the baths, and a memorial inscription in the same location records that he had, at his own expense, 'restored the Basilica, gates, and walls of the town (after the great earthquake); he had born the expense of the youth games; he had aided in the erection of a statue of the Emperor Vespasian; and an equestrian statue had been erected in his honour.'[8]

THE FORUM—CENTRE OF COMMERCIAL AND POLITICAL LIFE

✼

The ideal
Italian forum

The heart of commercial and political activities in Pompeii and Herculaneum was the Forum and its adjacent streets. According to Vitruvius in his treatise on architecture, Italian fora should not be constructed like the Greek agora 'because our ancestors handed down to us the custom of holding gladiatorial combats there; the columns must therefore be more widely spaced to allow a good view' and 'the width will be two-thirds of the length, the shape thus being rectangular, a more convenient proportion for shows.' He also directed how it should be built to make the transaction of business more convenient: 'Under the porticoes, the money-changers' stalls, and above, galleries'. The dimensions had to 'be proportionate to the size of the population, otherwise there will be a shortage of space, or the forum, too scantily filled, will look empty. The columns of the upper storey will be one-third less in height than those below, which being more heavily laden must be stronger.'[9]

The Pompeian Forum—a rectangular paved area 40 metres wide and 150 metres long, surrounded by a double colonnaded portico in white limestone,

Figure 6.3 View across the Forum to the Temple of the Capitoline Triad

Figure 6.4 Main road (decamanus major) of Herculaneum leading to the unexcavated Forum

Figure 6.5 Rectangular blocks to stop access of wheeled vehicles into the Forum

Figure 6.6 The Forum end of the main east-west thoroughfare of Pompeii (modern name: Via dell'Abbondanza)

featuring about forty statues of leading citizens and the imperial family, did not adhere exactly to Vitruvius's injunctions. It underwent a number of modifications during the town's history and at the time of the eruption, according to the latest evidence, was undergoing a comprehensive, vigorous and ambitious post-earthquake restoration. The Herculaneum Forum is, unfortunately, still buried under the town of Resina and the main artery leading to it has only been uncovered for a short stretch of its length.

Pompeii's chief meeting and trading centre was located where the main roads from Naples, Nola and Stabiae met, but it was closed to wheeled traffic. Access was barred by large rectangular blocks fitted solidly in the ground. There is also evidence that the area could be closed off by grilled gates during certain events. The deep wheel ruts worn into the volcanic stone blocks, used to pave the surrounding roads, attest to the amount of traffic focused on the Forum, particularly along the main business thoroughfare leading to it (the Street of Abundance: its modern name). Vehicles for the transportation of goods were quite solid judging from the remains of one in the Villa Regina in Boscoreale. They generally had two wheels—although a four-wheeled one was found at Stabiae—a wooden top and side panels, and were pulled by oxen or mules. A vehicle for transporting passengers, found in the House of Menander, was a gig with two high wheels, pulled by a horse. Its axle would have had had no trouble clearing the pedestrian crossings designed to protect

88
Modifications to Pompeian Forum over time

88
Adjacent streets, traffic and drainage

Figure 6.7 (left)
Stepping stones

Figure 6.8 Wheel
ruts caused by
constant traffic
near the Forum

the inhabitants from getting their feet wet. Except for a network of drains in the Forum, drainage water flowed down the streets to an outlet outside the walls. Herculaneum had no need of raised crossings as the town had an excellent drainage system.

❧

The bustle
of the Forum

On any day of the week, but particularly market day, the Forum and surrounding streets would have been filled with the lively bustle of shopkeepers and stall-holders, merchants, money-changers, customers, teachers and students, people wishing to pick up news or hear the latest gossip, as well as

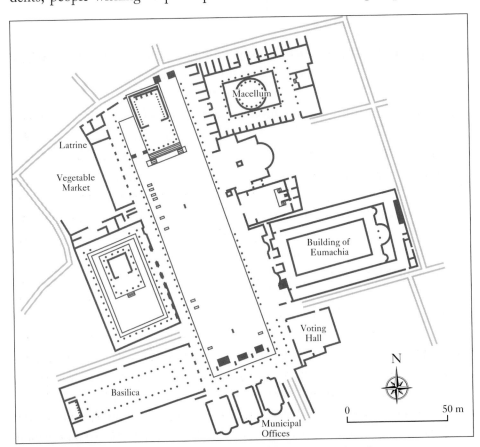

Figure 6.9 The buildings of the Pompeian Forum associated with business and commerce

those attending the law courts or holding political office. A frieze in the house of Julia Felix, depicting aspects of life in the Forum, is a valuable archaeological document.

Strange as it may seem to modern visitors who admire the white marble and tufa, the Forum buildings, roofed in red terracotta tiles, were brightly coloured, as were the statues that surrounded them, but unlike modern city dwellers, who deplore the defacing of public buildings, the Pompeian people covered the Forum walls, particularly the Basilica, with painted notices 'in vivid colours and large letters, the better to draw attention'.[10]

The labelled plan in Figure 6.9 shows the main Pompeian Forum buildings and their functions, which will be discussed later in the appropriate section of the text.

Colour and painted notices

COMMERCIAL LIFE

All the evidence points to Pompeii, unlike the quieter fishing/resort town of Herculaneum, being a bustling commercial centre in the years before its destruction, a town where making a profit and accumulating wealth was regarded as being favoured by the gods. Some of this evidence includes:

- the high number—about 600 so far excavated—of privately owned shops, workshops, bars and inns
- the city-controlled markets around the Forum
- the epigraphic evidence of the number of guilds of tradesmen and retailers
- the twenty or so maritime warehouses containing objects characteristic of a port area and buildings lined with wine jars
- paintings of cargo boats on the Sarno and porters carrying products to be loaded onto the vessels
- trade signs depicting various manufacturing processes
- inscriptions on walls and floors of houses and workshops paying tribute to the pursuit of profit: 'Profit is Joy' found in the mosaic entrance way of two wealthy men, Siricus and Numerianus; 'Welcome Gain' inscribed around the impluvium in the house of a carpenter and 'Here Dwells Happiness' scrawled on the wall of a bakery
- images of Mercury, the god of commerce, displayed everywhere to gain blessings: on a sign outside a shop, on a sales counter, as part of a set of scales or on the wall of a workshop.

Evidence of commerce

Desire for profit

The economies of Vesuvian towns (employment, trade, manufacture and profit) were largely based on agricultural production and fishing. The numerous medium-sized farmsteads and *villa rusticae* that dotted the Sarno plain, as well as the market gardens (*horti*) within the walls of Pompeii, provided the raw materials (wine, olive oil, cereals, fruit, vegetables, meat and wool) for much of the retail and industrial workforce. The fishing fleets—many from

Economy based on products of land and sea

Herculaneum judging by the volume of nets, hooks and other gear found—that plied the coastline of the Bay of Naples provided the much-valued crustaceans, molluscs and fish, the latter also used for making garum or fish sauce for which Pompeii was renowned. These industries spawned a host of others such as pottery, since terracotta and ceramic containers (dolia and amphorae) were needed for storage, and trade in wine, oil and garum.

THE WINE AND OIL INDUSTRIES

✦ Principal sources of income

Wine and oil were the principal sources of income for the people in the Vesuvian area. Generally, the profitable cultivation of both vineyards and olive groves could only be undertaken by wealthy landowners because of the cost of the long wait between planting and the first harvest, and the cost of wine and olive presses. Many of the landowners who had estates in the Vesuvian countryside lived in Pompeii or in Rome and only visited their estate villa irregularly, allowing them to be run by trusted dependants. For example, the rich Pompeian banker Lucius Caecilius Jucundus is believed to have owned the Villa of Pisanella at Boscoreale, an important wine- and oil-producing estate.

✦ Vineyards in town and country

Work carried out by Wilhelmenia Jashemski at Pompeii revealed evidence (2014 vine-root cavities) of a large commercial vineyard near the Pompeian amphitheatre, which today has been replanted. On the site was a room set up for wine pressing and a shed with embedded dolia which could each fill 40 amphorae. Smaller vineyards adjoining the Inn of Euxinus and the Inn of the Gladiators have been found; the grapes were pressed on the premises. In other areas, grapes were pressed by foot. Generally, however, wine doesn't appear to have been stored in large quantities in taverns and bars, but brought in from the farms and villas in the countryside when needed. These villas had rooms for pressing the grapes (*torcularia*), for fermentation (*cellae vinariae*) and storage. The *torcular* or press 'consisted of a solid wooden crossbar fixed at one end and pushed downwards by means of a winch with an arm lever'.[11]

Figure 6.10 A wine press (torcular)

Figure 6.11 A dolium

According to Pliny, 'districts with a mild climate store their wine in jars and bury them completely or partially in the ground thus protecting them from the weather . . . Spaces must be left between jars to prevent anything likely to affect the wine from passing from one to the other, as the wine very soon becomes tainted.'[12] The villas of Boscoreale—Villa of Pisanella and Villa Regina—possessed a huge storage capacity. The former had an internal courtyard of 120 dolia that could hold up to 50,000 litres, while the latter had 18 dolia holding 10,000 litres. The wine was transported to town in large leather wineskins (*cullei*), then decanted into amphorae or dolia for storage and serving in the numerous taverns and bars.

✖
Storage of wine

A wide variety of wines were produced in the Vesuvian area; a sign on a Herculaneum wine bar inviting patrons to 'Come to the Sign of the Bowls' advertised half a dozen types of wine and their vintages. Another tavern advertisement confirms that there was a wide range of wines sold in Pompeii: '. . . drink here for just one as; for two you can drink better, and for four have some really good Falernian wine.'[13] From Pliny's *Natural History*, and evidence from labelled wine jars, it seems the two most famous local wines were Vesuvinum and Pompeianum. Of the latter, Pliny said 'Wines from Pompeii are at their best within ten years and gain nothing from greater maturity', but he maintained that they were 'injurious because of the hangover they cause, which persists until noon the following day'.[14] Judging from a scrawl on the wall of a Pompeian bar, the quality of wine varied considerably: 'Inn-keeper of the devil, die drowned in your own piss-wine. You sell the inferior stuff but you keep for yourself, you swine, the good bottles.'[15]

✖
Varieties of wine

✖
Quality of wine

The same estates that produced wine also produced oil; the Villa of Pisanella kept enough storage jars for 5910 litres of oil. According to Pliny, more skill was 'needed to produce olive oil than wine, because the same tree produces different kinds of oil . . . The green olive, which has not yet begun to ripen, gives the first oil and this has an outstanding taste . . . The riper the berry the more greasy and less pleasant is the flavour of the oil.'[16] The oil from the green olive was also used in the manufacture of perfume which Pliny believed was 'the most pointless of all luxuries'.[17]

✖
Varieties of oils

Most of the pressing was done on the estates even though oil presses were found in Pompeian houses and in the Forum granary. Because 'the cause of oil is warmth',[18] presses and store-rooms had to be warmed by large fires. Cato, in his *Agriculture* (XXII, 3–4), recorded that Pompeian presses built from lava stone were the best. These (*trapeta*) were for the first pressing, to separate flesh from pip so that the oil did not get a bitter taste. A *trapetum* consisted of a circular basin with two mill wheels joined by a wooden beam which revolved on an iron spindle fixed into the sides of a basin. The second pressing was done with the same press as for grapes

✖
Oil presses

Figure 6.12 A wine shop

Figure 6.13 An olive press

(*torcular*). 'The first oil from the press is the richest, and the quality diminishes with each successive pressing . . . age imparts an unpleasant taste to oil and after a year it is old.'[19]

Within Pompeii, *officinae oleariae* retailed oil and it is believed that there may have been an olive market near or in the Forum *olitorium* or granary. Oil was used not only as the basic ingredient in perfume, but also for cooking, particularly in the *thermopolia* which provided a service to those who had limited cooking facilities in their homes, and for lighting. Oil was used in the *thermae* and *palaestra* for rubbing into bodies. Pliny disapproved of this practice which he blamed on the Greeks: 'The Greeks, progenitors of all vices, have diverted the use of olive-oil to serve the ends of luxury by making it available in gymnasia.'[20]

❈
Retail outlets and uses of oil

THE MANUFACTURE OF GARUM

❈
Highly valued

Pompeii was renowned for its garum, a fish sauce which was one of the main condiments used for flavouring Roman cuisine. According to Pliny, 'no other liquid except unguents has come to be more highly valued'.[21] There were various flavours depending on the type and quality of the fish used and its method of preparation. Apparently the valuable red mullet made the best garum, followed by tuna, mackerel and sardines, while anchovies were used for less refined sauces.

❈
A monopoly

The fisherman from Pompeii and Herculaneum sold their catches, both fresh and salted, in the Macellum (market) in the Forum, but prominent garum manufacturers such as Marcus Umbricius Scaurus may have obtained his fish more directly. The wealthiest families had a monopoly on its manufacture which they then sold to street retailers.

❈
Process

Garum was a potent mix, made from 'the guts of fish and other parts that would otherwise be considered refuse',[22] probably gills, intestines and blood, and the smell must have pervaded Pompeii. Although it was popular with most, some, like Seneca, hated its foul smell. The following quote gives a more detailed description of its manufacture:

> THE ENTRAILS OF SPRATS OR SARDINES, THE PARTS THAT COULD NOT BE USED FOR SALTING WERE MIXED WITH FINELY CHOPPED PORTIONS OF FISH AND WITH ROE AND EGGS AND THEN POUNDED CRUSHED AND STIRRED. THE MIXTURE WAS LEFT IN THE SUN OR A WARM ROOM AND BEATEN INTO A HOMOGENEOUS PULP UNTIL IT FERMENTED. WHEN THIS LIQUAMEN, AS IT WAS CALLED, HAD BEEN MUCH REDUCED OVER A PERIOD OF SIX WEEKS BY EVAPORATION, IT WAS PLACED IN A BASKET WITH PERFORATED BOTTOM THROUGH WHICH THE RESIDUE FILTERED SLOWLY INTO A RECEPTACLE. THE END PRODUCT DECANTED INTO JARS WAS THE FAMOUS GARUM; THE DREGS LEFT OVER WERE ALSO REGARDED AS EDIBLE AND KNOWN AS ALLEC.[23]

A product indispensable to the production of garum was salt. The Pompeians skilfully exploited a depression near the coastal road to Herculaneum to make a salt plant. Saltwater, washed up by the high tides, entered a channel into large shallow basins where it evaporated in the sun. As its concentration increased, it was allowed to overflow into progressively concentrated pools. Eventually, the pure crystallised salt was collected with spades from the final basin.

❈ Salt works

CLOTH MANUFACTURE AND TREATMENT

Wool was the basis of one of the most important industries in Pompeii, the washing and dyeing of wool and the manufacture of cloth. Associated with this was the laundering, bleaching and re-colouring of clothes. Both these activities were carried out in workshops and *fullonicae* or laundries.

❈ Steps in the manufacture of cloth

- The raw wool was first sent to an *officina lanifricariae* where it was degreased by boiling in leaden boilers.
- Once carded it was taken to the spinners and weavers, in private homes or in *officinae textoriae*.
- The cloth was next sent to *officinae tinctoriae* for dyeing, often in bright colours such as purple or saffron.
- The finished product was distributed to cloth merchants.

Laundries or *fullonicae* were scattered all over Pompeii—18, of which four, like the Fullery of Stephanus, were large. Some occupied the rooms of private houses (possibly rented) and were identified by a number of interconnected basins or tanks with built-in steps for washing and rinsing. Workers trod the cloth in a mixture of fuller's earth, potash, carbonate of soda and urine (because of its ammonia content). Although camel urine was the most prized, laundries usually had to make do with human urine and male passers-by were urged to supply their urine by filling the jugs hanging outside. There were special areas set aside for urine collection.

❈ Number of laundries

❈ Use of urine in washing

The fullers then rinsed, dried and brushed the cloth. Lucius Veranius Hypsaeus dried his fabric on brick pillars between the Corinthian columns of a large atrium, while another fuller, Stephanus, hung the wet clothes over canes on the upper floor and in the courtyard. Once dried, the cloth was bleached with sulphur and then dyed. A clothes press, a little under two metres high and over half a metre wide, was discovered in a shop attached to the House of the Wooden Partition in Herculaneum, and a painted sign over the Pompeian workshop of M. Vecilius Verecundus, an eminent mill owner and cloth merchant, showed the various processes involved in cloth manufacture.

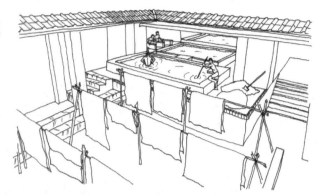

Figure 6.14 A Pompeian laundry

Wool was used also in the processing of felt to make slippers, hats, blankets and cloaks. It was impregnated with heated vinegar, creating a matted effect, and then pushed and pressed until it reached the right consistency.

The Guild of Fullers was a powerful organisation within the city. Its headquarters, as well as a possible wool market, were located in the Eumachia building on the eastern side of the Forum. This magnificent building, with the dimensions and layout of a temple, was paid for by the priestess/business woman Eumachia, who had married a wealthy owner of pastures and flocks of sheep and became the patron of the cloth-makers and dyers. She dedicated it in her own name and that of her son, Numistaeius Fronto, to the imperial family. Within the building was a statue of herself 'Dedicated by the Fullers to Eumachia, daughter of Lucius'.[24]

BAKERIES (PISTRINA)

The thirty or so bakeries (*pistrina*) that have been identified in Pompeii saved householders from buying the grain, milling it into flour and baking their own bread, which was a basic foodstuff. Because of the poor quality of the flour, the bread was very hard, and due to the lack of yeast, deteriorated quickly. Bakeries did their own refining of the grain in lava stone mills, usually three or four, set in a paved courtyard with a table for kneading the dough, and a brick oven. A mill was composed of three parts: a fixed conical block called a *meta*, a masonry base with a *lamina* for collecting the flour, and a hollow cylinder, *catillus*, into which was inserted a pole, turned by mules or donkeys. The ovens were heated by burning vine faggots and, once hot enough, they were cleaned out in readiness for baking the small round loaves of bread. These, marked off in eight sections for easy breaking, were dispatched to the various small shops and stalls in surrounding streets. A few bakeries had an adjoining area for selling their own bread, but most did not. In the bakery of N. Popidius Priscus, a member of a prominent Pompeian family (sometimes called the Bakery of Modestus because it was probably run by one of his freedmen), 81 loaves of bread were recovered, still on the oven where they had been placed on the morning of 24 August AD 79.

In Herculaneum, a baker known as Sextus Patulcus Felix appears to have specialised in cakes for 'twenty-five bronze baking pans of various sizes, from about four inches to a foot and a half'[25] (10 to 45 cm) were discovered in his premises.

Figure 6.15 A bakery with grain mills

Figure 6.16 A baker's oven

Figure 6.17 Loaves of carbonised bread

OTHER INDUSTRIES

From the evidence provided by epigraphy and popular painting, it is known that in Pompeii there were workshops of carpenters, plumbers, wheelwrights, tanners, tinkers, ironmongers, goldsmiths and silversmiths, marble-workers, stonemasons, gem-cutters and glassmakers. Many of their guilds played an influential part in politics. It appears that the commercial activity of Herculaneum was based on the work of skilled craftsmen, particularly carpenters, for whose work there was substantial demand.

❈ Numerous small workshops

Perfume manufacture was an important industry in Campania. Jashemski, in her *Gardens of Pompeii*, vol. 1 (1979) believed that the Garden of the Fugitives and Garden of Hercules were devoted to raising flowers for the perfume industry. She thought root cavities in the former garden probably represented rose bushes because of the irrigation channels. Fragments of terracotta perfume containers were also found there, and glass perfume bottles and terracotta unguent jars were discovered in the Garden of Hercules.

❈ The perfume industry

After the earthquake of AD 62, there was an increased demand for bricks and tiles for rebuilding. Many of the wine and garum producers who owned the kilns for making amphorae and dolia also owned the brick and tile factories.

❈ Pottery, bricks and tiles

Figure 6.18 Relief representing a workshop, possibly a tinker (Naples National Archaeological Museum)

MARKETS

☒
City-controlled
markets

On both sides of the Pompeian Forum were markets which were the property of the city, administered by two magistrates called *aediles* who made sure that:

- the markets ran smoothly
- goods were measured and priced accurately
- quality was maintained
- city regulations were upheld. For example, traders were only permitted to bring their goods to the market at dawn or in the evening to avoid traffic congestion; no wheeled traffic was permitted in the Forum at all.

☒
The Macellum

The Macellum, on the north-eastern side of the Forum, was a busy market specialising in the sale of fish and meat, and possibly fruit and vegetables. Its location was chosen so that its pedestrian traffic would not disturb the normal life of the main Forum square. It consisted of a large arcaded courtyard, with shops wedged between the marble columns of the portico on the southern side. In the centre was an unusual building; a large covered market called a *tholos* bounded by twelve columns. That this was a market is verified by a representation of a Roman market on a coin from the time of Nero. In

☒
A covered
fish market

its centre was a pool believed to be for live fish. Large quantities of fish scales and bones have been found in the underground channel that linked the pool with the sewers, so it was probably where fishmongers cleaned, filleted and sold their catch. As well as fish for eating and making of garum, and all kinds of molluscs and crustaceans, there was a variety of meats—lamb, beef veal, pork and poultry—for sale in the Macellum.

The Macellum also featured beautiful panelled painting in the 'fourth style'; a small raised temple; statues of an emperor and notable Pompeian dignitaries, probably those who had financed the building; a section that may have been used for sacrificial banquets or as an auction room, and a money changer's booth.

On the other side of the Forum was a market where dried cereals and pulses (*olitorium*) were sold to individuals and bakeries. Its entrance had eight openings to facilitate the movement of customers, and in a recess to the south was a weighing table (*mensa ponderaria*), a marble slab with nine circular cavities of different capacities—there were originally twelve—for inspecting and measuring the foodstuffs sold by shopkeepers. The beautiful Building of Eumachia on the east of the Forum was believed to have housed a wool and cloth market.

The documentary evidence (*Indices Nundinarii*) indicates that Saturday was market day in Pompeii. Itinerant pedlars sold an array of manufactured goods such as shoes, while local farmers from the countryside and owners of market gardens (*horti*) within the city, set up their stalls, in squares, under arcades and anywhere that was frequented by the inhabitants of the town, to sell their surplus agricultural and garden products. Polyculture was practised in Pompeii's horti; olives, vines, beans, cabbages, herbs and fruit were grown side by side, but Jashmenski also identified a large orchard of at least 300 trees.

With so much commercial activity centred on the Forum, and so many people milling around on market days, the Pompeian authorities were obliged to provide a public latrine adjacent to the granary. It was screened off by a vestibule and could accommodate 20 people at one time. Other public latrines (*foricae*) were located wherever people congregated, and incorporated into the various public bath complexes. 'The latrines annexed to the thermal baths in Pompeii preserve a certain aesthetic dignity' and some 'even came to assume the form of a monument'.[26]

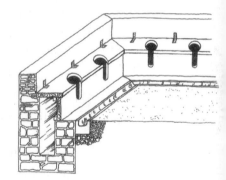

Figure 6.19 Public toilets near the Forum

Marginal notes:

✸ Other features of the Macellum

✸ Granary and weighing table

✸ Local market day

Shops (tabernae)

The main commercial thoroughfare in Pompeii was the road that ran from the Forum past the amphitheatre to the Sarnian Gate. Remains of shops along this road—and others—can be recognised by the wide opening onto the street, and the long groove in the stone threshold where a wooden shutter slid back during the day. Many had a back room, some a mezzanine—accessed by internal stairs—which was the living quarters of the shopkeeper. It is quite possible that the premises of a cloth merchant, a gemcutter or perfume vendor might be adjacent to a greengrocer, a garum seller, a wine and hot food bar, or a rag-and-bone vendor, all interspersed with entrances into grand residences in the insula behind. Shop and workshop owners advertised their business with painted trade signs, or paintings on the

✸ Location and appearance of shops

Figure 6.20 A thermopolium (snack bar)

outside of the walls. This busy street was also a prime location for painted political slogans.

❧
Fast-food outlets

About 200 public eating and drinking places have been identified in Pompeii. Some were simply fast-food snack bars and are recognised by the marble-covered counter in which large dolia, holding hot drinks and dishes, were encased (*thermopolia*). In most of these places food was taken away or eaten standing up. One of the largest found in Herculaneum, opposite the Palaestra, had two spacious entrances. Its counter was 'faced with irregular pieces of polychrome marble and eight large jugs (inserted into the counter itself) . . . Other jugs and amphorae may have been used for other types of oil or for sauce. A stove behind the counter was in use: varied dishes were kept simmering in terra-cotta casseroles over the charcoal fire.'[27]

❧
Bars and taverns

Wine bars and taverns (*cauponae*) were scattered throughout both towns, but in Pompeii they were more densely clustered near the entrance gates and around the amphitheatre. Some had a room or rooms at the back with benches for clients. In others there were couches for wealthier clients to recline on while eating and drinking. It seems that many Pompeians were heavy drinkers. Two graffiti declared 'Cheers! We drink like wineskins'[28] and 'Suavis demands full wine-jars, please, and his thirst is enormous.'[29] However, most people drank their wine diluted; they mixed it with water and added other ingredients such as 'honey, milk, ashes, lime, almonds and sea water' to enhance its flavour. They also sweetened sour wine with a 'sweet-tasting lead acetate syrup made by boiling the dregs of wine in lead-lined copper pans for several days'.[30] A particular favourite with Pompeians was hot wine.

One of the better-known establishments was that of a woman named Asellina who employed foreign waitresses called Smyrna, Maria and Aegle (some believe they were prostitutes). Sums showing customers' debts were scrawled on the inside walls of her inn, while political slogans, painted on the outside walls, revealed her interest in the forthcoming elections.

HOTELS

Visiting traders could find a bed for the night in one of the many hotels close to the port or within the city. A building named the Hostel of the Muses, after one of its dazzling paintings, was discovered on the bank of the ancient course of the Sarno, from where it would have had a view over the sea. Because of its unusual features—a small jetty, banqueting areas consisting of at least eight rooms with triclinia for eating and conversation, brilliant frescoes in the dining rooms, and an exceptionally large kitchen which could feed at least fifty guests—it is believed that it was a hotel for wealthy traders. Another hotel near the Forum could sleep fifty people, four to a room, while the two just inside the Herculaneum and Stabian Gates had dining rooms, bedrooms, stables, a water trough and a garage shed for wagons. It appears that the owners also provided for their guests' entertainment with upstairs rooms accessed by a side door for the discreet entry of local women.

❈ A port hotel

❈ City hotels

COMMERCIAL TRANSACTIONS AND MONEY

The Basilica, fronting onto the Forum, was not only the law-court, but an exchange where businessmen or speculators met clients and signed contracts. One man who would have frequented the Basilica was M. Caecilius Jucundus, the son of a freedman, L. Caecilius Felix, who, as a slave, belonged to a family of the Caecilii gens. He was manumitted—hence the name Caecilius—and acted as an agent for his former master. His son, Jucundus, accumulated great wealth by tax farming, lending money to merchants and renting and selling land, properties, businesses and slaves. He had a house in Pompeii and is believed to have been the owner of the Villa Pisanella at Boscoreale. In his Pompeian domus, 150 wax tablets were discovered: records of his various transactions between AD 52–62. Most were receipts (*apochae*) for rents and loans varying between 342 and 38,079 sesterces. If the Villa Pisanella belonged to Jucundus, the more than one hundred pieces of beautiful silverware as well as jewels and gold coins found in a chest confirm his wealth. The owner brought his possessions to the villa for safekeeping, possibly after the earthquake of AD 62.

❈ The Basilica

❈ A Pompeian banker

Figure 6.21 A sign indicating the house of Caecilius Jucundas

Figure 6.22, adapted from *Pompeii Revisited* (P. Carson), shows the main coinage denominations used in the Campanian region.

Figure 6.22 Coinage denominations

Name of coin	Material	Use
1 aureus ↑ 25 denarii	Gold	For major purchases such as slaves, land houses and payment of taxes
1 denarius ↑ 4 sestertii	Silver	
1 sestertius ↑ 2 dupondii	Bronze	Most widely used coin
1 dupondius ↑ 2 asses	Zinc orichaleium	For everyday use—shopping, trade and payment of wages
1 as ↑ 4 quandrans	Red copper	
1 quadran	Red copper	

OVERSEAS TRADE

❈ Imports

Pompeii certainly traded with other cities within Campania and the Italian peninsula, and it is known that although Pompeians produced their own wine and oil, they imported other varieties from Spain, Sicily and Crete, as well as pottery from Spain and Gaul (France), furniture from nearby Naples and lamps from Alexandria. However, it is not known with any certainty yet, just how extensive their exports were to other parts of the Roman Empire. The occasional Pompeian amphora, tile or fish container has turned up beyond Italy, but some scholars believe their export trade was minimal. Refutation or confirmation of this belief will depend on further work. At the time of writing, an Australian researcher attached to Macquarie University is investigating the pottery remains in Pompeii and her work may throw more light on Pompeii's overseas trade.

Figure 6.23 Reconstruction of the port of Pompeii

❈ Evidence of port activity

The port of Pompeii was less than a kilometre from the centre of the city. In the present area of Bottaro, a narrow strip of land has revealed not only the remains of 20 warehouses containing weights for anchoring boats and fishing gear, but amphorae and a statue of Neptune, god of the sea, to whom departing sailors made sacrifice. The port was an entrepot or trans-shipment point for local and foreign goods. Once the ships were unloaded, the goods were transferred to barges for the journey up the Sarno River to inland towns such as Nuceria, and onto wagons for the short trip into Pompeii.

LOCAL POLITICAL LIFE

Pompeii and Herculaneum, like all provincial towns, were self-governing in local matters, but subject to imperial decree from Rome. However, the emperor rarely interfered except where the empire's security or local order were threatened. After the revolt in the amphitheatre between Pompeians and Nucerians in AD 59 (see pages 7–8) the emperor, Nero, dismissed the two chief magistrates, had two more elected and appointed a law-giving prefect to supervise them. The inhabitants did not rail against such interference and constantly demonstrated their loyalty to the imperial family by constructing dedicatory statues, shrines, arches and buildings.

The epigraphic evidence suggests that political activity in Pompeii was intense, especially leading up to the elections in March of each year (Herculaneum probably a little less so). It appears from the thousands of electoral notices painted on the walls that most people, including women, were politically aware and enthusiastic. According to Cicero, competition for office was so fierce that it was harder to gain a seat in the City Council of Pompeii than in the Roman Senate. Michael Grant suggests this interest may have had its origins in a 'Samnite tradition of vociferous democracy'.[32]

Figure 6.24 summarises the organisation of Pompeian government.

MUNICIPAL BUILDINGS

The city council met in the lavishly decorated Curia chamber on the southern side of the Forum adjacent to the Comitium (People's assembly) in the south-eastern corner. The Comitium was a roofless building where town meetings were held during which the citizens could question the members of the government. The evidence for heavy gates suggests that some meetings might have been quite boisterous. It may also have been used on polling day. On the other side of the Curia was the small Tabularium where all the government business was recorded and filed, including tax records. Next door were the offices of the magistrates.

The Basilica was the seat of the judiciary and law courts, as well as a centre for business activities. It was one the finest buildings—if not the finest—in both towns. Basilicas usually followed a standard plan: a long rectangular central hall, flanked on either side by a colonnaded aisle and an apse at one end. The central hall in Pompeii's Basilica was two storeyed with light filtering through from the upper gallery. At one end, five doors linked the hall with the Forum and at the other was a raised podium where the magistrate, as judge, sat above the lawyers, witnesses, plaintiffs and defendants. It is believed that the tribunal podium was accessed by portable

❈ Autonomous in local affairs

❈ Political interest intense

❈ Structure of government

❈ Curia, comitium and tabularium

❈ Basilica and the law courts

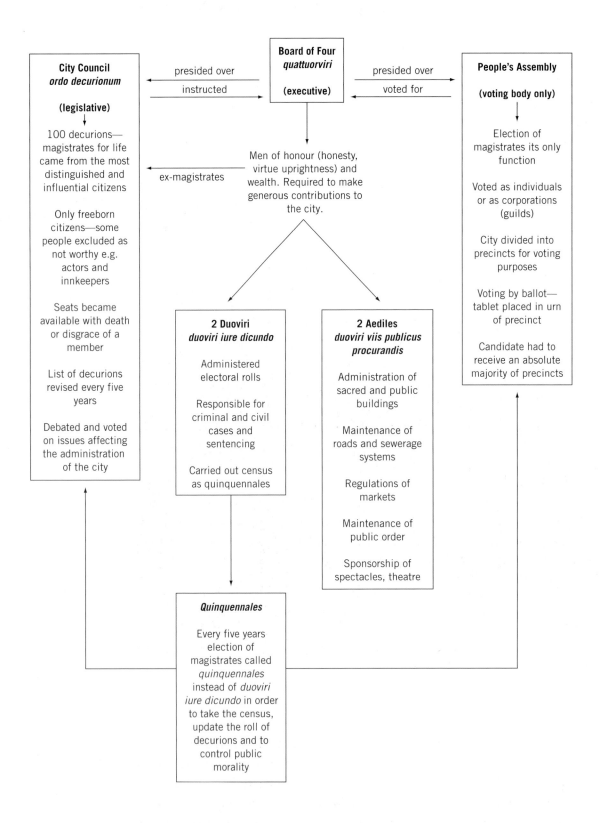

Figure 6.24 Organisation of Pompeian government

wooden steps which were removed during a session so that the public could not reach the judge.

The two *duoviri* (magistrates) made judgments about:

- unworthy decurions
- electoral candidates without the required qualifications
- inappropriate behaviour during elections
- misuse of public funds
- robberies
- murder.

They were responsible for sentencing, but could only give the death penalty to foreigners and slaves. In civil cases, they were limited to law suits whose value did not exceed 15,000 sesterces or defamatory trials whose limit was 10,000 sesterces.

⊗
Criminal and civil
duties of magistrates

Figure 6.25 The Basilica

ELECTION FEVER IN POMPEII

About half of the electoral manifestos and propaganda discovered in Pompeii related to the election of March AD 79. Earlier slogans were whitewashed over to make advertising room for the next group of candidates. To identify himself, a candidate wore a white toga (*candida*) and employed a slave to whisper his name to all with whom he came in contact (*nomenclator*). However, candidates did not:

⊗
Candidates

- write the manifestos themselves or sign them; this was done by family, friends, dependants or even particular trade guilds
- make electoral promises about tax cuts, road maintenance or a building program
- boast about what they did in the past.

What voters were interested in was the personal integrity and prestige of the candidate. Electoral manifestos usually included some references to these qualities: 'Worthy of the Republic', 'Most worthy', 'Most upright', 'Excellent', 'Virtuous', 'Lives a reserved life'. For example, 'Vesonius Primus urges the election of Gnaeus Helvius as aedile, a man worthy of public office.'[33] When C. Julius Polybius was running for office, a manifesto signed by two prostitutes, Zmyrina and Cuculla, appeared on a wall; he was furious and demanded that it be removed.

Many trade corporations jointly promoted a candidate. The pastry vendors backed Trebius Valente as aedile candidate;[34] the muleteers wanted to elect C. Julius Polybius as duovir[35] and the fruit merchants urged people to vote for M. Enium Sabinum as aedile.[36] Although women could not vote or stand for office, they were just as interested in campaigning as the men. Asellina the innkeeper and a group of women supporters who called themselves 'Asselinae' had an electoral slogan painted on the wall of her inn urging customers to vote for Caio Lolio Fusco as aedile. Even grandmothers were recruited to support a family member: 'Vote for Lucius Popidius Sabinus, his grandmother worked hard for his last election and is pleased with the results.'[37]

Judging by one graffito, teachers and students, joined in the campaigning: 'Teacher Sema with his boys, recommends Julius Simplex for the job.'[38]

Magistrates were not paid, but were expected to make generous contributions to the city and keep the people happy, which was usually achieved by sponsoring spectacular shows, dedicating buildings or statues, or presenting a large sum of his own money to the treasury.

Not everyone, however, was always happy with the chosen duoviri, and just as with modern cartoonists and voters, Pompeian graffitists drew caricatures and gave advice on how to run the city: 'Here's my advice, share out the common chest, For in our coffers piles of money rests'.[39] As in all political systems, there would have been a degree of corruption. The narrator in Petronius's novel of the freedman, *Trimalchio*, gives a fictitious (although realistic-sounding) account of such a case: 'No one gives a damn about the way we're hit by the grain situation. To hell with the aediles! They're in with the bakers—you be nice to me and I'll be nice to you. So the little man suffers . . . this place is going down like a calf's tail.[40]

Chapter review

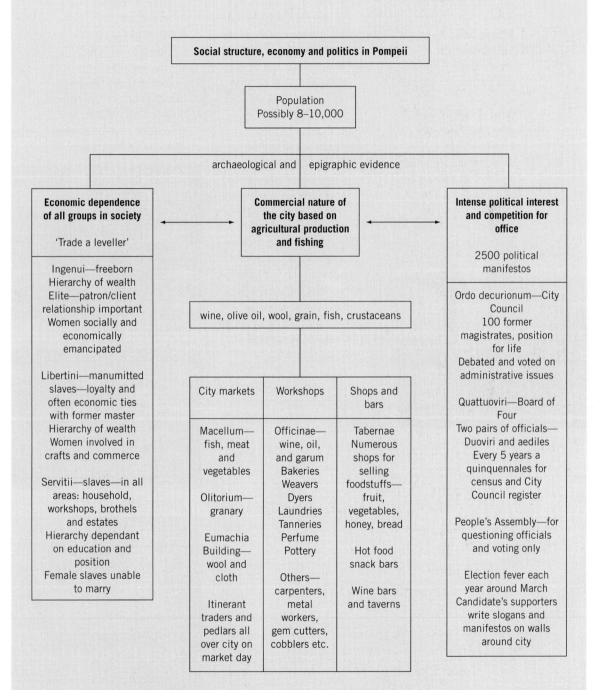

Social structure, economy and politics in Pompeii

Population
Possibly 8–10,000

archaeological and epigraphic evidence

Economic dependence of all groups in society

'Trade a leveller'

Ingenui—freeborn
Hierarchy of wealth
Elite—patron/client relationship important
Women socially and economically emancipated

Libertini—manumitted slaves—loyalty and often economic ties with former master
Hierarchy of wealth
Women involved in crafts and commerce

Servitii—slaves—in all areas: household, workshops, brothels and estates
Hierarchy dependant on education and position
Female slaves unable to marry

Commercial nature of the city based on agricultural production and fishing

wine, olive oil, wool, grain, fish, crustaceans

City markets	Workshops	Shops and bars
Macellum— fish, meat and vegetables	Officinae— wine, oil, and garum	Tabernae Numerous shops for selling foodstuffs— fruit, vegetables, honey, bread
Olitorium— granary	Bakeries Weavers Dyers Laundries Tanneries Perfume Pottery	
Eumachia Building— wool and cloth		Hot food snack bars
Itinerant traders and pedlars all over city on market day	Others— carpenters, metal workers, gem cutters, cobblers etc.	Wine bars and taverns

Intense political interest and competition for office

2500 political manifestos

Ordo decurionum—City Council
100 former magistrates, position for life
Debated and voted on administrative issues

Quattuoviri—Board of Four
Two pairs of officials— Duoviri and aediles
Every 5 years a quinquennales for census and City Council register

People's Assembly—for questioning officials and voting only

Election fever each year around March
Candidate's supporters write slogans and manifestos on walls around city

Activities

1 a Why was slavery so widespread in the Roman world?
  b Define the term 'manumission' and explain how it might occur.
  c What obligations and benefits came with manumission?
  d Write eight to ten lines on the occupations open to slave, freed and freeborn women in Pompeii and Herculaneum.

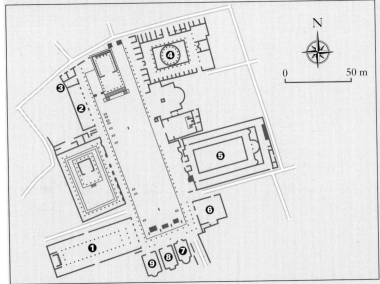

Figure 6.26 A view of the Forum as it is today

2 a Figure 6.26 shows part of the Pompeian Forum as it is today. Using the information in this chapter, explain how different its general appearance was in the early imperial period (after Augustus).
  b Identify the numbered buildings in the Pompeian Forum shown in Figure 6.27 and write one or two lines about the function of each.

3 Draw a mind map showing all the evidence provided in Chapter 6 that supports the claim that the wine and oil industry were probably the most significant sources of income for the people of the Vesuvian area.

4 'Papilius' breath is so strong that it can change the strongest perfume into garum.' (Martial, *Epigrams*, *VII*. 94)

a What is Martial saying in this quote?
b What was garum?
c How was it made?
d How important was it to the Pompeian economy?

5 Identify each of the objects below. Where might they have been found and what were their functions?

Figure 6.28

Figure 6.29

Figure 6.30

Figure 6.27

Activities

6 Read the following primary and secondary sources carefully and then answer the questions.

1 AULUS CLODIUS FLACCUS, SON OF AULUS, OF THE MENENIA VOTING GROUP IN ROME, THREE TIMES CHIEF MAGISTRATE, ONCE IN THE SPECIAL FIFTH YEAR, TRIBUNE OF SOLDIERS BY POPULAR VOTE [PROVIDED] IN HIS FIRST TERM DURING THE FESTIVAL OF APOLLO IN THE FORUM: A PROCESSION OF BULLS, BULL-GOADERS, SIDE KICKS, PLATFORM FIGHTERS (THREE PAIRS) BOXING IN GROUPS AND PAIRS, SHOWS WITH ALL THE MUSICIANS AND ALL THE PANTOMIMES, AND, [ESPECIALLY] PLYADES, AT THE COST OF 10,000 SESTERCES PAID TO THE CITY IN RETURN FOR HIS OFFICE.

C. Amery & B. Curren, *The Lost World of Pompeii*, p. 58

2 THE FULLONES ASK FOR VOTES FOR OLCONIUS PRISCUS AS AEDILE.

CIL IV 7164

THE GOLDSMITHS SUPPORT THE CANDIDATURE OF CAIUS CUSPIAS PANSA FOR AEDILE.

CIL IV 710

3 THE CITY ROADS WERE PUBLIC PROPERTY. NEVERTHELESS, THEIR MAINTENANCE AND CLEANING WAS PROVIDED BY THE COLLABORATION OF THE OWNERS OF THE HOUSES FRONTING THE ROAD, IN PROPORTION TO THE LENGTH AND WIDTH OF EACH HOUSE. (TABULA HERACLENSIS, 20; 32;50). THIS COLLABORATION WAS EXCLUSIVELY FINANCIAL, NOT DIRECT. THE MAINTENANCE WORK WAS OVERSEEN BY LOCAL MAGISTRATES (AEDILES AND CURATORES VIARIUM) WITHIN A SYSTEM OF TENDER.

E. Cantarella & L. Jacobelli,
A Day in Pompeii, p. 66

a Where might Sources 1 and 2 have originally been located in Pompeii?

b What was the purpose of each?

c What do Sources 1 and 2 indicate about the voting process?

d What does Source 2 indicate about the attitude of Pompeians to the political process?

e How many times had Clodius Flaccus been elected as magistrate?

f What were the names given to the four annually elected chief magistrates of Pompeii?

g What specific office did Clodius Flaccus hold in his first year as a magistrate?

h What is meant by 'once in the special fifth year'?

i What particular task assigned to an aedile is mentioned in Source 3?

j What other responsibilities did an aedile have to make sure the city ran smoothly?

k What were a magistrate's financial obligations to the city's inhabitants?

l If a magistrate did not get paid, why did he run for office, often not once but several times?

7 Topics for extended response, class discussion or oral presentations:

- The message 'Profit is Joy', found in the vestibule of a house of two wealthy men epitomises the commercial life of Pompeii.

- The contributions of notable men and women to the life of their respective towns.

Houses, villas and domestic life

7

THINGS TO CONSIDER

- Effect of topography, lack of space, economic changes and fashion on house types
- Common architectural spaces in atrium houses
- Differences between villas built purely for leisure and villa rusticae
- The composition of a familia and the power of the paterfamilias
- The patron–client relationship reflected in architecture and decoration
- The social, economic and political importance of the salutatio and dinner-party
- The roles of household slaves
- The house as a sacred space

Evidence and its limitations

There appears to be a large body of evidence for housing in Pompeii and Herculaneum in the 1st century AD; however, the limitations of architectural sources, discussed in Chapter 4, should be remembered when studying the urban *domus*. For example, it is difficult to know for certain the use of particular houses, especially larger ones, at the time of the eruption, or to know if they were occupied by one family or several. Also, the size of the house does not necessarily indicate the status of the owner. The following information is what is generally accepted at this point in time.

TOWN HOUSES

Changes in urban houses over time

The first impression of Pompeii—and to a lesser extent of Herculaneum—is what Wallace-Hadrill describes as an 'interlocking jigsaw of large, medium and small houses'.[1] Although a large percentage of the houses had architectural elements in common, each had its own particular features and, with time, the variations became more obvious. They reflected urban topography, the fashion of the day, growth in population, changes in economics and one or several earthquakes. Figure 7.1 illustrates some of the changes that occurred in housing over time.

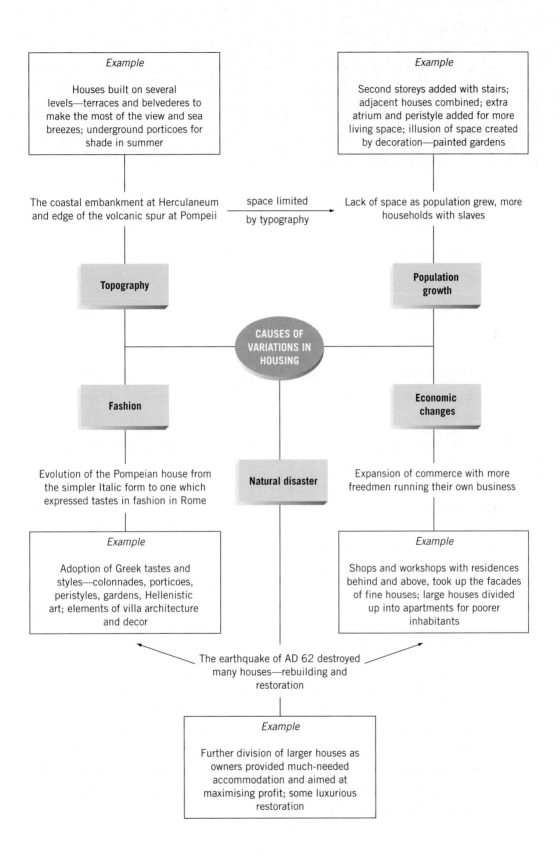

Example

Houses built on several levels—terraces and belvederes to make the most of the view and sea breezes; underground porticoes for shade in summer

Example

Second storeys added with stairs; adjacent houses combined; extra atrium and peristyle added for more living space; illusion of space created by decoration—painted gardens

The coastal embankment at Herculaneum and edge of the volcanic spur at Pompeii

space limited by typography

Lack of space as population grew, more households with slaves

Topography

Population growth

CAUSES OF VARIATIONS IN HOUSING

Fashion

Economic changes

Evolution of the Pompeian house from the simpler Italic form to one which expressed tastes in fashion in Rome

Natural disaster

Expansion of commerce with more freedmen running their own business

Example

Adoption of Greek tastes and styles—colonnades, porticoes, peristyles, gardens, Hellenistic art; elements of villa architecture and decor

Example

Shops and workshops with residences behind and above, took up the facades of fine houses; large houses divided up into apartments for poorer inhabitants

The earthquake of AD 62 destroyed many houses—rebuilding and restoration

Example

Further division of larger houses as owners provided much-needed accommodation and aimed at maximising profit; some luxurious restoration

Figure 7.1 Causes of variation in housing over time

Types of housing

Categories of houses

Wallace-Hadrill categorised the Pompeian houses into four groups on the basis of size, domestic and commercial function, architectural elements, and decoration.

1 shops and workshops with one- or two-roomed residences behind or above (*pergulae*—upper floor)
2 larger workshop residences of two to seven rooms on the ground floor, some with an atrium and even richly decorated
3 the average Pompeian house with between eight to thirteen rooms, most with an integrated workshop or shop, a fairly symmetrical plan and common architectural features such as decorated atria, tablina and colonnaded gardens
4 the largest houses designed 'for hospitality and large-scale admission of visitors'[2] with separate space for slaves. They often had two atria, large ornamental gardens—some with two peristyles—and were the most richly decorated.

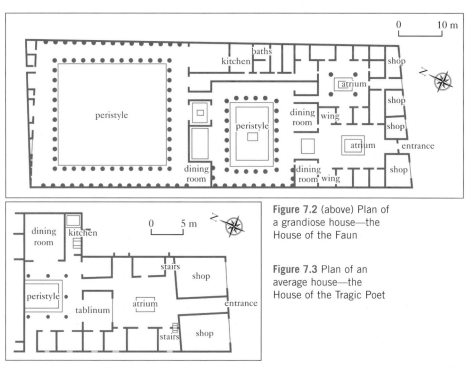

Figure 7.2 (above) Plan of a grandiose house—the House of the Faun

Figure 7.3 Plan of an average house—the House of the Tragic Poet

Flats and terraces

Other forms of accommodation—a result of the tendency to build upwards and divide up large houses—were found in both Pompeii and Herculaneum: middle-class apartments as well as small, one-roomed flats for poorer people. Two-storeyed 'terraced houses' with a small garden at the back were built near the Pompeian amphitheatre. In Herculaneum, a flimsy 'jerry-built' house, constructed in response to growing population and lack of space, amazingly survived the eruption with its furnishings intact and some of the red paint still on its walls. It appears to have been crudely constructed with a

Cheaper forms of construction

wooden skeleton made up of square frames filled with stones and mortar. The House of the Trellis—as it is called, for its style of construction—was built as a two-family residence, one on the ground floor and the other on the first floor. Its facade was narrow, a mere seven metres wide with two entrances, one leading to a staircase. The two families shared a cistern for water and a small courtyard which provided ventilation and light.

Figure 7.4 Lavish decoration in the House of the Vettii (Naples National Archaeological Museum)

Figure 7.5 Stairs leading to the upper floor in the House of the Beautiful Courtyard

Figure 7.6 House of the Trellis in Herculaneum

FEATURES OF TOWN HOUSES

Wallace-Hadrill's categories 3 and 4 include all the elements that are commonly associated with Pompeian and Herculanean houses.

The exterior

Houses opened directly onto the raised pavements of busy streets and because they were built to face inward, their facades were rather austere. There were few, if any, windows on the street side, and the entrance, even of a grandiose house, was often located between shops or workshops with

Facades

Figure 7.7 A shop and house—the House of the Beautiful Courtyard in Herculaneum

Figure 7.8 Facade of the House of the Wooden Partition in Herculaneum

Figure 7.9 Impressive entrance to the House of the Great Portal in Herculaneum

no indication of the rich decoration or elegance beyond. Most doors were made of wood, although there were a few monumental doorways flanked by brick and stucco half-columns. The red tiled roofs were usually flat or gently sloping.

Once the visitor entered the narrow corridor off the street (*fauces*—'throat') and entrance hall (*vestibulum*), he or she was offered a vista into the residence through the soaring, splendidly decorated atrium, with its shallow central pool (*impluvium*) and roof aperture (*compluvium*), through to the elaborately decorated master's reception room (*tablinum*—'record room') and on to the colonnaded peristyle and cool and peaceful garden beyond. Where space was limited, decoration was often used to create an illusion of spaciousness.

All public spaces in the house were designed and decorated to impress the visitor with the owner's wealth and status, which were indicated by certain architectural and decorative features alluding to public and sacred buildings. For example, 'columns, whether in an atrium or a peristyle or within a room, have the effect of marking out space as prestigious'.[3] They suggested a public portico or Greek stoa. An apse with its vaulted canopy alluded to the public baths; triangular pediments (*fastigia*) and second-storey clerestory windows were characteristic of temples and the classical basilica, while a central swimming pool (*piscena*) in a peristyle suggested the athletics ground (*palaestra*).

Figure 7.10 View through atrium to peristyle

Figure 7.11 Interior of the House of the Samnite in Herculaneum with Greek-inspired loggia above the atrium

Figure 7.12 Entrance mosaic of a chained dog from the House of the Tragic Poet in Pompeii

The fauces and vestibulum

According to Vitruvius, 'buildings having magnificent interiors' should also have 'elegant entrance courts to correspond: for there will be no propriety in the spectacle of an elegant interior approached by a low, mean entrance'.[4] In some houses, the front door led directly into the vestibule on the side of which was a small room, for the doorkeeper (*ianitor* or *ostiarius*) and possibly his dog. The mosaic floors of some vestibula featured a snarling dog and the words 'Cave Canem' or 'Beware of the dog'. The entrance corridors and vestibules were usually beautifully painted, for this was where the owner's clients waited for an audience to discuss business or political matters.

The atrium, tablinum and peristyle

In the earliest houses, the atrium or spacious rectangular hall off the vestibule, had no opening in the roof and was the centre of domestic activity focused on a hearth. The name 'atrium' is believed to come from 'ater' meaning 'dark black' because of the smoke-blackened walls.

88
Earliest atria

With the development of the impluviate atrium, sunlight shone through the square aperture that pierced the ceiling, and the shallow pool below collected water from the roof gutters. This was stored in a cistern underneath the impluvium. Vitruvius identified a number of impluviate atria:

88
Impluviate atria

- the Tuscan—the most common in Pompeii—with no columns and four roof pitches which converged towards the compluvium
- the tetra with four supporting columns at the corners of the compluvium
- the corinthian (Greek style of column)

The atrium eventually developed into a space that was more ceremonial and sacred. The family shrine (*lararium*), dedicated to the household deities (*lares familiare*), was usually located in the atrium, although it could be found elsewhere in the house. In some of the larger houses, rooms on either side of the entrance might contain figures of the lares. Portrait busts of the owner and sometimes wax masks of the family's ancestors (*imagines maiorem*) were also displayed. This was a space through which visitors and clients circulated.

88
Sacred nature of atria

The floors were often covered in black and white mosaics in geometrical patterns, and the ceilings—although few have survived in Pompeii—probably featured, painted and decorated stucco and massive wooden beams in oak or beech, which in the more gracious homes may have been gilded and inlaid. Even in the smaller houses, brilliant paintings covered the walls. Furniture was minimal in Pompeian houses. 'Interior architecture sometimes included built-in furniture . . . This made it possible to appreciate the pictorial decorations of the room integrally.'[5] There might have been a cupboard (*armaria*), a bolted chest (*arcae*) as well as a marble table (*cartibulum*) at the back.

88
Decoration and furnishing of atria

Sometimes, when a household became overcrowded, a second atrium might be added—if space were available—to provide for the activities of the family as opposed to the public activities carried out in the main atrium and tablinum. The House of the Faun and the House of the Vettii at Pompeii had two atria: one large, one smaller.

88
A second atrium

Figure 7.13 A tetrastyle atrium

Figure 7.14 Mosaic floor

Figure 7.15 Timber ceiling

❧
The tablinum for
reception of guests

At the end of the atrium, on the same axis as the vestibule, was the *tablinum* or main reception room where the owner (*dominus*) conducted daily business and where the family and commercial documents were held. It was probably in the tablinum that the *solium* or high-backed chair for the pater-familias would be found, with a wooden or bronze bench footrest.

❧
Changes in use
of tablinum

This room was open to the atrium and was usually the most richly deco-rated space in the house. In some homes it was still used as a dining room, study and bedroom for the master and could be closed off with curtains or wooden partitions for privacy. In the elegant but modest House of the Wooden Partition in Herculaneum, one of these has survived: a double door with three beautifully decorated panels. There was a tendency in the 1st century AD to open up the tablinum or even replace it with magnificent audience rooms and to focus on the peristyle rather than the atrium. In some houses the atrium disappeared altogether, replaced with a multiplicity of reception rooms—five in the House of Menander—suitably decorated to indicate their public nature.

❧
Alae

In the basic house there were usually two 'wings' (*alae*) at the far corners of the atrium. These originally were to let light in from side windows and were probably used for a variety of purposes, but particularly as a work space for the dominus's clerks and secretaries.

❧
Development of
the peristyle

In most houses, the peristyle—a colonnaded portico or large cloistered area overlooking a garden (*viridaria*)—replaced the original kitchen garden (*hortus*) where vegetables and fruits were cultivated and even wine and oil produced for the family. It was the favoured way to expand the house and bring more light into it, as well as to provide a place of contemplation. Some of the grander houses had two or even more peristyles: the Pompeian House of the Citharist had three.

❧
Love of gardens

Peristyles began to be incorporated into houses in the 2nd century BC with the Roman adoption of the Hellenistic taste for colonnades and porti-coes. About the same time 'Greek horticultural experts began arriving in Italy to create pleasure gardens',[6] particularly water gardens. To those who were ini-tiates of Bacchus (Dionysus), god of nature as well as wine, a garden was the earthly form of the promised afterlife, one of the reasons for the profusion of statues of the god scattered around the garden, and Dionysiac masks and reliefs on peristyle walls which might also be painted with murals of fruits trees, flowers, birds and animals.

❧
Types of garden
plants

According to Vitruvius (VI, 5, 2), the garden was an essential feature for the homes of people holding public office and there appears to be evidence of many of the finer houses transforming kitchen gardens into ornamental gardens with sacred groves (*sylvae*) and covered walkways (*ambulationes*); ornamental beds of flowers (violets, roses and hyacinths) and medicinal herbs; trees (narcissus, bay, acanthus, ivy, oleander, myrtle, box and yew and juniper), and cypress clipped into a variety of shapes. However, this was not always the case: the House of Pansa and the estate of Julia Felix also contained large produce gardens.

Figure 7.16 The peristyle of the House of the Vettii

Figure 7.17 Garden in a seaside mansion in Herculaneum

While modest houses had one fountain, more luxurious residences had many: the House of the Vettii had 14 interconnected fountains in the peristyle. After the earthquake a medium-sized atrium house—the House of Octavius Quartio, also called the House of Loreio Tiburtino—was renovated extensively and featured waterworks of all kinds: spouting jets, gushing waterfalls, channels, pools and a nymphaeum (monumental fountain dedicated to the nymphs with niches in the form of a grotto).

In those houses without a peristyle, due to lack of space, a room next to a small garden might be decorated with elements from nature. Even in the cramped residences of the artisans and shopkeepers, the owner's love of nature might be expressed in a garden painting on a back wall, a pergola covered in vines, a small vegetable garden, or even a low masonry wall built around an impluvium and filled with soil where plants might grow.

✽
Water gardens

✽
Alternatives to peristyle gardens

Figure 7.18 A nymphaeum

Figure 7.19 A multicoloured mosaic depicting fruit, flowers, peacock and deer on the walls of the summer dining room in the House of Neptune and Amphitrite in Herculaneum

Triclinia and cubicula

✠
Location and size
of triclinia

A separate dining room or *triclinium* ('three couches') was introduced after the Roman adoption of the Greek practice of reclining while dining. It was usually located off the atrium or looking onto the peristyle. Some larger residences had two triclinia, one for summer adjacent to the garden and one for winter, usually next to the tablinum. Where a second storey had been added, it became the custom to take meals on the upper floor overlooking the garden. Most triclinia were fairly small, with just enough space for the three couches—each of which held three people—the small, low, wooden, bronze or marble table placed in front of the couches (*mensa*), and the larger rectangular serving table. Some triclinia were built in, and the stone bench was covered with mattresses and colourful cushions. Others were more elegant, curved wooden pieces (see page 126 for seating arrangements).

✠
Example of a
summer triclinium

One of the best preserved summer dining rooms was found in Herculaneum in the House of the Mosaic of Neptune and Amphitrite, in which the owner compensated for lack of a peristyle by extensive use of multicoloured mosaics depicting festoons of fruit and flowers, peacocks and deer.

✠
Sleeping areas

Smaller rooms called *cubicula* may have had many uses, but are generally thought to have been rooms for sleeping. They could be located at different parts of the house, but were usually adjacent to the main reception area or secondary atrium if there was one. Many of these were windowless, but richly decorated, often with erotic scenes. In some houses there was a suite of rooms—bedroom and reception rooms—for the master of the house overlooking the garden or the sea, with an antechamber for the master's personal slave. According to Michael Grant 'the position of the beds was often indicated by a special configuration of the floor mosaic and by a lower vaulted ceiling forming a sort of a niche.'[7] Beds often ranged from the simple: a stone podium covered with mattress and cushions, to the sumptuous: a wooden version, with base of wooden cross pieces, strips of cloth or leather and decorated with bronze, silver or ivory.

Service areas

✠
Marginal spaces

The urban domus was 'a curious mix of gracious and ungracious living'.[8] The service areas of the house—for tasks such as cooking, washing and the private living and sleeping quarters of the slaves—were often marginalised and accessed down long, dark narrow corridors. In some houses, like the House of the Vettii, the service area, entered from the side of the atrium, had its own courtyard leading to the kitchen, lavatories and an assortment of store rooms and small sleeping rooms. In more modest houses, where space did not allow marginalisation of these quarters, the decoration, or lack of it, served the same purpose.

✠
Small kitchens

The kitchen (*culina*) in most houses was quite small, often only large enough for one or two slaves. It contained a stone hearth with podium and a recess for firewood or charcoal. Some had a small brick oven, running water and a sink. As there were no chimneys, with smoke simply escaping through a hole in the roof, they would have been badly ventilated, with fires a constant problem.

The latrine—rather unhygenically—was directly adjacent to or opened off the kitchen, as both rooms used the same pipes for water supply. Its paved floor sloped towards a pit covered with a wooden seat with a hole in it. In better homes, piped water flushed the toilet, in others, kitchen overflow did the job. Waste from upstairs rooms ran through pipes to be discharged through the latrine into the sewerage system, or a trench underneath the streets. Public latrines may have compensated for any shortage of domestic facilities, although it seems that there was a city-wide lack of toilets judging by the graffiti urging people not to defecate in the streets. Domestic bathing facilities were limited, although some of the more luxurious houses incorporated a bathing area which, on a small scale, reproduced the architectural elements of the public thermae.

✛ Toilets and bathing facilities

Water supply

After the construction of the Augustan aqueduct and its Pompeian branch, both Pompeii and Herculaneum were supplied with water from the springs of Acquaro 26 kilometres away. Previously, households had relied on underground cisterns and cylindrical or marble wells adjacent to the impluvium. By

✛ The Augustan aqueduct

Figure 7.20 Water tower

Figure 7.21 Terracotta pipes

Figure 7.22 Lead pipes

Figure 7.23 Well beside an impluvium giving access to the underground cistern

Figure 7.24 Public fountain

✖️
Cisterns and
water pipes

the 1st century AD, most houses are believed to have had some water connection. In Pompeii, the aqueduct reached the city at its highest point near the Vesuvian Gate where a huge cistern, the *castellum acquae*, redistributed the water through three large lead mains which ran under the footpaths. Branching off the main lines, smaller pipes fed the water into other distribution structures in the shape of pillars, usually built near crossroads. The water was forced up into lead tanks within these water towers, reducing the pressure in the pipelines. An elaborate system of variously shaped pipes (*fistulae*) supplied the service areas, gardens and fountains of private homes as well as public baths, latrines and the forty or more public fountains located in the streets, usually no more than 70 to 80 metres apart. The water flowed day and night through decorative spouts, providing for those who could not afford to have water connected to their homes.

✖️
Public fountains

Cooling, heating and lighting the house

✖️
Coping with
the climate

Many poorer families, in their cramped accommodation, probably suffered from the stifling summer heat, but wealthier families designed their homes, especially those overlooking the sea, with terraces to catch the summer sea breezes, and with roofed loggias and covered porticoes for shade. There were airy rooms adjacent to the gardens with their trees, fountains, fish ponds and grottoes, vaulted underground rooms and marble and travertine floors. The strong, cold north-easterly winds and rains of winter rain required more careful planning for those lucky enough to face the sea. For example, in finer houses there were opaque windows of crystallised gypsum or sulphate of lime and crude glass in the form of thin plate, 4–6 millimetres thick, inserted in a bronze or wooden frame which turned on a pivot. Wooden partitions and shutters which folded or slid into the walls, curtains or nets were also used to protect and warm the house. Winter dining rooms were often painted with a black background which would have absorbed any heat in the house. The charcoal burning braziers probably filled the house with smoke in the winter months.

✖️
Common forms
of lighting

Artificial lighting, even in the grandest houses, was always inadequate, especially when shuttered against the rain and winds. In the public areas of the house, natural light entered via the compluvium, windows and peristyle or courtyard, but service areas were stuffy and darker. There was a variety of artificial lighting, ranging from oil lamps, lanterns and candles. The most common form was the terracotta, bronze or even glass lamp filled with oil, with a wick and handle. Some had two or more necks for greater light and many were decorated with images of gods, gladiatorial contests and erotic subjects. The wealthy were always searching for unique and elaborate forms. Lanterns with semitransparent sides of horn or bladder and candles made of 'tallow fat rolled around a twisted wick'[9] were widely used. Important and valuable elements in domestic furnishing were the lamp supports, sometimes in the form of bronze statues known as 'torchers', and bronze candelabra, some with four wicks for use at banquets. In the House of the Wooden Partition in Herculaneum, bronze lamp supports took the form of a ship's figurehead.

Smoke and the smell of oil must have permeated the house at all times, and the evidence—references to eye troubles—suggests that many people may have suffered eye strain due to the poor light. 'A lamp consisting of a single candle gives only one hundredth as much light as a 60 watt bulb.'[10]

Figure 7.25 A lamp

Security

Although the houses looked inwards and had few or only high and narrow windows on the street side, the fact that the main entrance opened directly onto the busy streets appears to have made house owners security conscious. Not only did the main doors have a bronze lock (*claustrum*) with an L-shaped keyhole, but there is evidence that in some houses there was a bolt on the inner side of the door fitted into holes in the door jambs with a possible diagonal bar fitted into a cavity in the floor for added protection. Occasionally, it appears, an iron grating was fixed across the compluvium to prevent thieves gaining access via the roof.

❀ Locks and bolts

❀ Atria grills

VILLAS

The remains of about 100 villas have been discovered, some only a few hundred metres apart, scattered across the Sarno Plain. On the maritime hillside at Stabiae, five kilometres south of Pompeii where Pliny the Elder's friend Pomponianus lived, at least 12 villas have been excavated. On the other side of Pompeii at Boscoreale and Boscotrecase were some of the more palatial residences: the Villa of Pisanella, the Villa of Publius Fannius Sinistor, and one believed to belong to Agrippa Postumus (the grandson of the emperor Augustus).

❀ Numbers discovered in the area around Pompeii

Villas varied in scale, architectural features and luxury, and unlike the urban domus they did not look inward but were designed to take in the view over the sea or rolling countryside

❀ The villa and the landscape

VILLAS BUILT PURELY FOR LEISURE (OTIUM)

These were often built on different levels with terraces and belvederes, a subterranean portico (*cryptoporticus*), expansive gardens, groves, grottoes, water displays, thermal baths and large swimming pools.

The Villa of the Papyri, on the coastal outskirts of Herculaneum, was the epitome of a villa built for leisure. It is believed to have belonged to the Pisones, a notable Roman aristocratic family, who loved to surround themselves with the most refined friends, philosophers and men of letters and 'it remains one of the greatest testaments to the cultural level reached by the Roman during the Hellenistic age'.[11]

❀ Villa of the Papyri

✺
Ideal location

This maritime villa was sheltered from the north winds by the woods of Vesuvius and cooled by the sea breezes in the heat of summer. According to Amadeo Maiuri, it had

> . . . NO BUILDINGS TO OBSTRUCT ITS VIEW, AND BELOW IT WAS A LARGE GARDEN DESCENDING TO THE LITTLE PORT THAT MUST HAVE SERVED THE OBLIGATORY LANDING PLACE FROM THE SEA; ABOVE IT RAN THE PUBLIC COAST ROAD THAT LED TO THE CITY'S DECUMAN, AND IT MUST HAVE COMMANDED ALL THE FREEDOM AND BREADTH OF VISTA THAT ITS FORTUNATE POSITION COULD OFFER.[12]

✺
Dimensions

✺
Bronzes and marbles

✺
Library of papyri

The villa had the dimensions of an imperial residence; it has been estimated at 33,465 square metres (245 by 137 metres). A colonnade of 36 columns circled the peristyle, and a continuous portico allowed the owners and their guests to walk around the extensive gardens, filled with statuary and fountains—supplied by system of hydraulic pipes—without ever once leaving the protection of the portico. A terrace overlooking the sea ran the entire length of the villa and a circular belvedere, giving a 360-degree view, was paved with one of the finest mosaics ever discovered. A total of 87 marble and bronze sculptures from the Greek archaic period (7th–6th centuries BC), some originals, others superb copies, were found in the garden and rooms of the villa. The sculptures included gods, nymphs, famous orators and philosophers, athletes and forest animals. It also contained the largest papyrus library ever found: 1800 rolls, almost entirely the writings of Epicurean philosophers and more specifically the work of Philodemus of Gadara. Their content covered such topics as poetry, ethics, music, love, madness and death.

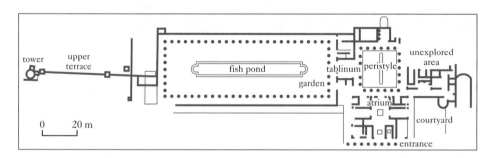

Figure 7.26 Plan of the Villa of the Papyri

✺
Examples of suburban villas

✺
Terraces, galleries and cellars

The two Pompeian suburban villas: the Villa of Mysteries and the Villa of Diomedes, not constrained by the spatial limitations of the more luxurious houses within the city, were built on several levels, providing the ideal lifestyle of outdoor/indoor living.

The Villa of Mysteries built on a slope facing the sea, had extensive porticoes facing south, east and west, and hanging gardens high above a subterranean vault (*cryptoporticus*). The Villa of Diomedes also had a series of terraces on several levels overlooking 'the largest garden in the whole

Pompeian region'.[13] This sunken walled garden with fish pond and pergola was surrounded by a continuous shady gallery extending out from a crypto-porticus used as a cellar, where members of the household had unsuccessfully sought refuge during the eruption. On the corner of the colonnade, two belvederes gave a view of the coast.

The entrances of both villas, unlike urban houses, led directly into the peristyle according to the precepts of Vitruvius. He considered this the most appropriate form for a country estate. Both villas also had their own bath suites with a succession of frigidarium, tepidarium and cadarium (see Chapter 9). The tablinum and triclinium in the Villa of Mysteries were painted in life-size figures, including the famous and controversial continuous fresco which appears to show an initiation rite into the Dionysiac mysteries. Another painting, with black background and Egyptian-style motifs, is the best example of the 'third style' of wall decoration discovered.

❋ Private thermae

❋ Wall paintings in the Villa of Mysteries

Figure 7.27 Painting from the Villa of Mysteries

VILLA RUSTICAE

Wealthy Romans and Pompeians annexed country farms and added elaborate residential quarters—*pars urbana*—for the owner to stay in when visiting. Although these villas were luxurious, their primary focus was agricultural production (vineyards, olives and rearing of livestock) and the villa included professional facilities set aside for the treatment and conservation of produce (*pars fructuaria*); a threshing floor, barn for storage of fodder; a large room containing presses for the production of wine and oil (*torcularium*); cellars or courtyards with terracotta jars (*dolia*) buried into the floor for storage; stables, tool sheds, and cramped quarters for labourers and slaves (*pars rustica*, see Chapter 6).

Unfortunately, most of these villas have only been partially excavated—some officially, when remains came to light during building work, farming projects, gravel extraction or quarrying, and some unofficially by landowners. In most cases the site was filled in following the excavation.

❋ Mix of the gracious and rustic

❋ Few remains

✿
Paintings in the Villa
of Fannius Sinistor

Two of the most famous villa rusticae are the Villa of Publius Fannius Sinistor and the Villa of Pisanella, both at Boscoreale. Nothing remains of the former with the exception of two of its spectacular rooms now reconstructed in the Metropolitan Museum of Art in New York and the Naples National Museum. These rooms featured outstanding wall paintings: in one the amazing architectural decoration appears 'to penetrate the walls and open up impossible prospects of buildings, balconies and terraces, pergolas and fountains among trellises and garlands of flowers'.[14] The frescoes in the other room feature allegories of Asia and Macedonia, one perhaps announcing the birth of Alexander the future conqueror of Asia.

✿
A hoard of silver in
Villa of Pisanella

The Villa of Pisanella appears to have been a little more rustic, although its owner certainly wasn't, judging by the rich hoard of silverware, jewels and coins found hidden in a well in the torcularium. The courtyard was surrounded by porticoes on three sides onto which faced the dining room, sleeping quarters and torcularium. The centre of the house was a large kitchen from which a door led to a heated bath—a sign of luxury—in close proximity to the stables.

DOMESTIC LIFE

The home was the centre of family life, personal religion, as well as business and political dealings.

THE FAMILIA

✿
As a legal and
social unit

The Roman familia included all those people who came under the control of the the paterfamilias. As a legal unit it included children—no matter their age or whether they lived under the same roof or not—over whom he had *patria potestas* (power), and slaves to whom he was master or dominus. From the legal point of view, his wife was not under his control—she remained part of her father's familia—and his freedmen were his clients. However, in a wider social framework they all comprised the familia.

✿
Power of the
paterfamilias

The power of the paterfamilias over his children began several days after their birth and continued while ever he lived, no matter whether they were adults or not. Soon after the birth of a child—when the midwife announced it was healthy and fit for rearing—it was placed at his feet and he had the choice of picking up the child, a gesture indicating that he or she was now part of the family, or not accepting it, in which case the child was put outside the circle of the family. Even adult children were subject to his disciplinary power: both sons and daughters required his permission to marry and he could break up their marriages if it suited him, but usually he consulted with family members before taking serious action.

The upper class girl brought a dowry to her marriage although her father

Figure 7.28 Fresco of Paquis Proclus and his wife (Naples National Archaeological Museum)

kept total control over her other financial affairs, and if she divorced, the dowry had to be returned. If she was caught in the act of adultery, her husband was obliged to divorce her, but her children remained as 'property' of their father. Men were permitted to have sex with prostitutes—hence the number of brothels in Pompeii—but forbidden to have relations with unmarried or widowed freeborn women. On the death of her father, a girl or woman was put under the guardianship of another male. Although she could inherit a share of his estate and make a will on the same basis as a brother, she could not freely dispose of her inheritance. However, after Augustus, a freeborn woman with three children and a freedwomen with four could legally act on her own behalf in financial affairs.

✗ Daughters and wives

Though an adult son had political rights, election to one of the magistracies could be difficult to achieve without the financial backing of the paterfamilias, from whom he received an allowance and who 'owned' all possessions in the family.

✗ Adult sons

To the paterfamilias, the daily visit of associates, clients and dependants (*salutatio*) was vital for business and any political ambitions he may have had. They arrived in the early morning after a frugal breakfast (*jentaculum*) of milk, water, a piece of bread and cheese, taken at sunrise. Some came in litters carried by slaves, others on foot, wearing the heavy white woollen toga, folded and draped over the left arm (a garment reserved for outdoors and formal situations as opposed to the shin-length woollen tunic worn while relaxing at home). A man's personal slave, if he had one, would probably have spent the

✗ Importance of clients

previous evening preparing his toga. The slave doorkeeper (*ostiarius*) ushered them into the imposing vestibule and atrium and the master's accountant (*dispensator*) and secretary or clerk (*notarius*) were in attendance to keep a record of proceedings. According to Vitruvius, the houses of patrons reflected their social position, whereas 'men of everyday fortune' did not need houses 'built in the grand style, because such men are more apt to discharge their social obligations by visiting others than by having others visit them'.[15] With the end of the morning rituals, many of those who attended might accompany their patron to the Forum, continuing to contribute to his standing as an important citizen.

Although there were huge social contrasts in Pompeii and Herculaneum between the owners of houses such as that of Menander and that of the wealthy freedmen Aulus Vettius Conviva and Aulus Vettius Restitutus, and those who rented a tiny upstairs apartment or lived in a room at the back of a small workshop, the gulf was bridged by living in close proximity and dependence on each other. This interconnectedness between all groups is reflected in the architecture of both individual houses and insulae.

For much of the day the men were out of the home either in the Forum conducting business or widening their networks. They may have returned home for lunch (*prandium*) taken about midday which was a reasonably modest meal of cold meats, eggs, vegetables, bread and leftovers from the previous evening's dinner. Not all Pompeians and Herculaneans ate at home. Some out of necessity, others out of preference, frequented the numerous hot food bars. In the afternoon the men generally attended the public bathing complexes before returning home to dinner (*cena*) or to attend a special dinner party.

The main domestic tasks for a well-to-do woman were attending to her children, supervising slaves and perhaps spinning and weaving. She had no need to feed or look after a new-born baby as there were slaves to suckle (wet nurses—*nutrices*), and take care of the child once it was weaned. These nurses were usually chosen for their health and refinement and were an important part of the household, often being manumitted later. Wealthy families had a large staff of cooks, bakers, carvers and servers. Cooks were highly valued because dinner parties 'were an essential tool of social and political control'.[16] According to Grant, 'a cook cost the price of a horse . . . though he was still only worth a third as much as an expensive fish'.[17] Certainly the cook's knowledge of gastronomy had to be substantial if his master was to impress his guests.

If the women of the household were literate, they might spend part of the day reading. Although it is not known how many females could read and write, it is believed that upper-class girls were educated in the home, probably by a slave tutor. The frescoes showing women with pen and tablet or with a book in their hands suggest that literacy was a mark of status and that such an accomplishment might have made a woman more desirable as a marriage partner. According to Pliny the Younger, his third wife Calpurnia was 'highly intelligent and a careful housewife'. He believed that her devotion to him gave her an interest in literature:

> SHE KEEPS COPIES OF MY WORKS TO READ AGAIN AND AGAIN AND EVEN LEARN BY HEART . . . IF I AM DOING A READING, SHE SITS BEHIND A CURTAIN NEAR BY AND GREEDILY DRINKS IN EVERY WORD OF APPRECIATION. SHE HAS EVEN SET MY VERSES TO MUSIC AND SINGS THEM TO THE ACCOMPANIMENT OF HER LYRE.[18]

Figure 7.29 Fresco of a girl with a stylus and wax tablet (Naples National Archaeological Museum)

It is possible that a small percentage of women in other classes had a basic knowledge of reading and writing, especially wives of rich freedmen, but for the majority of the female population it was probably not a priority. The boys of the household were put in the hands of an educated family slave (*pedagogue*) who supervised their lessons and accompanied them to the Forum or to the home of a teacher. Dexter Hoyos in *Inscription, Graffiti and Literacy* says that recent scholarship points to as little as 'twenty percent of males and ten percent of females'[19] in Pompeii being able to read and write. This is probably based on the number who are believed to have had enough money to have their children educated. However, the number of graffiti, electoral slogans and verses from Roman literature written on the city's walls suggests there might have been more.

✲
Education of boys

Upper-class women had their own personal attendants (*pedisequae*) to help them with their toilette, hair and clothes. While at home, a woman wore soft leather sandals (*soleae*), a vest-like garment against the skin (*tunica interior*), covered by an ankle-length woollen tunic caught at the shoulders. If she left the house she added a colourful *stola*—a loose woollen garment tied at the waist with a belt, probably added some jewellery and replaced the light sandals for a sturdier outdoor pair (*calcei*). When the weather was particularly bad, she would protect her shoulders and head with a loose cloak (*palla*).

✲
Female dress

DINNER PARTIES

Dinner was the main meal of the day and could begin about four o'clock in the afternoon. In well-to-do homes this meal was divided into three phases:

✲
Three courses

- *Gustatio* consisted of tasty dishes to whet the appetite. This might include eggs, vegetables, olives and sausages accompanied by honeyed wine (mulsum).
- *Fercula* ('dishes that are carried') comprised several courses of fish, shellfish, poultry, stuffed roasts of meat (pork, lamb, kid and wild boar) and vegetables. Wine was served with these courses.
- *Mensae secundae* (dessert) included fresh and dried fruit, nuts, cheeses and cakes, often followed by salty dishes such as snails, oysters and olives so that the guests would drink copious amounts of wine after the meal.

Although many inhabitants of Pompeii and Herculaneum could not afford such extravagances and delicacies, others may have thrown banquets almost as outrageous as those satirised by some of the literature, such as Petronius's *Satyricon*. His character, the wealthy freedman Trimalchio, depicted as 'stupid, greedy, gluttonous and extremely pretentious'[20] threw a feast which included honeyed dormice, sows' wombs, and cakes stuffed with live thrushes. The 'convenient' form of Epicureanism, or living life to the full identified at Pompeii, may have gone too far on occasion, leading to over-indulgence.

A more realistic account of the food favoured by Romans can be found in the five hundred or so recipes in a cook book by Apicus (*On Cooking*). The Romans liked their food sweet (addition of honey) and spicy. The popularity of fish sauce is evidence of their love of food with a strong flavour. Apicus's recipes used imported spices such as pepper, ginger, cinnamon, nutmeg and cloves, as well as native herbs like oregano, coriander, mint, aniseed and fennel, and he made his own garum from the much prized red mullet.

Dinner parties were part of the ritual which bound a patron to his large network of clients and on these occasions he had an opportunity to display his collection of silver and glassware and to boast of the skills of his cook.

An influential slave within the household was the *vocator*, who sent out the invitations and arranged the seating for a maximum of nine people including the host and his wife. Women, unlike their Greek counterparts, joined their husbands at dinner parties and guests often brought their own slaves to serve them and guide them home safely through the unlit streets. Slaves of the host were expected to 'wash and dry the feet of the guests' and 'spread a linen cloth on the cushions of the couches'.[21] Each couch held three people, separated by cushions, but seating was not ad hoc; it followed a strict

Figure 7.30 Silver cup (Naples National Archaeological Museum)

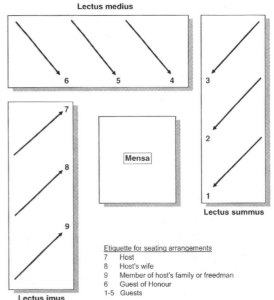

Lectus medius

Mensa

Lectus summus

Etiquette for seating arrangements
7   Host
8   Host's wife
9   Member of host's family or freedman
6   Guest of Honour
1-5 Guests

Lectus imus

Figure 7.31 Triclinia—dining arrangements

etiquette. If any guest was unhappy with his placement the master could always blame the vocator.

The diners, wearing fine white togas (*synthesis*), reclined obliquely facing the low table (*mensa*), supporting their left elbow on a cushion. As the Romans did not use forks—although knives and spoons were used occasionally—a slave known as the *scissor* cut up the food before it was placed on the mensa by the male food servers (*ministri*). Guests held a plate in their left hand and ate with their right. Young, handsome male wine waiters (*pueri a cyatho*), one to each guest, kept the wine flowing during the meal, according to etiquette. Evidence from the black painted walls of the winter dining room of Marcus Epidius Hymenaeus and Gaius Arrius Crescens (the House of the Moralist) suggest there may have been a code of behaviour expected by some of the more refined hosts. 'Don't cast lustful glances, or make eyes at another man's wife. Don't be coarse in conversation. Restrain yourself from getting angry or using offensive language. If you can't, go back to you own house.'[22]

Etiquette

Apart from animated conversation, these dinner parties were enlivened by a variety of entertainment provided sometimes by the guests themselves—called upon for a poetry recitation or song—and by household and professional entertainers: readers, dancers, acrobats, jugglers, actors and poets. After-dinner drinking was often heavy and dinner parties could last well into the evening.

Entertainment

At Pompeii and Herculaneum the nights were pitch black and full of dangers. 'Those who did not want to run the risk of breaking a leg or having an unpleasant encounter would be accompanied by a servant with a torch . . . those who had no one to accompany them had to make do with a candle and make their way with a little fear', avoiding other revellers and drunks who had stayed late at the taverns, as well as garbage raining down from above as 'plebeian houses took advantage of the dark to get rid of their rubbish'.[23]

Late night dangers

THE HOUSE AS A SACRED SPACE

According to Cicero the 'most sacred, the most hallowed place on earth is the home of each and every citizen . . . the very centre of his worship, religion and domestic ritual.'[24] All family ceremonies were conducted by the paterfamilias as chief priest, and religious observances in the home were associated with:

Paterfamilias as chief priest

- the household gods as well as any other gods that may have been selected by the family as household guardians. There was an 'assimilation of divinities (even foreign gods) into Roman domestic religion'[25] such as Venus, Bacchus/ Dionysus and Isis.
- the sacred hearth
- the ancestors
- rites of passage; birth, marriage, death.

(See Chapter 9 for details of private worship.)

Household guardians, the hearth and ancestors

Chapter review

Urban housing
Looked inwards, opened directly onto street; some spatial limitations

Types
Small and medium—sized taberna houses
Average-sized (8–13 rooms) atrium houses
Grandiose atrium houses designed for large numbers of visitors
Terraced houses
Apartments of various sizes in insula houses

Variations in housing reflect urban topography, lack of space, economic factors, fashion and a natural disaster

Architectural spaces and features of atrium houses
Fauces and vestibulum; atrium; tablinum; peristyle and garden, triclinium; alae; cubiculm; oecus; exedra and marginal areas (kitchen, latrine and slaves quarters)

Mosaic floors, wall paintings (frescoes), decorative pieces in garden, minimal furniture, water supply, lighting, heating and security

---

Villas
Designed to be one with the landscape and to make the most of the view, some, a combination of luxury and the rustic

Types
Villa of otium (relaxation and leisure)
Best example is Villa of the Papyri at western end of Herculaneum and the magnificent suburban villas just outside Pompeii—Villa of Diomedes and the Villa of Mysteries.

Villa rusticae (a working estate combined with an elegant living area)
Good examples at Boscoreale—Villa of Pisanella, Villa of Fannius Sinistor and Villa Regina
Over one hundred excavated

Architectural spaces and features
Villa of otium—often built on different levels with terraces, subterranean porticoes, belvederes, water displays, extensive gardens and porticoes, thermal baths, swimming pools
Marble floors, outstanding wall paintings, bronze and marble statues.

Villa rusticae—luxurious residences for owner and area for agricultural production (torcularium, stables, storage) and slaves

---

Domestic life
The home a centre of a family life, personal religion, business and political dealings

Roman familia—a legal and social unit of wife, children (unmarried and married), slaves and freedmen
Patria potestas—power of paterfamilias; dominus (master) of his slaves
Importance of patron/client relations—morning salutatio as a tool of social and political control and business dealings
Duties of household slaves—nurse, pedagogue, cook, dispensator, vocator, personal attendants etc.
Food and etiquette at a dinner-party or banquet—a way of further networking
Religious observances and practices—shrine (lararium) of household gods (lares, penates, genius); the sacred hearth; the ancestors; family rites of passage (birth, marriage, death); magico/religious amulets

Activities

1 a Name the spaces or rooms numbered on the plan shown in Figure 7.32.

b Into which of Wallace-Hadrill's categories of houses does this one fit?

c Which of the numbered spaces were open to the owner's clients?

d What would a visitor in the 1st century AD expect to find in the numbered parts of the house?

2 AT ONE END IS A LARGE NYMPHAEUM WITH A CENTRAL APSED NICHE FLANKED BY TWO SMALLER NICHES . . . THE ENTIRE NYMPHAEUM IS COVERED WITH MOSAIC FLORAL DESIGNS, WHICH SURROUNDED TWO PANELS OF DEER BEING CHASED BY HOUNDS. FESTOONS OF FRUIT AND FLOWERS ARE SURMOUNTED BY PEACOCKS. SCALLOP SHELLS FRAME THE EDGES, AND COLOURED MASKS CAP THE PEDIMENT.

Joseph Jay Deiss, Herculaneum: Italy's Buried Treasure, *p. 92*

a Identify the house and room described in the source.

b What is a nymphaeum?

c Why was it built into this particular house?

d What is an apse and a pediment? Why were apses and pediments often included in the houses of Pompeii and Herculaneum?

e What other architectural features were included in prestigious houses?

4 THE VILLA . . . IS AT ONE WITH THE LANDSCAPE: IT IS LAID OUT IN SUCH A WAY THAT WITHOUT GOING OUT OF IT THE INHABITANTS COULD ENJOY AT ANY TIME OF THE DAY AN INFINITELY VARYING SPECTACLE OF LIGHT AND SHADE UPON THE NATURAL SURROUNDINGS OF THE HOUSE, AND UPON THE SEA AS FAR AS THE HORIZON.

Marcel Brion, Pompeii and Herculaneum *p. 151*

3 Use Figure 7.33 to help explain what the poet Horace is referring to in the quote below.

THE FISHES FEEL THE OCEAN NARROWING FROM ALL THE RUBBLE THROWN INTO THE DEEP AND STILL CONTRACTORS AND THEIR WORKMEN FLING CEMENT TO IT, FOR ONE WHO CANNOT KEEP TO SOLID EARTH.

Figure 7.33 Fresco of a villa at Stabiae (Naples National Archaeological Museum)

a Make a list of all the features of a villa built for leisure which illustrate the secondary source above.

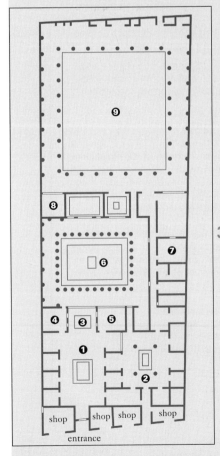

Figure 7.32 Plan of the House of the Faun

Activities

b Compile another list which shows the ways in which villa rusticae differed.

5 Draw a diagram showing the slaves that might be found in a well-to-do household and the tasks for which they were responsible.

6 Study the menu from Trimalchio's feast in Petronius's *Satyricon* and answer the following questions.

　a What evidence is there from this menu that Pompeians liked their food sweet.

　b What other evidence, apart from this menu, is there for their liking for spicy foods.

　c What was the point of including salty dishes like snails and oysters in the mensa secundae?

　d What items on this menu are unlikely to have been on the menu of most banquets held in Pompeii and Herculaneum?

　e What evidence from Trimalchio's menu reveals his gluttony and need to 'show off' to his guests?

f What was Petronius's purpose in writing about Trimalchio and his feast?

g What part did banquets play in Pompeian and Herculanean society?

8 Write a paragraph for each, explaining the powers and responsibilities of the paterfamilias with regard to his:
　a wife
　b daughters
　c sons

d slaves
e freedmen/clients

9 Topic for extended response, class discussion or oral presentation: 'The urban domus "was a curious mix of the gracious and ungracious".'[26]

Gustatio
Black and green olives; honeyed dormice with poppy seeds; grilled sausages; dark Syrian plums and pomegranate seeds; *beccaficos* (tiny figpecker birds) in spiced egg yolk inside pastry eggs. Honeyed wine

Fercula
Served on round plate with different dishes for each sign of the Zodiac: *Aries*: ram's chick-peas; *Taurus*: beef; *Gemini*: kidneys and testicles; *Cancer*: crown of myrtle; *Leo*: African figs; *Virgo*: sterile cow's womb; *Libra*: scales supporting tarts and honey cakes; *Scorpio*: scorpion fish; *Sagittarius*: hare; *Capricorn*: lobster; *Aquarius*: goose; *Pisces*: two red mullets.

Roasted fattened fowls, sow's wombs and hare; roast whole wild boar with dates, suckled by piglets made of cakes stuffed with live thrushes; boiled whole calf stuffed with sausage and black pudding. Wine (the jars labelled 'Falernian wine, 100 years old')

Mensa secundae
Fruits and cakes; oysters and scallops; snails; bone fattened chicken and goose eggs; pastries stuffed with raisins and n quince apples and pork disguised as fowls and fish.

Figure 7.34 Menu for Trimalchio's feast[27]

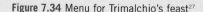

Relaxation, entertainment and sport

8

THINGS TO CONSIDER

- The abundance of evidence for physical and aesthetic forms of entertainment
- The part played by wealthy individuals and magistrates in promoting drama and spectacles
- The architectural features of buildings devoted to leisure and sport
- The status and popularity of those involved in public performances

It appears that 'pleasure came easily'[1] to the people of Pompeii and Herculaneum judging by the number of graffiti relating to gambling, drinking, sex, celebrity gladiators and actors, as well as the number of buildings associated with sport, entertainment and relaxation. Perhaps the popularity of Epicureanism and the worship of Dionysus/Bacchus, both prevalent in Campania, encouraged the inhabitants to seek happiness and release from the cares of the world. Also, the Roman adage, borrowed from the Greeks—a sound mind in a sound body (*mens sana in corpore sano*)—contributed to their passion for physical exercise and the baths. Their addiction to the theatre and the bloodthirsty spectacles in the amphitheatre were made possible by the large number of days in the Roman calendar for religious festivals and civic holidays, as well as the financial backing of magistrates and the generosity of those aspiring to political office.

Pleasure and passion

VISITING THE BATHS

For the people in all Roman towns, a visit to the municipal or privately owned bath complexes (*thermae*) was a social occasion as well as an 'opportunity to satisfy not only the well-being of the body, but also of the spirit'.[2] Archaeologists have identified four thermae in Pompeii: the Stabian Baths (the oldest), the Forum Baths, the Central Baths (still under construction at the time of the eruption) and the Sarno Baths. There was also the small privately run bath of Julia Felix. In Herculaneum, two have been discovered, the Suburban and Forum Baths.

Satisfying body and spirit

LAYOUT AND DECOR OF BATH COMPLEXES

Generally the bath areas were divided into sections for men and women. If there were no separate areas, males and females attended at different hours. However, in some places there was mixed bathing until the time of Hadrian, despite criticisms from writers at its inappropriateness. Although the decor of each complex may have differed, most were vaulted, the walls and ceilings covered in elegant stucco work and the floors in mosaic, often with a marine theme.

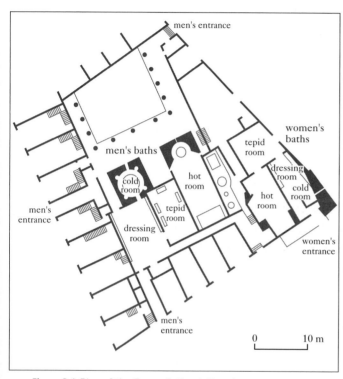

Figure 8.1 Plan of the Forum Baths at Herculaneum

Figure 8.2 Decoration of the tepidarium in the Forum Baths in Pompeii

The chief bathing elements were identical. There was:

- a *vestibule*, often in the form of an exercise yard with portico
- an *apodyterium* or changing and waiting room with benches and small niches or shelves for storing clothes
- a *frigidarium* or room with circular cold bath
- a *tepidarium* or warm room used as a transition space so bathers' bodies could adjust to the temperature changes. Sometimes off the tepidarium was a *laconicum* or sweating room, heated by a brazier.
- a *caldarium* or hot room with a rectangular heated bath (*alverus*) at one end and a large circular basin (*labrum*) for cold-water ablutions between sessions in the hot bath, at the other. The alverus was lined in marble with steps for sitting and could usually hold about ten people at one time.

The heating system was provided by a charcoal-burning furnace located at the back of the caldarium, between the men's and women's sections. Hot

Figure 8.4 The fountain at the far end of the men's caldarium in the Forum Baths in Pompeii

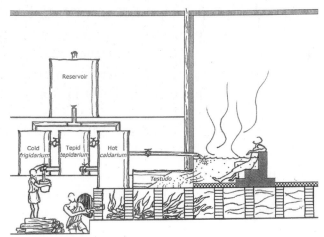

Figure 8.5 A marine mosaic in the Forum Baths in Pompeii

Figure 8.3 Waiting room for men in the Forum Baths in Herculaneum with basin for washing hands

air circulated through the interstices (*hypocaustum*) under the marble floor which was raised about 70 to 90 centimetres on brick pillars (*suspensure*), and through air ducts built behind the walls. To prevent the bathers suffering the nuisance of cold condensation dropping onto them, the ceiling had grooves in the plaster which collected and channelled the condensation down the walls. Vitruvius described how the water for the hot bath was heated (see page 148).

Figure 8.6 Heating system in the thermae

THE ULTIMATE IN LUXURY

The Suburban Baths in Herculaneum, supposedly financed by Marcus Nonius Balbus, were an elegant and graceful complex which would not have been out of place among the magnificent buildings of Rome. They featured an 'architecturally notable vestibule'[3] and the waiting room was 'one of the great finds of archaeology'.[4] Features of the waiting room included:

- walls of varied-coloured marbles, framed white stucco panels containing bas-reliefs of naked warriors in various poses, winged cupids and a red spiral stucco frieze running around the room

❈ Suburban Baths at Herculaneum

- a floor of black marble squares divided by narrow bands of white marble
- magnificent wooden panelled doors
- a vaulted roof with light coming through a glass-enclosed ceiling niche.

ACTIVITIES AT THE BATHS

✿
Benefits of a visit
to the baths

As well as enjoying the benefits of the warm, hot and cold baths, visitors could practise physical exercise and play sport, indulge in a range of therapies such as massage, stroll in the gardens, listen to music and poetry recitals and read in the library, conduct business, and receive invitations.

✿
Sexual activities

Pornographic graffiti suggests that even some sexual activities may have taken place in the baths. Apparently a masseur in Pompeii was 'accused of taking liberties with women'[5] and at Herculaneum 'pimps and prostitutes began to make a nuisance of themselves'.[6] In the town's Suburban Baths, a back room at the end of a corridor seems to have been used for sex. 'Two companions were here; and after the bad guidance of Epaphroditus in everything, they tardily threw him out. Then with the girls they joyfully consumed one hundred and five and a half sesterces.'[7] Another graffito describes Apelles the waiter dining 'most pleasantly with Dexter the slave of Caesar', and then both screwing 'at the same time'.[8] It seems that they may have had other companions with them as another scratching says they 'lovingly screwed the two twice'.[9]

The baths opened at midday after the furnaces had been lit and an afternoon visit became a daily routine for many people. From the discovery of hundreds of lamps in the Forum Baths and Stabian Baths, it appears that the complexes stayed open at night for those unable to make it during the day. They were bustling, lively places. Seneca described the noises coming from a bath complex adjacent to his lodgings.

HERE I AM SURROUNDED BY ALL KINDS OF NOISE (MY LODGINGS OVERLOOK A BATHHOUSE). CONJURE UP IN YOUR IMAGINATION ALL THE SOUNDS THAT MAKE ONE HATE ONE'S EARS. I HEAR GRUNTS OF MUSCLEMEN EXERCISING AND JERKING THOSE HEAVY WEIGHTS AROUND; THEY ARE WORKING HARD, OR PRETENDING TO. I HEAR THEIR SHARP HISSING AS THEY RELEASE THEIR PENT BREATH. IF THERE HAPPENS TO BE A LAZY FELLOW CONTENT WITH A SIMPLE MASSAGE I HEAR THE SLAP OF HAND ON SHOULDER; YOU CAN HEAR WHETHER IT'S HITTING A FLAT OR HOLLOW. IF A BALLPLAYER COMES UP AND STARTS CALLING OUT HIS SCORE, I'M DONE FOR. ADD TO THIS THE RACKET OF A COCKY BASTARD, A THIEF CAUGHT IN THE ACT, AND A FELLOW WHO LIKES THE SOUND OF HIS OWN VOICE IN THE BATH, PLUS THOSE WHO PLUNGE INTO THE POOL WITH A HUGE SPLASH OF WATER. BESIDES THOSE WHO JUST HAVE LOUD VOICES, IMAGINE THE SKINNY ARMPIT-HAIR PLUCKER, WHOSE CRIES ARE SHRILL SO AS TO DRAW PEOPLE'S ATTENTION AND WHO NEVER STOPS EXCEPT WHEN HE'S DOING HIS JOB AND MAKING SOMEONE ELSE SHRIEK

FOR HIM. NOW ADD THE MINGLED CRIES OF THE DRINK PEDLAR AND
THE SELLERS OF SAUSAGES, PASTRIES AND HOT FARE, EACH HAWKING HIS
OWN WARES WITH HIS OWN PARTICULAR PEAL.[10]

Many were accompanied to the baths by slaves. Some, according to Juvenal's *Satires*, took a 'mob of rowdy retainers', like 'that show-off Tongilius, who was 'such a bore at the baths' with his 'outsized oil flask of rhinoceros horn'.[11] Slaves carried their master's or mistress's oil, soda and strigil (a curved bronze or bone scraper) for cleaning and massage. Soap, which Pliny the Elder said was 'an invention of the Gauls'[12] was not in general use. The slaves may have helped their master and mistress disrobe in the change room where clothes and valuables were placed in small cupboards. 'Women wore a two-piece or more modest costume (*balnearis vestus*), men wore leather trunks or bathed naked.'[13] Often before taking to the baths, people engaged in exercise, one popular form with men being a game called bladder-ball (*pila*) which was 'played with inflated animal bladders often painted green'.[14] Both males and females indulged in massages and used perfume liberally.

After a relaxing and invigorating session in the thermae, visitors might enjoy a light snack, read a book in the library or stroll among the gardens in conversation with friends or business acquaintances.

✻ Bathing equipment

ATTENDING THE THEATRE

Although the people of Pompeii were not as addicted to the theatre as much as to the bloody gladiatorial spectacles, theatrical performances of all kinds (traditional Greek and Roman tragedy and comedy, Oscan farces, mime and pantomime) were extremely popular. Evidence of this can be seen in the theatre complex at Pompeii and the magnificent theatre at Herculaneum, the number of theatrical motifs used in the decoration of well-to-do houses, and the graffiti written by fans about local and visiting actors.

✻ Evidence

THEATRE DESIGN AND DECORATION

Two theatres, essentially Greek in design, have come to light in Pompeii. The larger of the two is believed to be older than any theatre in Rome and was probably built at a time when Hellenic influence in Campania was still strong. During the Augustan age it was renovated and embellished in marble by the architect Marcus Artorius Primus. He also increased its seating capacity to 5000 to allow more people to enjoy the popular entertainment (comedies, tragedies and farces) for which it was used. The horseshoe-shaped auditorium (*cavea*) was divided into three horizontal areas: the section nearest the stage (*ima cavea*) was reserved for authorities and important visitors, and the highest section (*summa cavea*) appears to have been occupied by women. Up until the time of Augustus, women had sat with the men. Other

✻ The great theatre of Pompeii

members of the public were seated in the media cavea. The stage (*proscenium*), which provided the back drop for the performance, was ornamented with columns and statues and connected by three doors to an area behind, possibly the actors' change rooms.

❈
The covered Odeon

The small covered theatre or Odeon was built later (early 1st century BC) and had 'the stamp of the late Hellenistic architectural tradition'.[15] Its construction was instigated by two local magistrates who had been followers of Sulla and had settled in Pompeii when it became a Roman colony. Because it was to be used for more serious performances such as concerts, lectures and poetry recitals, its features—roof, steep cavea and size—made it acoustically perfect. Vitruvius, in his chapter on theatres, says:

❈
Acoustics according
to Vitruvius

> THE VOICE IS A FLOWING BREATH OF AIR . . . IT MOVES BY THE ENDLESS FORMATION OF CIRCLES, JUST AS ENDLESSLY EXPANDING CIRCLES OF WAVES ARE MADE IN STANDING WATER WHEN A STONE IS THROWN INTO IT . . . IN THE SAME WAY THE VOICE MAKES CIRCULAR MOTIONS; HOWEVER ON THE SURFACE OF WATER THE CIRCLES MOVE HORIZONTALLY, WHILE THE VOICE AT ONCE ADVANCES HORIZONTALLY AND MOUNTS UPWARDS STEP BY STEP . . . SO LONG AS NO OBSTACLE INTERFERES WITH THE FIRST WAVE . . . ALL OF THEM WILL REACH THE EARS OF THE SPECTATORS WITHOUT ECHOING, THOSE IN THE LOWERMOST SEATS AS WELL AS THOSE IN THE HIGHEST. THEREFORE THE ARCHITECTS OF OLD, FOLLOWING IN NATURE'S FOOTSTEPS, PERFECTED THE STEPPED SEATING OF THEATRES AFTER THEIR RESEARCH INTO THE RISING OF THE VOICE.[16]

Adjacent to both theatres was a spacious foyer (*quadriporticus*) where spectators could stroll between performances.

❈
Theatre at
Herculaneum

The theatre of Herculaneum, which could hold about 2500 people, was one of the little town's most impressive buildings. When first discovered it was in perfect condition, but the earliest 'excavators' used it as 'a quarry for ancient art and marbles'.[17] Unlike the Pompeian Greek-style theatres built into the hillside, it was free-standing with a two-storey facade of arches and pillars. On the top of the theatre stood gilded equestrian statues and larger than life bronzes of emperors

Figure 8.7 The Odeon. Notice the wider tiers reserved for prominent individuals.

Figure 8.8 The quadriporticus, often referred to as the Gladiators' Barracks

and other influential individuals. Its proscenium was decorated with red and yellow porphyry columns and cornices of green serpentine with niches for statuary. Two boxes at either end of the orchestra were reserved for the very highest officials like Nonius Balbus. At one end of the theatre was a portico which allowed spectators to have a view over the countryside during intervals.

PERFORMANCES

Theatrical performances were organised for religious festivities, often to celebrate the dedication of a monument or achievement. Magistrates tendered out the staging of the performance to an impresario and the program was advertised with or without a *velarium* (awning) and *sparsiones* (perfume showers). A coloured awning was sometimes stretched across the auditorium to provide light shade, and water was sprayed from a tank located at the highest point in the theatre, but spectators had to bring their own cushions for the long performance.

Entry was free to all, but admission could be gained to the theatre only by having a small piece of bone or ivory as a token which indicated where the holder was to sit. Some of these were 'in the form of fish, birds, skulls or theatre masks'.[18] Those with the image of a bird (a dove or pigeon) indicated the highest seats against the wall.

All classes attended the theatre although there is some doubt about slaves. If they were not permitted to attend in the 1st century AD, they certainly seem to have been in the days of Plautus, a Roman comic poet who lived c.254–84 BC. In a play he comments on the noise made by women and babies brought to the theatres by their slave wet nurses. Of course these lines could have been merely to entertain rather than to portray fact. 'Tell the wet nurses to take care of the babies at home and not bring them to the theatre' to avoid them 'bleating like sheep. Let the matrons be silent as they look on and laugh, and let them keep their shrieks and chatter for home.'[19] Theatres were certainly noisy. Audiences, particularly at performances of comic farces and pantomimes, were excitable, sometimes raucous and often impatient.

Although actors had a low social status, they were popular. For example, an actor of the late 1st century BC, Norbanus Sorex, was recognised by a bronze portrait found in the Temple of Isis. Judging by the graffiti, many actors appear to have acquired large fan clubs, like the pantomime stars Theorus and Pierus, as well as the much acclaimed Pilaid, Actius and Paris. The fans of Actius Anicetus called themselves Actiani Anicetiani and left graffiti about their regret at his leaving the city. By far the most popular was Lucius Domitius Paris, a favourite of the theatre-loving emperor Nero, who was called 'Paris, pearl of the stage' and 'Paris the sweet darling'.[20] Other graffiti mentions 'Comrades of the Paris Club'.[21] Although there were generally no female actors (males played female roles), women did seem to take part in

✵ Staging a theatrical performance

✵ Velarium and sparsiones

✵ Seating

✵ Attendance

✵ Popularity and status of actors

✵ Women and mime

mimes and pantomimes and there is a graffito of an actress called Histrionica Rotica (Erotica), perhaps a name indicative of what she did on stage.

✼
Features of
traditional drama

By the 1st century AD, it was probably only the upper classes in Pompeii and Herculaneum who appreciated the traditional tragedies and comedies. It seems that performances were infrequent and 'tended to be put on for private groups'.[22] During such performances wigs, and masks which amplified the voice, were worn and use was made of all the traditional devices for effect and surprise: a curtain with painted scene and figures which was raised vertically from the ground; the machine for use in plays that featured gods and supernatural forces; trapdoors and the various methods of making thunder, lightning, rain and smoke which signalled the appearance of divine apparitions.

Figure 8.9 (left) Mosaic of a theatre mask (Naples National Archaeological Museum)

Figure 8.10 Fresco of a theatre mask (Naples National Archaeological Museum)

✼
Oscan farces

Most popular with the majority of people were the Oscan farces (*Atellanae*) that originated in the Campanian town of Atella, and mime and pantomime, introduced in the 1st century BC. The Atellanae, with their bawdy characters—Pappas the old fool; Maccus the glutton; Buccho the hunchback and Dossenus the crafty one—plus their crude dialogue bordering on the obscene attracted a huge following in the towns of Vesuvius. The audience loved these humble characters and the unexpected situations in which they found themselves: Pappas standing for office, Maccus becoming a banker and Buccho as a general or gladiator.

✼
Mime

✼
Pantomime

Ancient mimes depended for effect on short amusing plots, ludicrous actions and obscene gestures. The actors did not wear masks, as in traditional theatre, performed barefoot and wore striking clothes. Women appeared on stage and often did some form of a striptease in response to the audience. Pantomime was based loosely on mythological themes, and actors were accompanied by singers and musicians. No masks were used and there were no words spoken. So that the audience could recognise the characters' ages and status, actors wore wigs and different coloured clothes.

DEVELOPING THE BODY AND PLAYING SPORT

Every Roman town had its open-air sports ground (*palaestra*), as well as exercise facilities at the thermae. The importance of sport to the inhabitants of Pompeii and Herculaneum can be gauged by the size of the main palaestra which tended to follow a similar design. The Large Palaestra in Pompeii, opposite the amphitheatre, was a 107 by 141-metre rectangle, surrounded by a portico on three sides, shade trees and enclosed by a wall. In the centre was a large swimming pool. The Herculanean palaestra occupied a whole block with a street frontage of approximately 110 metres and depth of 70 metres with a swimming pool in the shape of a cross about 50 metres in length with its cross arm about 30 metres. Like its Pompeian counterpart, this palaestra was surrounded by trees—the roots of which have been found—and the field itself outside the pool was large enough for practising all the traditional sports of athletics, wrestling, javelin and discus throwing. Its main entrance was 'like a majestic columned cella, or inner portion of a temple . . . all was spacious and imposing'.[23] Deiss suggests that in this room sacrifices were made prior to any competition and that in a niche probably stood a magnificent statue of Hercules, patron of the town. Adjacent to this vestibule were other rooms off the portico with wall paintings, one of a young bronzed athlete lying on a couch with a beautiful woman.

✦ Features of a palaestra

Figure 8.11 The Pompeian palaestra

Figure 8.12 Bronze runner from the Villa of the Papyri in Herculaneum (Naples National Archaeological Museum)

It is certainly possible that the sports grounds of both Pompeii and Herculaneum featured statues of young men with the ideal male body, probably copies of classical Greek statues. Somewhere in the palaestra would have stood a statue to Hypgeia, goddess of health.

In order to promote physical excellence, virtue and loyalty to the state, Augustus formed associations of young people (*collegia*) who competed in

✦ Augustus's youth organisations

athletic competitions or Youth Games (*Ludi Iuventus*) before their elders. The local unit in Pompeii was known as Iuventus Pompeiana and is believed to have comprised young men and women from the age of 11 to 17.

ENJOYING THE SPECTACLE OF THE AMPHITHEATRE

Evidence for the gladiatorial contests and wild animal hunts held in the Pompeian amphitheatre is in the form of numerous graffiti; wall paintings and reliefs in public and private buildings (amphitheatre, taverns, funeral monuments and private houses); various forms of ceramic art such as lamp bases; terracotta statues; and gladiatorial equipment. Paintings of *munera gladiatoria* (gladiatorial games) in private homes became widespread during the reign of Nero but unfortunately many of these have disappeared and are only known 'from the descriptions made by the archaeologists who discovered them [Fiorelli and Sogliano] and from the drawings made at the time of the excavations.'[24]

Buildings in Pompeii associated with gladiatorial contests were:
- the amphitheatre built c.70 BC at the expense of the *duoviri quinquennali*, C. Quinctius Valgus and Marcus Porcius
- the barracks dated from the time of Augustus to 62 AD. This building appears to have been originally a private home converted to hold the members of the *familiae gladiatoriae*, possibly between 15 and 20 men.
- the quadriporticus (originally associated with the theatres) which was adapted for gladiatorial accommodation in Nero's reign possibly due to destruction of the original barracks during the earthquake, or perhaps because of increased numbers of gladiators
- the schola armaturium, believed to have been a depository of gladiatorial armour, although it is also thought to have been a school for the 'Pompeian Youth' (*Iuventus Pompeiana*)

THE GREAT AMPHITHEATRE

✖
Size

This great gladiatorial venue could hold 20,000 people; prior to its construction, spectacles were held in the Forum. Its seating capacity, plus evidence from Tacitus (the fight between Pompeian and Nucerian spectators in AD 59, see pages 7–8) suggest that people from the towns and countryside around Pompeii regularly attended the performances.

✖
Location

It was built in the south-east of the city 'to take advantage of the embankment that ran along the back of the fortification wall'[25] and to avoid congestion; the south-east was not so densely populated. Its outer facade featured a series of blind arches and access to the highest levels (*summa cavea*), was via two double and two single stairways (see Figure 4.3). As with the theatre, this was where the women were seated on the orders of Augustus. The middle sections (*media cavea*) were reached by a covered gallery leading from the western side. The *ima cavea*, reserved for city authorities and distinguished guests, were divided from the rest of the cavea by a barrier 80 centimetres high and the stone tiers in this area were larger and shallower to allow for the portable seats (*bisella*) of the elite who were protected from the activities in the arena by a parapet 2.18 metres high. Access to the arena was through two paved vaulted tunnels, which allowed carts with equipment for the spectacle to enter, and since, unlike most amphitheatres, it did not have a subterranean area, four spaces at the end of each of the two entrance corridors were probably used for gladiators and wild animals. As for the theatre, a velarium was provided. Part of the system by which the awning was anchored can still be seen at the top of the back wall. Also, sparsiones, which according to Seneca, fell in droplets from perforated pipes surrounding the outside perimeter of the amphitheatre, helped mitigate the smells from wild animals and the crowds. Some scholars believe these sparsines may have been gifts of fruit and coins.

Figure 8.13 The amphitheatre

Figure 8.14 Cavea of the amphitheatre. Notice the separate section at the front reserved for prominent individuals.

STAGING A SPECTACLE (MUNERUM)

The games' sponsors, called *editores munerum*, were expected to fully or partly finance the production. The surviving *edicta munerum* (programs advertising the spectacles) record the names of nine public officials, civil and religious, in the last years of Pompeii who took on this responsibility. Possibly the most famous was Cn. Alleius Nigidius Maius, described as 'prince of the games'[26] on account of the lavish nature of the spectacles he presented. The editor had to employ the services of an agent (*lanista*), an entrepreneur who sold or rented his gladiators for the munus.

🎯 Sponsors

The going price for a gladiator depended on his success in the arena. It is difficult to identify many of these agents because the word 'lanista' from 'lanius', meaning 'butcher' was never used on the programs. Despite the wealth of many of these agents, it was regarded as a shameful career; the

🎯 Agents

lanista was 'considered a vendor of human flesh'.[27] However, from the surviving inscriptions, it appears that the most famous agent active in Pompeii during the time of Claudius and Nero was Numerius Festinus Ampliatus, whose company of gladiators seems to have gained a great reputation not only in Pompeii but in areas further afield. Sometimes a lanista not only ran his own *ludus* (school), but was able to successfully negotiate for the performance of well-known gladiators from one of the imperial schools in Rome such as the Iuliani or Neroniani. An agent's job was not easy, as he had to be able to provide large numbers of gladiators, constantly recruit and train new members to replace those who died or retired, and deal with city authorities.

❀
Programs

The editor commissioned the advertising in the form of edicta munerum painted on walls and the distribution of pamphlets sold on the street (*libelli munerari)*. These programs included:

- the name of the magistrate and his official position
- the reason for the spectacle
- the number of gladiators
- other events such as beast hunts
- the date (usually held over one day, sometimes four, in Spring—March to June because of weather
- the provision of a velarium and sparsiones.

> TWENTY PAIRS OF GLADIATORS OF DECIMUS LUCRETIUS SATRIUS VALENS, PERPETUAL FLAMEN [PRIEST] OF NERO CAESAR, SON OF AUGUSTUS, AND TEN PAIRS OF GLADIATORS OF HIS SON, DECIMUS LUCRETIUS VALENS, WILL FIGHT AT POMPEII FROM APRIL 8—14. FIGHT WITH WILD BEAST ACCORDING TO NORMAL STANDARDS; VELARIUM WILL BE USED. [CIL IV. 3884]

Another sponsor of the games (and theatrical performances) was A. Clodius Flaccus, a wealthy local aristocrat. The program of two of his spectacles is outlined below.

DUOVIR:	FOR THE FEAST OF APOLLO. A PROCESSION (POMPA) THROUGH THE FORUM. PRESENTED BULLS, TORREROS, BOXERS AND THREE PAIRS OF PONTARII.
QUINQUENNALIS:	FOR THE FEAST OF APOLLO. A DAY OF CONTESTS BETWEEN THIRTY PAIRS OF WRESTLERS AND FORTY PAIRS OF GLADIATORS IN THE AMPHITHEATRE. A HUNT WITH WILD BOARS AND BEARS AND BULLFIGHTS.

Usually the names of the gladiators were not included unless someone had reached such a height of popularity that he would add prestige to the sponsor and increase turnout. 'Felix will fight against bears'.[28]

Since the spectacles lasted from dawn till dusk, the aediles gave permission for itinerant pedlars to set up food and drink stalls beneath the portico. A tavern nearby also appears to have done a roaring trade. As there are no remains of toilets in the amphitheatre, spectators probably used the latrines in the nearby palaestra, judging by the number of gladiatorial graffiti. Others must have attempted to relieve themselves in the open as there are many warnings throughout the city against this behaviour.

✦
Facilities

The spectacle began with a procession (*pompa*) featuring a variety of musicians and all the participants dressed in ornate garments. The morning session was often devoted to *venationes* (animal hunts) although these were not mandatory at every spectacle. The *venatores* and *bestiarii* would fight against wild exotic animals or animal would be pitted against animal. These savage contests in which beasts tore each other to pieces probably served to increase the bloodlust of the spectators.

✦
Animal hunts

The gladiators warmed up in front of the crowd and then subjected themselves to a weapons check. There would be great interest in the contest if one of the gladiators was freeborn or involved in his first fight (designated *tiro* or T in the graffiti). Death—except in the case of criminals—was not necessarily

✦
Gladiators

Figure 8.15 Categories of gladiators

Category of gladiator	Equipment and weapons
Most gladiators fought bare-chested and wore the *subligaculum* (loincloth tied to a belt).	
Thratex or Thracian	Arm band on right arm (*manica*); two high leggings decorated to the knee; short sword; either curved or angles (*sica*); helmet topped with a tall crest decorated with the head of a griffin and feathers
Hoplomachus	Leggings; horizontal bandages over thighs; helmet with upturned brim and feathers; small round shield and straight sword
Murmillo	Right arm protected by a *munica*; left leg protected by short laced leggings; helmet with visor and angular crest decorated with horsehair or feathers; curved, rectangular shield one metre high in wood covered with leather, and the only weapon, a short sword (*gladius*)
Secutor	Heavy gear—metal leggings, long, rectangular shield, small, round helmet with nothing projecting and only holes for eyes; sword
Retiarus	Net, trident and short sword, armband on the left, not right arm to successfully manoeuvre the net; a rectangular bronze plate (*galerus*) of 12–13 cm tied to his left shoulder to protect bare head
Others	Eques fought on horseback with lance and small round shield; Provocator carried a king of cuirass to protect his chest; Essedarius fought on top of a cart
Venatores and bestiarii fought against wild beasts	Short tunics; wooden spits or poles with iron tips and leather whips; sometimes a cap-shaped helmet and small, straight sword

the desired outcome from these contests, either for the bulk of the population who had their favourites, or for the lanista who had spent vast sums of money on recruiting and training his men. Although it was entirely up to the editor or emperor to grant mercy (*missum*, shown as M in some of the graffiti) they usually took notice of the wishes of the spectators who would either raise their index finger or wave a handkerchief and call out for the loser to be spared, or give the thumbs down sign. Losers were often left to fight another day according to the graffiti which showed the number of fights and wins of each gladiator, but there were 'special munera sine missione in which the editor would refuse to spare any of the defeated gladiators'.[29] The lanista was prepared for the death of his men, however, with a 'reserve bench' or *supposticii* to take over. The editor had to pay the lanista for those he did not spare. The victorious gladiators (shown as *vicit* or V in the graffiti) received a palm as a sign of victory and money, the amount decided on before the contest. Figure 8.15 summarises the different categories of gladiators and their equipment. The Thrax or Thracian seems to have been the most popular.

Figure 8.16 Access tunnels under the cavea of the amphitheatre   **Figure 8.17** Bronze helmet worn by a murmillo (British Museum)

❧
Status of gladiators

Gladiators were prisoners-of-war, slaves, freedmen, criminals condemned to death, and occasionally *ingenui*, fallen on hard times. Although the majority were slaves, there are references to free men in the inscriptions (CIL IX. 466): six free men to twenty slaves appeared on one occasion in the arena. Despite the lack of archaeological information, some of the literary sources also mention women fighting in the arena: 'The same year witnessed gladiatorial displays on no less magnificent scale than before, but exceeding all precedent in the number of distinguished women and senators disgracing themselves in the arena.'[30] However, there is no evidence from Pompeii and these instances should not be considered the norm. The gladiators were regarded as *infames*. Like actors, such infamy was attached to anyone who made his or her living performing in public, but in the case of a gladiator there was also the brutality and stench of death associated with them.

On the other hand, there is no doubt from the graffiti about the celebrity status of many who became favourites with the crowds, admired for their courage and adored by women, even by upper-class matrons. Juvenal sends up this female obsession of gladiators in his satires, wondering what were the attractions of Sergius that compelled Eppia, wife of a Roman senator, to abandon her husband and children and risk being labelled a 'she-gladiator'. After all, Juvenal says, Sergius was already over forty, with a wounded arm, deformed and scarred face, a bulging nose and a weeping eye. 'But then he was a gladiator! It is this that transforms these fellows into hyacinths!'[31]

Popularity

Two who boasted about their prowess with women and competed against each other in egotistical scribblings were the Thracian, Celadus, and the retiarius, Cresces. Celadus described himself as 'heartthrob of the girls'[32] and 'pride of the girls',[33] while Cresces went further and bragged about being the 'doctor to night-time girls, morning girls and all the rest'.[34]

Gladiators and women

Proven gladiators might be given a *rudis* or a wooden sword to mark the end of a successful career in the arena with some going on to become instructors or even a lanista.

GAMBLING AND PROSTITUTION

Gambling was a passion in Pompeii and Herculaneum, as elsewhere in the Roman world. 'Set out the wine and dice. To hell with him who cares for the morrow.'[35] Games of chance with dice, astragals (bones from the feet of sheep with different configurations and values) and a type of chess board and pawns appear to have been carried out in any number of establishments: taverns, small wine bars and—from evidence provided by a fresco—even among the sausages, onions and other foodstuffs hanging from the ceiling of a shop. In a tavern owned by one, Salvius, were paintings showing two men arguing over a game of dice, accompanied by comic-strip type wording. 'I've won.' 'It's not a three. It's a two.' 'You criminal! Three! I've won!' 'Ortus, you foul-mouthed cheat.' Eventually Salvius is forced to throw them out: 'Out you go. Fight outside!'[36] The authorities regarded taverns as dishonest places.

Passion for dice

Prostitution was regarded as a business in Pompeii and Herculaneum and by the time of Caligula, profits from it were taxed. Prostitutes were supposed to be registered with the aediles and 23 April each year was set aside as a holiday for them. Because 'moral values were set by men'[37] prostitution was seen as a normal part of their everyday sex life and there was no stigma attached to visiting a brothel or a tavern where dancing girls—usually exotic foreigners—seduced the male customers while they reclined on couches drinking. 'A tavern girl from Syria . . . an artist with her sinuous hips, keeping time to the castanet—after a few drinks she dances seduction in the smoky tavern, elbows flashing to the shrill of the flute.'[38] Sometimes taverns functioned as brothels

Prostitution a recognised business

Seduction in taverns

and there is no doubt about the occupation of a woman called Hedone ('pleasure' in Greek) who ran one.

Despite the acceptance of prostitution, those who engaged in sex for payment were stigmatised. One of the names given to them was 'lupa' or wolf and they prowled the streets in their scanty clothing, with heavy make-up and brightly coloured hair, luring men to small, dank rooms somewhere, with nothing more than a stone bunk covered in a straw mattress. Others provided their services in the back streets; in fact the word 'fornicate' comes from the Latin word 'fornix' meaning 'arch'. Some prostitutes were employed by 'pimps' or brothel owners (*lenone*).

The largest brothel (*lupanar*) in Pompeii—and the only one excavated so far that was exclusively for this purpose—was owned by a man named Africanus. It is a two-storey building of 10 rooms (*cella meretricae*), five running off a corridor on the ground floor with a latrine at the end, and five more upstairs with a separate entrance. The walls of this lupanar are still covered in erotic paintings showing couples in various positions, but it is believed that these were used simply to stimulate the men, rather than advertise the various services provided.

Most prostitutes were foreigners, judging by the names in the graffiti and most of their customers came from the lower classes. The cost varied from between 16 asses to as little as two assess, or the price of a loaf of bread or jug of wine. Wealthy men had no need to visit a brothel. They could invite a prostitute to their homes, use one of the household slaves, or visit the home of a high-class courtesan, skilled in the art of lovemaking.

Chapter review

RELAXATION, ENTERTAINMENT AND SPORT

Baths

- range of features
  - gymnasium — masseurs
  - social meetings places
  - cold, warm and hot baths, sweat rooms
- both men and women attend
- municipal thermae
- decor
  - painted stucco walls
  - mosaic floor
  - vaulted roofs

Theatre

- Pompeii
  - large theatre (5000) — popular theatre
  - small covered Odeon (1300) — recitals, lectures
- Herculaneum (2500)
- auditoriums
  - tiered—ima cavea, media cavea, summa cavea
  - velarium and sparsiones
- sponsors
  - traditional drama, Oscan farces (Atellanae), mime and pantomime
  - celebrity actors

Palaestra

- open sports ground
  - Youth Games
  - athletics, wrestling, javelin, discus
- porticoes swimming pool, trees

Amphitheatre

- editores
  - lanista
  - familia gladiatoria
  - infamy but celebrity status
  - edicta muneria
- Pompeii (20,000)
- spectacles
  - dawn till dusk
  - velarium and sparsiones
  - gladiatorial contests
  - animal hunts

Taverns, brothels

- gambling
  - dice, astragals
  - seductive dancers
- prostitution
  - high-class courtesans
  - business—taxed under Caligula
  - brothels (lupinar); lupa (she-wolves)
  - foreigners—slaves and freed women
  - pimps

Activities

1 Read the quote from Vitruvius's *De architectura*, examine the sketch and photograph, and then answers questions that follow.

Figure 8.18

First of all, choose as warm a site as possible. that is, one facing away from the north wind and the north-east wind. Then the caldaria and tepidaria will have light from the west in wintertime. or, if the nature of the site prevents this, at least from the south, as the most common time for bathing is generally from midday to evening. Care should also be taken that the men's and women's caldaria are connected and placed in the same area. In this way it will be possible for them both to share a common furnace for the tubs. Three bronze tanks should be assembled above the furnace, one a caldarium, one a tepidarium, one a frigidarium, and they should be so placed that however much hot water flows from the tepidarium into the caldarium, as much cold water is coming in from the frigidarium to the tepidarium in the same fashion.

This is how to make a suspended floor of the caldaria. First, the floor is laid with one and one-half foot tiles that incline towards the furnace . . . In this way the flames will circulate more freely under the suspended floor. On top of this piers of eight inch tiles should be placed so that two foot tiles can be placed over them. The piers should be two feet high . . . and over them place the two foot tiles which will hold up the pavement.

The washbasin [in the caldaria] in particular should be built beneath the window so that those standing around it will not obscure the light by casting shadows. The alcoves for the washbasin should be made spacious enough so that once the first comers have taken their place, the rest of the bathers stand around comfortably and watch.

Vitruvius, De architectura, *5.10.1, 2, 4.*

a Where, according to Vitruvius, should bath complexes be located and why?

b What was a caldarium?

c Why should care be taken to make sure the men's and women's caldaria were placed in the same area?

d How was the water for the hot pool and the room itself heated?

e Identify the object shown in Figure 8.18.

f What was the procedure for bathers before entering the caldarium? What happened in the caldarium?

g How does the sketch of the room shown in Figure 8.19 conform to Vitruvius' injunctions?

Activities

Figure 8.19 Activities in a caldarium

Figure 8.21

2 a Describe what is happening in the mosaic pictured in Figure 8.20. What evidence is there that this does not depict a mime or pantomime. What type of theatrical presentation does it depict?

   b Describe the most popular forms of entertainment held at the Large Theatre in Pompeii.

   c To what object does the following quote refer? Where would such an object have been used?

   . . . WATCH THE YELLOW AWNINGS. THE REDS, THE PURPLES SPREAD ON POLES AND BEAMS IN SOME GREAT THEATRE, WHERE THEY FLUTTER, BILLOW, STIR, OVER THE AUDIENCE . . .
   Lucretius, De rerum natura, *4.75–83 I*

   d What other facilities were provided at the theatre for the comfort of the audience?

   e Where did women sit in the theatre?

   f Who sat in the very front rows?

   g How was the Odeon in Pompeii designed to suit its particular purpose?

3 Identify the structure shown structure in Figure 8.21 and explain what purpose it served in Pompeian society.

Figure 8.20 Mosaic from the House of the Tragic Poet (Naples National Archaeological Museum)

Activities

4   The graffiti shown in Figure 8.22 was discovered on a tomb in the Pompeian necropolis outside the Nucerian gate. It shows two contests, one between a free man and a Neroniani or member of one of the imperial gladiatorial schools in Rome, and the second between the same free man and another experienced gladiator.

a   What is the name of the freeborn fighter?

b   What evidence is there that it was his first fight in the arena?

c   What was the name of his first opponent and what evidence is there that he came from one of the Roman imperial schools?

d   How many successful fights had he had?

e   What evidence is there that a loser in the arena could live to fight another day?

f   What evidence is there that his second opponent was even more successful than his first?

g   What were the outcomes of both contests?

h   Who decided if a defeated gladiator was spared?

i   Why was death not usually the desired outcome of these contests?

j   What reward did a successful gladiator receive?

5   Topic for extended response, class discussion or oral presentation: 'Pleasure came easily to the Pompeians'.

Figure 8.22 Graffiti of gladiatorial contests

Religion and death

Roman religion had been greatly influenced by the Greeks of Campania from the 6th century BC, and various gods were adopted and adapted to suit the Roman needs at particular times. In Pompeii and Herculaneum, the people worshipped a range of deities: Roman adaptations of the Greek pantheon, nature and household protectors, and eastern gods and goddesses, in both the public and private sphere. With the advent of the imperial age, another religious element was added: the cult of the emperors, by which Augustus, his family and successors were integrated into religious practices as a means of securing loyalty and unifying the empire.

Range of deities

OFFICIAL RELIGION

'The most characteristic feature of Roman religion was its essentially political orientation.'[1] Priestly offices were political appointments, and each citizen had a political duty to scrupulously carry out the correct rituals to the gods (sacrifice and prayer) to ensure prosperity, good luck and protection for the state and its people. Just as priests presided in temples, so the paterfamilias, as priest, presided over the domestic shrine.

Political nature of official religion

Although no temples have been excavated at Herculaneum, sanctuaries at Pompeii, as well as other public buildings, private homes, taverns and shops in both towns, reflect the degree to which religion was integrated into social and political life.

No temples found in Herculaneum

The plan of the Forum and surrounding area in Figure 9.1 shows the location of major temples and buildings associated with the imperial cult.

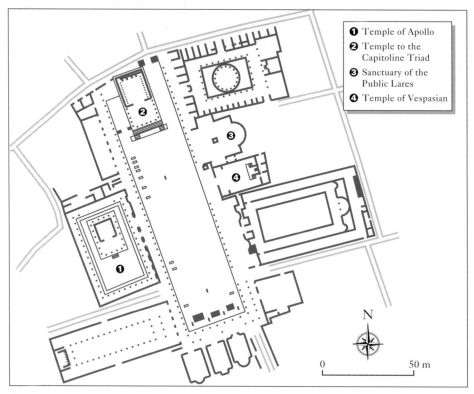

❶ Temple of Apollo
❷ Temple to the Capitoline Triad
❸ Sanctuary of the Public Lares
❹ Temple of Vespasian

N

0   50 m

Figure 9.1 Temples around the Pompeian Forum

THE CAPITOLINE TRIAD

⚘
Jupiter, Juno,
Minerva

The triad of gods Jupiter (protector of the state), Juno (protector of women) and Minerva (patroness of craftsmen) were identified with the Greek Zeus, Hera and Athena. A temple dedicated to the triad dominated the Pompeian Forum and games were held in their honour on the first of September every year.

⚘
Capitolium

Their temple was modelled on the Capitolium in Rome—although smaller—and was the symbol of Rome's power in Pompeii from the time it became a Roman colony (80 BC). It stood on a podium 3 metres high with columns supporting a gabled pediment. Statues of the three deities shared a single cella in a colonnaded hall and the massive temple base held sacrificial equipment and the town's public treasures. Unfortunately, like many structures in Pompeii, it was extensively damaged during the earthquake of AD 62 and any subsequent seismic activity. The bas-relief of Caecilius Jucundus provides evidence of its damage. It was formerly believed that the worship of the triad was moved to a smaller sanctuary dedicated to Jupiter Meilichios near the theatre district after AD 62, but work in the Forum over the last decade has shown that it was repaired and in working order when the eruption occurred.

HERCULES, APOLLO AND VENUS

Hercules was worshipped from a very early date in Herculaneum where he was regarded as the town's founder, and at Pompeii, where his cult was popular with sailors and traders because of his legendary journeys. Michael Grant believes that interest in his mythological exploits became fashionable during the 1st century AD because 'emperors, notably Nero, liked to be regarded as reincarnations of Hercules'.[2]

🕸 Early worship of Hercules and Apollo

Worship of Apollo, the oracular god, is believed to have been introduced into Pompeii during the 6th century BC from Cumae, the leading Greek city on the Bay of Naples. During the 2nd century, the god's sanctuary on the western side of what became the Forum was replaced with a temple built according to Hellenistic models, although the dais reached by a central flight of stairs was an Italic element. Other changes were made at the time of Augustus, who adopted Apollo as his patron and associated this brilliant god of light with his new 'Golden Age'. Also, as god of music, Apollo was enthusiastically embraced by the lyre-playing Nero.

🕸 Augustus and Apollo

Venus, the Roman equivalent of Aphrodite goddess of love, was worshipped in pre-Roman days as a nature goddess, Venus Fisica, and it is to this form of the goddess that the Latin poet Lucretius wrote:

🕸 Venus as goddess of nature

> DARLING OF GODS AND MEN, BENEATH THE GLIDING STARS
> YOU FILL RICH EARTH AND BUOYANT SEA WITH YOUR PRESENCE.
> FOR EVERY LIVING THING ACHIEVES ITS LIFE THROUGH YOU . . .
> EVERYWHERE, THROUGH ALL SEAS, MOUNTAINS AND WATERFALLS,
> LOVE CARESSES ALL HEARTS AND KINDLES ALL CREATURES
> IN OVERMASTERING LUST AND ORDAINED RENEWALS.[3]

Since she was believed to have been born from the waters, she is often depicted nude reclining in a sea shell, accompanied by nereids (water nymphs), dolphins and cherubs, or even leaning on a rudder. She was worshipped by sailors who sought her protection and her temple stood on a terrace looking out to sea.

Figure 9.2 Venus floating in a sea shell from the House of Venus in a Sea Shell in Pompeii

Figure 9.3 Paintings of Hercules from the Basilica of Herculaneum (Naples National Archaeological Museum)

❧
Venus as patroness
of Pompeii

With the establishment of Pompeii as a Roman colony in 80 BC, Venus became the patron goddess of the city and, as such, was expected to bring well-being and success in everything to the community. Her image, in various forms, was endlessly repeated in houses, taverns and shops around the city. It appears that all classes of people worshipped her in one way or another. She was urged, via graffiti, to support candidates for office, to grant success in love and even to get rid of a rival. However, she was just as readily blamed when things did not turn out as expected. One graffitist wrote on the basilica, that he wanted to 'smash her head in with club'.[4] In an ironic twist, the temple to Venus, protectress of Pompeii, was one of the most severely damaged buildings in the city.

THE IMPERIAL CULT

❧
Worship of genius
of the emperor

❧
Augustales

Close by the temple to the Capitoline triad were four buildings which, during the 1st century AD, became linked with the imperial regime. The cult of the emperor's genius (generating force) was first introduced at the time of Augustus as a form of homage, and a new religious college of 21 part-time priests called *Augustales*, predominantly recruited from freedmen, was set up to supervise the cult. These associations were formed in cities throughout Italy including Pompeii and Herculaneum. Later Julio-Claudian emperors took more obvious steps at deification and the imperial cult flourished in Campania. Excavations at Herculaneum have brought to light the magnificent Collegium Augustalium, headquarters of these cult priests. This building throws light on the practise of the cult, as do the reliefs on an altar in the so-called temple to the genius of Vespasian in the Forum at Pompeii. (See page 164 for a more detailed view of the altar.)

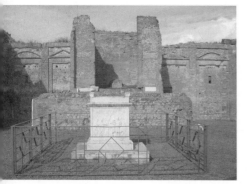

Figure 9.4 The remains of the Temple of Vespasian in the Forum of Pompeii

❧
Public lares and
Augustus

As a public representation of the *lares* (deities) worshipped in the home, the *Lares Publici* were protectors of the crossroads (*compita*). They became linked to the emperor himself and in the Pompeian sanctuary's central apse was the statue of the genius of Augustus alongside ten young dancers representing the Lares.

❧
Religion and
politics

The remains of a temple close to the shrine of the lares was originally dedicated to the goddess Fortuna, but in 3 BC the epithet 'Augusta' was added, associating the new imperial regime with the deity of good fortune. It was erected by the duumvir Marcus Tullius at his own expense on his own land in honour of Augustus, perhaps to repay an imperial favour. It contained a statue to Fortuna Augusta and statues of the imperial family. This building reveals the link between religion and politics.

❧
Private sponsorship
of imperial cult

Another private building in the Forum linked to the cult of the imperial family was the Edifice of Eumachia, sponsored by the priestess of the same name. Although it is thought to have housed a wool market and the headquarters of the cloth and wool merchants, it was a celebration of the Julian clan to which Augustus belonged, and honoured the 'Concordia and the Pietas Augusta'.

PUBLIC RITUAL

Part of the ritual carried out by the *flamens* (specialised priests to a particular god or gods) and Augustales on behalf of the population, was the sacrificial banquet. The offering of an animal (*sacrificium*) to the god was done according to strict ritual from which there was no deviation. The presiding priest, with head veiled, exhorted those present to be absolutely silent and initiated the ritual slaughter by coating the sacrificial knife and head of the animal with *mola salsa* (in Rome this was a mixture prepared by the Vestal Virgins). The killing followed precise rules: the entrails, dedicated to the god, were burned and offered up, and the rest of the flesh was divided among the participants according to status. Priests and magistrates sat apart from the public and were given the superior cuts of meat. The inferior cuts were handed out in order of precedence with some participants receiving only a tiny portion of the sacrificial animal.

✖
Sacrificial banquets

MYSTERY RELIGIONS

The cults of the Hellenistic world (those areas which incorporated a mix of Greek and Eastern culture ruled by the successors of Alexander the Great) were introduced into Italy with Rome's conquest of Greece, Macedon and the East in the 2nd century BC. They were brought back by merchants, soldiers and slaves and included the Dionysian, Eleusinian and Orphic mysteries and the cults of Cybele, Isis and Mithras. Because official religious practices tended to be impersonal and the 'decrees of Fate and Fortune' oppressive,[5] those seeking a more emotional involvement with a god were attracted to these cults, which promised their devotees happiness, salvation and resurrection through initiation.

✖
Arrival of cults from the East

The two most popular foreign cults in Pompeii and Herculaneum were of Isis and Dionysus/Bacchus. It appears that at first they were popular with women and the lower classes of slaves and freedmen, but eventually became far more widespread throughout society, judging by the motifs, objects and paintings associated with both cults found in private homes.

THE CULT OF ISIS

Egyptian influence was strong in Pompeii in the religious, aesthetic and commercial spheres, possibly because of trade contacts between the great Hellenistic city of Alexandria and the ports on the Bay of Naples, and the annexation of Egypt as an imperial province under Augustus. It is not known whether the worship of Isis came directly from Egypt or via the Hellenistic

✖
More female worshippers of Isis

East, but Louise Zarmati in *Women and Eros* suggests that it came with 'foreign women'[6] and since prostitutes, many of whom were foreign slaves, worshipped the goddess, this seems probable. Although the cult was open to men and had a professional body of priests, 'nearly one-third of worshippers mentioned in the inscriptions are female'.[7] It soon spread among the elite with some, like Julia Felix, incorporating shrines dedicated to the goddess into their gardens with statuettes and paintings of Egyptian deities. In the House of the Gilded Cupids was a chapel (*sacrum*) dedicated to Isis, Serapis (Hellenistic god with the attributes of Osiris) and Anubis.

✼
Egyptian myth of Isis and Osiris

According to Egyptian myth, Isis was the sister/wife of Osiris, popular king of Egypt, who was locked in a chest by his jealous brother Seth and cast into the Nile. The chest washed up on the coast of Lebanon at Byblos where Isis found it. She became pregnant to the dead Osiris by magical means and gave birth to a son, Horus. She took her husband's body back to Egypt and hid it in the Nile delta where Seth found it and cut it up into fourteen pieces which were scattered all over Egypt. Isis and her sister, Nephthys, went in search of the pieces, and with her own magical powers, help from Anubis and special words from Thoth, she and her sister put the pieces together. After turning themselves into birds they fanned life back into Osiris who was resurrected as God of the Underworld.

✼
Fusion of Greek and Egyptian

In the 3rd century BC, the Graeco-Egyptian ruler of Egypt, Ptolemy I, fused Greek and Egyptian elements into the cult of Isis and Osiris/Serapis. In the Roman world, Isis offered consolation from suffering, happiness and salvation while her husband promised resurrection, and Anubis, sometimes integrated with Mercury, guided the soul to the next life.

✼
Daily services

There were two daily services in the Temple of Isis, which appears to have been open all day, unlike other sanctuaries. Evidence for these rites comes from the high-quality wall paintings that once adorned its walls. They featured Egyptian-style landscapes, exotic

Figure 9.5 A fresco from Herculaneum depicting one of the rituals associated with the cult of Isis (Naples National Archaeological Museum)

beasts, scenes from Egyptian and Greek mythology, and the priests performing their duties. Priests, priestesses and initiates wore white linen robes, sandals of papyrus and headbands featuring the Egyptian cobra (*ureaus*), and ceremonies were accompanied by burning of incense, chanting and music.

Before sunrise, the worshippers gathered in front of the temple where the image of the goddess was presented to them to the accompaniment of the *sistrum* (the sacred rattle). The participants remained in prayer until the sun rose, when they uttered an invocation for its daily rebirth. At 2.30 in the afternoon, water supposedly from the Nile was consecrated and sprinkled around by the priest as a symbol of life.

During the year there were two major festivals in honour of the goddess.

❈
Yearly festivals

- The 'Navigation of Isis' on 5 March, during which a procession of priests, priestesses and worshippers carried a small boat to the sea shore, purified it with water and sulphur and prayed for the protection of all sailors.
- The 'Isia' between 13 and 16 November commemorated the discovery of Osiris's body. It is believed that this was when the secret initiations took place during which the participants experienced a rebirth, committing themselves to leading purer lives.

The outstanding paintings, decorations and furniture found in the Temple of Isis in Pompeii, and the fact that it was one of the first public buildings to have been totally restored after the earthquake, point to the sig-nificance of the cult. The cult complex, which was surrounded by high walls to maintain the secrecy of the ceremonies, included the temple on its podium, a shrine giving access to a subterranean cistern holding holy Nile water, an initiation and banquet hall, a repository for equipment and remains of sacri-fices, and lodgings for the priests.

❈
Temple features

Figure 9.6 Fresco from the Temple if Isis in Pompeii showing the goddess receiving Io at Canopus in Egypt (Naples National Archaeological Museum)

Figure 9.7 A cult building and altar in the precinct of the Temple of Isis

THE CULT OF DIONYSUS/BACCHUS

The cult, centred on Dionysus—Greek god of wine and fertility—swept through Greece in the 6th century and 300 years later became enormously popular in southern Italy as the cult of Bacchus. It offered 'an escape from worldly reality into mystic communion with the god and the promise of a blessed life after death'.[8] The cult incorporated an account of the rescue of Ariadne, who had been abandoned on the island of Naxos by Theseus, and her sacred marriage to Dionysus, which endowed her with eternal life. A fine painting in the House of the Vettii illustrates this myth, showing the god approaching the sleeping Ariadne.

Originally the cult was attended only by women on three days of the year, but it was supposedly transformed 'on the initiative of a Campanian priestess named Annia Paculla'[9] who admitted men and extended the celebration of the rites to five times a month. According to Livy, the cult spread 'like a contagious disease' and 'to the religious content were added the pleasures of wine and feasting'.[10] While under the influence of wine, the worshippers supposedly committed all kinds of debaucheries. 'Men, apparently out of their wits, would utter prophecies with frenzied bodily convulsions: matrons attired as Bacchantes, with their hair dishevelled and carrying blazing torches, would run down to the Tiber, plunge their torches in and bring them out still alight . . .'[11]

The Roman Senate believed that the secret and excessive nature of the Bacchanalia (Latin name for the rites of Bacchus) was a threat to public order and provided opportunities for political conspiracy. In 186 BC a senatorial decree authorised the consuls to suppress Bacchic societies, although worship of the god by individuals was not forbidden. However, the cult continued to flourish in Campania and there is ample evidence of its popularity in Pompeii and Herculaneum. While some worshippers, such as the owners of the Villa of Mysteries, appear to have had a deep and serious attachment to the god, most in Pompeii seem to have been more light-hearted in their attitude: 'This cult at its least exacting level, tended to succumb to mere sensuality, with the afterlife pictured as a sexy debauch; and many were the drinking and dining clubs that assumed the exalted patronage of Bacchus.'[12] Petronius parodied this in his *Satyricon*, when Trimalchio had a boy dressed up as Bacchus at his dinner party.

Dionysus/Bacchus was identified in the wall paintings with vine leaves in his hair and carrying a staff or *thyrus* tipped with a pine cone. He is often accompanied by satyrs, creatures in Greek legends that inhabited the forests and mountains. They were half man, half beast (a man's body with goat's ears, horns, hoofs and tails), lazy and lascivious. The older ones were called Sileni, the younger Satyrisci. They were often depicted playing a lyre or pipe.

In the Villa of Mysteries just outside Pompeii is possibly the best group of paintings that have survived from the ancient world. Dated from the time of Augustus, this enigmatic and much debated megalography appears to depict rituals associated with the cult of Dionysus/Bacchus, perhaps similar to an initiation undertaken by the mistress of the villa herself. This series of paintings is believed to have been a copy of earlier ones on the walls of the Dionysiac sanctuaries of Pergamum and Smyrna in the Hellenistic east.

The 35-square-metre room in which the paintings were found is believed to have been part of the private quarters of the owners of the villa. The central panel, which is slightly damaged, shows a seated Ariadne holding a reclining Bacchus flanked by a silenus and a young satyr and a woman removing a phallus, symbol of fertility, from a basket. Beyond her is a winged female raising a long whip, perhaps to scourge the initiate who has to undergo various ordeals before the Sacred Marriage. A woman in bridal yellow is making preparations, and another with a veil over her head may represent a priestess. Four other female figures seem to be involved in a sacrificial rite accompanied by a silenus playing a lyre and a faun playing a pipe, while another woman with raised hand whirls around in what appears to be an orgiastic dance. Scholars differ, not only in their interpretation of the paintings, but in the purpose they believed they served.

8
Possible rituals associated with the cult

Figure 9.8 A scene from the Dionysian wall paintings in the Villa of Mysteries showing Dionysus lying in the lap of Ariadne. This portion of the painting is damaged.

Figure 9.9 A scene from the Dionysian wall paintings in the Villa of Mysteries showing a female initiate or one being initiated into the cult

PRIVATE WORSHIP AND OBSERVANCES

Together with the *lares* (protectors of the household), *penates* (protectors of the stores) and *genius* of the paterfamilias (generating force), many households incorporated other gods into their family worship. As well, the power of Vesta extended over all hearths and altars, so 'every prayer and sacrifice ends with this goddess because she is the guardian of innermost things'.[13] Figure 9.10 summarises the features of *lararia* (household shrines) and the household guardians.

8
The household as a sacred space

8
Lares, penates, genius and Vesta

The souls of the dead were believed to live on after death in a world of malevolent and benevolent forces. A family's ancestors, represented by wax masks kept in the house, were honoured on every family occasion as they were the protectors of the family's lineage.

8
Honouring the ancestors

There were family ceremonies associated with all rites of passage, such as birth, marriage and death. A sacrifice of incense and cake was made at the family shrine when a new-born was accepted into the family by the paterfamilias, and on the eighth day after birth, he or she was named in a ceremony (*lustratio*) 'when any pollution associated with the birth was cleansed away'.[14] Relatives, friends and clients of the paterfamilias crowded into the atrium to congratulate the parents and wish the child good fortune. When a girl was to

8
Rites of passage

THE LARARIUM

Type of lararia	Household guardians	Worship and offerings
• A wall niche found in poorer homes with painted back wall and figurines • Aedicula, a 3-dimensional miniature temple set on a podium, lined with marble or painted stucco with statuettes; found in richer homes • A wall painted to look like an aedicula with the household gods also painted	• Lares: protectors of the household, originally protectors of the farm and its boundaries; a pair of dancing youths in short, country-style tunics, holding in one hand a drinking horn in the shape of an animal's head or a horn of plenty, and in the other a dish (patera) or a wine bucket • Penates: a name derived, according to Cicero, from 'penus' which meant a store of human food of any kind, and the penates were supposed to reside in the recesses of the house (penitus) • Genius: the essential spirit of the head of the house • Bacchus and Mercury: sometimes added to the lararium • Snake and altar: the snake (Agathodemon), shown rearing its head or wrapping itself around an altar, protected the hearth and brought fertility	• Ritual conducted by paterfamilias as chief priest • Regular daily offerings and special monthly celebrations • Offering of a wreath, portion of a meal such as fruit and eggs; crumbs dropped on the floor were left as an offering • On important occasions a lamb might be sacrificed

Figure 9.10 Private worship of household gods

be married, omens and sacrifices were taken, and on the day of her marriage her father offered a banquet, after which she was taken in a torch-light procession to her husband's house, during which the virility of the groom was lauded by his friends and 'walnuts were thrown over the couple to wish them fertility'.[15] Once across the threshold of her future home, the bride made an offering of water and fire. Death was marked by a rite called *conclamatio* by which the gathered relatives invoked the deceased's name out loud. Usually the body was prepared (washed, oiled and preserved) by the women, a coin was placed under the tongue to pay Charon the ferryman, who bore the soul to the next life, and the body laid out in the atrium for visitors to show their respect (see page 161–162 for funerals).

✖
Magico/religious
amulets

The Pompeians and Herculaneans also propitiated the gods for good luck and fertility by a variety of amulets, depicted as objects or paintings. The *mani pantee* was a votive hand—usually in bronze—with thumb, index and middle finger raised in a sign of benediction and an image of the Eastern god, Sabatius, seated in the palm with other symbols of deities: snake, toad and beetle. An image of a mother and child at the wrist suggests these may have been amulets intended to protect maternity and breast-feeding. Snakes, regarded as benevolent, were believed to bring peace and prosperity, but by far the most common amulet was the erect phallus, symbol of virility and fertility. It was found everywhere in houses as decorative bas-reliefs and even on lamps and children's rattles. The purpose of a Priapus—god of fertility and abundance—just inside the entrance of the house of the wealthy Vettii brothers, with its enormous phallus weighed against a bag of money on a pair of scales, was to ward off the evil eye and bring prosperity to the owners.

Figure 9.11 An aedicula form of lararium

Figure 9.12 A painted lararium in the thermopolium of L. Vetutius Placidus

DEATH AND BURIAL

Except perhaps for those deeply involved in the mystery/salvation cults, most people probably had no clear concept of life after death, despite the fact that they were constantly reminded of the brevity of life and urged to enjoy it while they could. Guests at banquets were confronted with reminders of death: skeletons and skulls were common images in triclinia, others engraved on drinking cups such as the goblets found in the Villa of Pisanella at Boscoreale, which featured groups of skeletons, one with a butterfly, symbol of the human soul, and a heavy purse which is labelled 'wisdom'. At Trimalchio's banquet in Petronius's *Satyricon*, a slave brings in a silver jointed skeleton and after it is thrown about the table, Trimalchio makes a pompous speech about the shortness of life: 'Man's life, alas is but a span, So let us live while we can. We'll be like this when dead!'[16] Graffiti also urged the people to live life to the full because nothing lasts forever.

Despite their enjoyment of life, each time the inhabitants left or returned to the city they were confronted by the reality of death. Lining the streets leading to the Herculaneum, Nucerian, Vesuvian and Nolan Gates were the tombs of their ancestors.

After the family rites were performed, it was up to the paterfamilias to make sure that the deceased, whether an immediate family member, slave or freedman, received the proper burial rites. Those who didn't were believed to live on in the next life as malevolent entities. For this reason, those without families or who were too poor often belonged to a funeral club, to which they paid a fee while alive. This ensured they would be cremated and interred in a mausoleum with others in the same club. In this way they would not be forgotten.

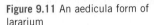

Reminders of the brevity of life

Necessity of proper burial rituals

✤ Cremation

In the 1st century AD most people were cremated, although burials were still carried out. No cremation or *inhumation* (burial) was permitted within the city walls, and legally there was supposed to be a belt of approximately 30 metres left free around the city's perimeter. However, sometimes important individuals were given permission to build their tomb within this space.

✤ Ancestors and the funeral

The funeral procession included musicians and professional mourners (*praeficae*) who wailed and scratched their faces. Members of the family wore the wax masks of their ancestors (*maiores*) so that the protectors of their lineage were also present at the funeral and there was a continuing link between the living and the dead. After the cremation, the ashes of the deceased were preserved in urns of terracotta or even glass, and incorporated into the structure of the tomb or buried at its foot. Tombs rarely belonged to an individual, and a popular type had niches in its facade for the urns of all members of the household. Sometimes the letters STTL were carved into the monument: 'Sit, Tibi Terra Levis' or 'May the earth be light upon you'.

✤ Cremation urns

✤ Variety of tombs in necropolis

Tombs varied from the plainest enclosure made of brick to the most elaborate monument with sculptural decoration. The tomb of the Istacidii family, owners of the Villa of Mysteries, comprised a large funerary chamber or podium surmounted by a circular temple with statues of the most prominent family members set up between columns. In front of it was the semicircular (*schola*) tomb of the priestess of Venus Mamia, daughter of Publicus, whose place of burial was given by decree of the decuriones. Some tombs were of a simpler altar type, but the one belonging to the Augustale Caio Calventio Quieto sat on a stepped pyramid surrounded by an enclosure. The monumental tomb of the priestess Eumachia and her family is the most impressive in Pompeii.

✤ Evidence from tombs

Tombs provided an opportunity to remind passers-by of the achievements and social status of the deceased. Some were decorated with bas-reliefs which recalled their occupations and contributions to Pompeian society. For example, the tomb of the famous garum manufacturer Umbricius Scaurus featured a decorative scheme inspired by the games held in the amphitheatre for which he was probably a sponsor, while the tomb of the Augustale, mentioned above, featured the *bisellum*, or seat in the front row of the theatre reserved for distinguished individuals. The tombs lining the street outside the Herculaneum gate alternate with shops and aristocratic villas, such as the Villa of Cicero.

Figure 9.13 (left) Mosaic skeleton (Naples National Archaeological Museum)

Figure 9.14 (centre) Engraved glass funeral vase found in the necropolis (Naples National Archaeological Museum)

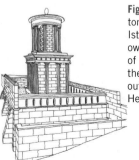

Figure 9.15 The tomb of the Istacidii family, owners of the Villa of Mysteries, in the necropolis outside the Herculaneum gate

Chapter review

RELIGION AND DEATH

Public religion

Mystery cults
- 'Imported' from Hellenistic East
- The cult of Isis
  - Evidence from Temple of Isis, paintings and decorations in private houses
  - Originally popular with women and lower classes but spread through society
  - Emotional appeal—more personal involvement through initiation
- The cult of Dionysus/Bacchus

Official cults
- Impersonal
- The Capitoline triad
  - Jupiter, Juno, Minerva
- Hercules, Apollo and Venus
- Greek gods adopted and adapted over time
- Correct rituals to the gods
- Flamens and Augustales
- Imperial cult to the genius of the emperor
- Lares Publici

Private worship

Ancestors
- Wax masks

Private worship

Household duties
- Lares, penates, genius
  - Lararia
  - Sacred hearth
    - Vesta
- Provided for family, slaves and freed slaves
  - Paterfamilias

Death

Tombs
- Streets of tombs outside city games
- Rarely for individuals
  - Opportunity to remind people of deceased's achievements and status
- Family tombs varied in style—schola, exedra, altar

Funeral
- Rituals for dead at the tomb
- Correct rites essential for all—connection between living and dead
- Cremation and burial outside city boundary
- Burial clubs—to provide for poor and those without families

Activities

1 Figure 9.16 shows the remains of the Capitolium.

   a Where was it located?

   b What triad of gods were worshipped there?

   c When and why was it built?

   d What other gods adopted and adapted from the Greeks were worshipped in Pompeii?

2 a What do the following graffiti reveal about the relationship of the people of Pompeii with the goddess Venus?

   'PORTUMNUS LOVES AMPHIANDA, JANUARIUS LOVES VENERIA. WE PRAY VENUS THAT YOU SHOULD HOLD US IN MIND. THIS ONLY WE ASK YOU.'[17]

   CALLING ALL LOVERS! I WANT TO BREAK VENUS' RIBS WITH CLUBS AND CRIPPLE THE LOINS OF THE GODDESS. IF SHE CAN POUND MY SOFT CHEST, WHY SHOULDN'T I BE ABLE TO SMASH HER HEAD IN WITH A CLUB.'[18]

   b Under what other forms was the goddess worshipped in Pompeii?

3 a In which temple was the bas-relief shown in Figure 9.17 found?

   b To whom or what was this temple dedicated?

   c Identify the priest and describe what is happening in this scene.

   d To which college of special priests would this one belong?

Figure 9.17 A bas-relief on a marble altar

   e In one paragraph, describe the rites that would follow.

   f What purpose did the imperial cult serve in the Roman empire?

Figure 9.16 The remains of the Temple of the Capitoline Triad

Activities

4 a Compare the remains shown in Figure 9.18 with the fresco depicted in Figure 9.5. What part of the ancient temple do these remains represent?

   b List five other features of the ancient temple.

   c Who was the goddess Isis and where did she originate?

   d Why did her worship flourish in Pompeii, especially among all classes of women?

   e With evidence from the fresco depicted in Figure 9.5, describe what an eyewitness might have seen in this part of the temple at sunrise and early afternoon each day.

5

Figure 9.19
Bacchus/Dionysius from a lararium in the House of the Centenary

   a What features allow identification of the god in Figure 9.19?

   b Name one significant piece of archaeological evidence from Pompeii and one significant literary reference to the worship of this god in the Vesuvian area.

   c What can be learnt from these two sources about the worship of this god?

   d Not everyone took the worship so seriously and yet the image of the god was found everywhere in Pompeii. Why?

6 Use the following sources to describe in several pages the attitude of the people of Pompeii and Herculaneum to death.

Figure 9.20 A mosaic from a workshop in Pompeii (Naples National Archaeological Museum)

NOTHING IS MORE ABSURD THAN TO POSSESS FINELY FURNISHED HOUSES WHILE WE LIVE AND NOT TO THINK OF THE ONE IN WHICH WE SHALL HAVE TO RESIDE FOR SO MUCH LONGER.

Petronius, Satyricon, *35*

Figure 9.18 The remains of the temple of Isis in Pompeii

The influence of Greece and the Hellenistic cultures of the east on Pompeii and Herculaneum—a research topic

10

⚸ This chapter is in the form of a piece of research, since the influence of Greece and the Hellenistic cultures has been discussed throughout the text. Figure 10.1 indicates where the information can be found in the text.

Figure 10.1 References in this text to the influence of Greece and Hellenistic cultures

Chapter	Influences of the Greeks and cultures of the Hellenistic East
1	Toponym of Herculaneum is Greek—Heracles; Influences of the Greeks in the 6th century BC; Greek architect Hippodamus laid out geometric grid of Pompeii; Roman expansion into the East in 2nd century BC—adoption of Hellenistic culture
4	Hellenistic pictorial schools; Early wall painting 'styles' based on Hellenistic themes; Decoration of atria and peristyles based on Hellenistic motifs; Silverware found in House of Menander embossed with scenes of Greek myths and traditional Hellenistic landscapes
6	Greek and Eastern slaves in households and estates; Foreigners employed in taverns; Trade with Alexandria
7	Parts of the house that copied or alluded to Hellenistic architecture; Size of grand houses based on Hellenistic 'palace' model; Greek horticultural experts—gardens and water gardens
8	Theatres essentially Greek in design; Odeon had the 'stamp' of the Hellenistic architectural tradition; Traditional Greek tragedies and comedies performed—masks; Keeping the body fit at the palaestra (Greek gymnasia)—featured Greek-style statues of young athletes; Prostitutes—many from the Hellenistic East
9	Religion influenced by early Greeks in Campania—adoption and adaption of Greek pantheon of gods: Zeus (Jupiter), Hera (Juno), Athena (Minerva), Aphrodite (Venus) and Apollo; Mystery cults—Dionysus/Bacchus and Isis

RESEARCH

Use the information in this text, the additional source material and suggested reading to research this topic.

- Explain the terms 'Hellenic' and 'Hellenistic cultures'. Show that you are aware of the differences.
- Explain how and when Pompeii and Herculaneum came into contact with Greece and the Hellenistic East, including Egypt.

- Show how private and public architecture in Pompeii and Herculaneum reflected these influences.
- To what extent did the Hellenistic world influence wall paintings, mosaics and furnishings?
- Explain how both the Greek pantheon of gods and the mystery cults of Isis and Dionysus/Bacchus became part of the religious life of Pompeii and Herculaneum. Why did the mystery cults eventually become so popular with all classes of people.

You must include visual material, but you can present your information in any form that you consider appropriate.

SOURCE MATERIAL

1 The Hellenisation of Roman lifestyle and the advent of 'Asian luxuria' in Roman houses of the Republic had a great influence on the architectural transformations of the classical home with an atrium, by introducing innovations such as high vestibules, wide atriums and peristyles, extremely large gardens and porticoes, as well as libraries, picture galleries and basilicas.

2 The House of the Faun is a remarkable illustration of the influence of the Hellenistic East on both the architecture and art of the large Pompeian residence in the 2nd century BC. Its luxurious mosaic panels (*emblemata*), which recall the colourful world of Dionysus and the Greek theatre, adorned a number of rooms in the house. At the threshold between the entrance vestibule and the Tuscan atrium was an emblem with a rich festoon of flowers and fruit adorned by two tragic masks with long curly wigs. The next room depicted a double emblem depicting a cat capturing a partridge and Nilotic ducks with lotus flowers in their beaks. In a dining room was an emblem depicting Dionysus as a child riding a tiger in the centre of a vegetable frame with theatrical masks, and in a bedroom, an erotic emblem depicting a satyr and a nymph. On the threshold of the exedra was the large magnificent mosaic of an exotic Nile scene filled with ducks, snakes, crocodiles and a hippopotamus. This scene is an introduction to the main decoration of the hall, which is centred around the celebration of Alexander the Great and the founding of Alexandria. In this monumental mosaic Alexander is depicted defeating Darius at Issus, the battle which assured Alexander's conquest of Asia, and his entry into the rich delta region of Egypt. These mosaics were the work of the skilled Alexandrian craftsmen, active in Italy between the end of the 2nd century BC and the beginning of the following century, during which the imposing restructuring of the Pompeian grand residences took place; their size and sumptuousness evoking the magnificence of the oriental Hellenistic palaces.

3

Figure 10.2 Floor mosaic of Alexander the Great defeating Darius at the Battle of Issus, from the House of the Faun

SUGGESTED READING

Robert Etienne, *Pompeii: The Day a City Died*, trans. Caroline Palmer, 1997, Documents: The Boscoreale Treasure, pp. 192–7

Ernesto De Carolis, *Gods and Heroes in Pompeii*, trans. Lory-Ann Touchette, 2001. This book is excellent for examples of paintings with themes associated with the love life of the Greek gods, the tragic stories of the Greek myths, and themes related to *The Iliad*.

Erich Lessing & Antonio Varone, *Pompeii*, 1996. Especially chapters 'In Search of an Identity' and 'The New Roman Society'.

Colin Amery & Brian Curran, *The Lost World of Pompeii*, 2002. Especially the chapters 'The Pompeian House' and 'Life and Art'.

Figure 10.3 Mosaic of Plato and the Athenian Academy

PART 4

Investigating, Reconstructing and Preserving the Past

IN PART 4 STUDENTS LEARN TO:

- describe and assess the significance of key people and the methods they used in the excavation of the sites from 1863 until 1961
- understand the importance of investigations carried out between the 1970s and the present time in challenging earlier interpretations of the finds
- evaluate the part played by specialists in other disciplines to greater understanding of Pompeii, Herculaneum and the Vesuvian area
- describe the destructive forces that plague Pompeii and Herculaneum
- understand the issues of conservation, preservation and restoration
- discuss ethical issues relating to the display of human remains and custodianship
- present findings in a variety of diagrammatic, written and oral forms.

IMPORTANT TERMS

anecdotal evidence
autoCAD
conservation
digital imagings
ecofacts
ethics
false assumptions
'new excavations'
one-layer site
political context
preservation
regions
replicas
restoration
stratigraphic sampling
structural phases

Changing archaeological methods and interpretations

11

THINGS TO CONSIDER

- Evolution of archaeological methodology in the 19th and 20th centuries
- The influences of political and cultural context on excavation and interpretation of material remains
- The ongoing work of retelling the story of the site
- The use of new technologies and scientific advancements in archaeology

---

OUR PICTURE OF POMPEII HAS CHANGED OVER THE YEARS ACCORDING TO THE QUESTIONS PEOPLE HAVE CHOSEN TO ASK OF THE EVIDENCE AVAILABLE TO THEM AND THE ISSUES THEY HAVE CHOSEN TO ANALYSE THROUGH NEW ARCHAEOLOGICAL EXPLORATION.

Alison E. Cooley, Pompeii, *p. 11*

CONTRIBUTIONS OF 19TH- AND 20TH-CENTURY ARCHAEOLOGISTS

The beginning of a more scientific approach

From 1860 to 1960, archaeology at Pompeii came of age under the leadership of men such as Giuseppe Fiorelli, Vittorio Spinazzola and Amedeo Maiuri. They adopted a more systematic and scientific approach to excavation and the documentation of finds.

Royal link with archaeology challenged in the early 19th century

In the mid-19th century, after approximately one hundred years of Bourbon dominance, the close link between the court and archaeology was about to be challenged. No longer was it acceptable to have:

- a haphazard excavation method motivated by the need to find precious objects and beautiful paintings
- a jealously guarded royal collection in the Naples Museum
- a monopoly by the Herculaneum Academy in publishing finds
- a site for select visitors only.

GIUSEPPE FIORELLI (1860–1875)

In 1860, with the unification of Italy (the Kingdom of Naples was annexed to the Kingdom of Italy) and the demise of the Bourbon dynasty, a new era in Pompeian excavation began. Giuseppe Fiorelli was appointed as inspector of the excavations and three years later was given direction of the Naples Museum as well as the superintendency of Pompeii. According to Alison Cooley in *Pompeii* (2003):

✕ Fiorelli's impact

> IT IS HARD TO EXAGGERATE HIS IMPACT ON THE HISTORY OF POMPEII.
> WHETHER HE WAS PRIMARILY A POLITICAL PRAGMATIST, ADMINISTRATOR
> OR ARCH INNOVATOR, FIORELLI ARGUABLY REMAINS THE INDIVIDUAL
> WHO HAD THE GREATEST IMPACT UPON THE WAY IN WHICH POMPEII HAS
> BEEN BOTH EXCAVATED AND PERCEIVED.[1]

To some extent, his innovations were the result of a gradual process which had begun over ten years before. Fiorelli wanted to:

✕ Aims

- introduce a more cohesive and systematic approach to excavation as a whole
- ensure more effective controls on publication of the results of excavation
- open the site up to more visitors
- incorporate the site into the teaching program at Naples University
- set up an antiquarium on the site to house those more ordinary objects not wanted at the Naples Museum.

Fiorelli's achievements

1 He was responsible for introducing a uniform numbering and naming system by dividing the topography of the site—including those areas not yet excavated—into nine regions (*regiones*) each of 22 town blocks (*insulae*) and entrances to houses and shops within each insula. He allocated a number to each, instead of the arbitrary naming that had been the practice. For example, the House of the Faun, which had had eight different names, became VI-xii. 2,5,7. This system made it easier to draw up plans and to locate individual structures. Although lay visitors to the site today still refer to houses by a name, as does this text, Fiorelli's system, with some modifications, is still used by those working on the site and in their publications.

✕ Division of site into regions, insulae and houses

2 He introduced a more systematic approach to excavation, unlike the haphazard digging

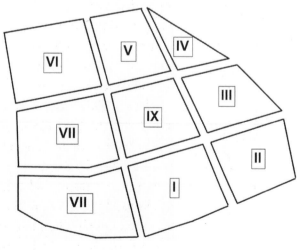

Figure 11.1 Fiorelli's regions

of his predecessors who had excavated wherever the site seemed most promising. He organised a workforce of 500 people and, following the line of the roads, connected different parts of the site. According to August Mau, 'he first set about clearing the undisturbed places between the excavated portions; and when in this way the west part of the city had been laid bare, he commenced to work systematically from the excavated part to the east.'[2]

3 He realised that his predecessors had lost or overlooked a lot of precious information by digging straight down through the layers of debris and pumice to the ground level of AD 79, extracting anything of interest and shovelling the material aside. Artefacts had been documented with no understanding of their context, and information about collapsed upper storeys was lost. He imposed a system of slowly uncovering the houses from the top down, collecting data to help restore the ancient buildings and their interiors and gain a better understanding of the process of burial. 'Although Fiorelli's method was still a far cry from modern stratigraphic digging techniques . . . it was a first step in the right direction.'[3] Wherever possible, he left paintings in situ, although the best continued to be cut from the wall and shipped off to Naples. Other objects were removed for display to a small antiquarium built on the site.

4 He made a discovery that contributed more than anything else to his fame: his recognition of the significance of cavities in the deposits of hardened ash as impressions of the victims' bodies. With the passage of time, the ash had solidified around the body contours as it decomposed, and an

Figure 11.2 Plaster casts of victims

impression was left. He devised a method of injecting liquid plaster into the cavities, enabling him to recover not only the shapes of humans and animals as they died, but other objects made of perishable material. Today, a similar process of casting is used but plaster has been replaced with a semi-transparent epoxy resin which allows the bones and any small objects worn or carried by the victim to remain visible.

5 He introduced a new system for recording the work in progress. Day books or diaries were to include the date, the number of workers employed, the time the job started and finished, the exact place of excavation, and a precise description of the number, type and quality of the objects found. An architect had to add his observations and a superintendent stamped every page before it was submitted to the inspector of the excavations.

※ Careful documentation

6 He made 'a fundamental shift in approach to the antiquities of Pompeii'[4] by attempting to focus on its overall history rather than on individual objects, buildings and art, and he pointed out that archaeological evidence rather than the textual sources could be used to reconstruct history.

※ Attempts to see the 'big picture'

7 He contributed to the education of archaeological students as well as the public. A school of archaeology at Pompeii was set up; it was eventually replaced by a national Italian School of Archaeology in 1875. By charging an entrance fee, a wider cross-section of visitors gained access to the site and an awareness of the importance of the work being done there. The first tour of Italy was launched by Thomas Cook in 1864.

※ Attempts to introduce education at the site

By the time he was promoted to the position of Director General of Antiquities throughout Italy in 1875, three-fifths of the site had been excavated and he believed that the town could be completely unearthed in little over 70 years if the excavations continued at the same rate.

During Fiorelli's tenure, systematic approaches were being used in other areas of Pompeian research, which was 'part of a general revolution in the field of ancient history and archaeology'.[5] These included a complete catalogue of all painted panels from Pompeii (W. Helbig 1868) and a collection of Pompeian painted and incised inscriptions as part of the Corpus Inscriptionum Latinarum (K. Zangemeister 1871). This was followed in 1873 and 1882 by August Mau's history and classification of Pompeian wall painting. This famous art historian, who worked for the German Archaeological Institute in Rome, visited Pompeii and, using Fiorelli's systematic work and comments made by the ancient architect Vitruvius on pictorial styles, developed a sequential classification of wall paintings from the 2nd century BC to the imperial age. Although there have been various adjustments to his original subdivision, his four chronological 'Pompeian styles' have been retained. Mau believed it was a mistake to cut the best pictures from the walls while leaving the decorative framework intact, because the pictures needed to be viewed as a whole. He thought the whole painting should be left in situ while providing it with whatever protection was necessary.

※ Others follow the systematic approach— cataloguing and classifying

FIORELLI'S SUCCESSORS (1875-1905)

Those who followed Fiorelli in the last years of the 19th and early 20th centuries faithfully carried on his work, but proceeded more slowly because of the greater care taken for the preservation of the remains. Roofs of timber and tile were restored to protect floor mosaics and the frescoes still remaining on the walls.

Under the supervision of the architect director Michele Ruggiero (1875–93) and the epigraphist director Giulio De Petra (1893–1901), excavation predominantly focused on the northernmost quarters of the city where they unearthed the Central Baths, the House of the Centenary, the House of the Vettii, the House of Lucretius Fronto and other buildings in regions V, VI and IX. They both began to investigate the area outside the city walls. Ruggerio was 'responsible for the consolidation and restoration in situ of over six hundred paintings and of the atria of the House of the Silver Wedding and the House of the Balcony'[6] while De Petra was responsible for restoring roofs, covering atria and recreating several gardens. These men helped to bring the city to life. The historian Ettore Pais (1901–1905) continued to excavate, finding the remains of the Vesuvian gate and water tower, but Antonio Sogliano (1905–1910) devoted himself primarily to conservation and many of the techniques he devised are still in use today.

During the directorship of Ettore Pais, Charles Waldstein, reader in classical archaeology at Cambridge, launched a program to gain international support to cover the cost of reopening Herculaneum for excavation, which had been suspended in 1780. Despite getting the interest of some of the world's richest men, at the last minute the Italian government pulled out of the scheme feeling their prestige was being undermined by the international effort. Herculaneum was not reopened until 1927.

VITTORIO SPINAZZOLA (1910–1923)

Vittorio Spinazzola, as director, was more interested in 'the realities of town planning' than with the possibility of 'extraordinary discoveries'.[7] Between 1912 and 1914, he chose to move his investigations away from the northern quarters of the town and focus on a 600-metre length of the main commercial road—the Via dell'Abbondanza or Street of Abundance—that ran west to east through Pompeii, linking the Forum with the amphitheatre and the Sarnian gate. This resulted in a more unified approach and these 'New Excavations' as they came to be called, 'revealed a Pompeii that had been scarcely

❧
Discovery of shops,
workshops, graffiti
and wall writings

dreamed of'[8] with its election posters, popular paintings and numerous shops and workshops, such as the Laundry of Stephanus and the Inn of Asellina, interspersed with fine houses. His meticulous excavation method showed how the buildings along the main east–west street had been buried, and allowed him to reconstruct their facades as fully as possible, particularly the upper floors, with their windows, balconies and roofs. Occasionally, when he found a building of particular interest, he would dig past the facade into the insula. In this way he discovered houses such as that of the Cryptoporticus and Octavio Quartio (or Loreius Tiburtinus) with its extensive gardens and waterworks.

However, criticisms can be made of Spinazzola's work. By focusing on unearthing the frontages only, he had to shore them up to prevent them collapsing from the weight of the earth behind. Also, he could only guess at the exact function of many of the shops.

Spinazolla's directorship was caught up in the bureaucratic reorganisation and political changes associated with the rise of the Fascist government of Mussolini in Italy, and in 1923 he was forced to retire. However, by that time 'the town's most important business artery had been cleared over almost its entire length'.[9] It was left up to his successor, Amadeo Maiuri, to bring it to the condition that visitors enjoy today.

8
Criticism of his method

Figure 11.3 The Via dell'Abbondanza today

AMEDEO MAIURI (1924–1961)

Amedeo Maiuri took over the directorship of Pompeii in 1924 and remained in charge until his retirement in 1961. He has often been described as the most productive, determined and controversial director in the history of the excavations. Guido Piovene in his book *Travels in Italy* (1958) went further, calling him 'this prince among archaeologists'. Most of those who have worked at Pompeii—and Herculaneum after 1927—would probably agree with Andrew Wallace-Hadrill that he was a 'towering figure . . . endlessly energetic, learned and imaginative'[10] and that 'his massive presence lies behind the excavation, publication and interpretation of the majority of houses'.[11]

8
Status as an excavator

His most productive period corresponded with the Fascist government of Mussolini—the twenties through to the outbreak of World War II—when Italian archaeology as a whole benefited from an injection of state funds. Excavation ceased during the war, and Pompeii suffered serious damage from the 160 bombs dropped by the allies in 1943. Digging was resumed in 1947, and from 1951 until 1961 there was intensive activity at Pompeii with over ten insulae totally cleared. However, much of the latter work was hurried and chronically underfunded. Despite his wide-ranging excavations, by the time he retired, 26 hectares of the total site area of 66 hectares were still not excavated. Figure 11.4 summarises the achievements of Amedeo Maiuri.

Figure 11.4 The achievements of Amedeo Maiuri

1	Continued the work of Spinazzola along the famous Via Dell' Abondannza in an attempt to uncover the insulae on either side and gain a view of the whole
2	Excavated the House of Menander with its famous silver treasure
3	Completed work on the Villa of Mysteries outside the wall of Pompeii
4	Studied the structure of the walls and towers
5	Cleared and restored the area behind the Triangular Forum which revealed the terrace houses on the steep flank of the Pompeian mound
6	Deepened the excavations at significant locations (Forum, temples and oldest houses) to investigate pre-Roman levels
7	Restored public buildings such as the tribunal of the Basilica and the roofs of many houses
8	Supervised the re-openings of the excavation at Herculaneum
9	Discovered the House of the Bi-centenary in Herculaneum—the town's largest and richest residence—containing 18 wax tablets
10	Resumed excavations after the WWII with the Villa Imperiale discovered under the damaged Antiquarium and a pre-Roman temple to Dionysus found in a bomb crater
11	Explored regions I and II and brought to light the House of Julia Felix which had been originally uncovered in 1775 and then reburied
12	Cleared the necropolis outside the Nucerian Gate

Influences on Maiuri's interpretation of the finds

1 Mussolini and the Fascists ruthlessly exploited the potential of Italy's imperial past in order 'to create a model for a new imperialist Italy'.[12] Archaeology and Maiuri benefited from the dictator's financial support. Whether consciously or not, Maiuri followed the political line by excavating glorious monuments such as the House of Menander and the Villa of Mysteries, which were a testament to the magnificence of Italy's past.

When he excavated the House of Menander between 1927 and 1933, the evidence (wall paintings and silver treasure hoard) convinced him of ownership at the highest level of society, probably a member of the Poppaea gens to whom Poppaea Sabina, Nero's second wife, belonged. Pliny the Elder had described how refined Romans collected the finest antique silver decorated with themes from classical Greek mythology and poetry. 'In Maiuri's interpretation the House of Menander became an illustration of Pliny's text.'[13]

2 After 1926, he became interested in the historical debate engendered by Michael Rostovtzeff's *The Social and Economic History of the Roman Empire* in which he focused on the rise of the commercially and industrially based bourgeoisie in early imperial Italy. Rostovtzeff was a Russian exile who became professor of ancient history and archaeology at Yale University. For his history, he had drawn on his knowledge of Pompeii which he had visited several times. In fact, he had written his thesis years before on 'In the light of the New Excavations'. It is believed that Maiuri drew on Rostovtzeff for his interpretation of the archaeological finds in Pompeii and Herculaneum.

🎕
Impact of
Rostovtzeff's
history on Maiuri's
interpretations

Maiuri looked for physical evidence of economic and social change in both towns. To him the 'often surprising juxtaposition of rich and poor, beautiful and commercial, luxurious and squalid, suggested patrician classes in decline' with a 'brutal invasion of the commercial world'.[14] He formulated a thesis of a major social and economic transformation of the early empire, which developed into a crisis after the earthquake of AD 62, when he believed patricians left the city and retreated to their country estates, leaving a 'motley crowd of enriched merchants, second hand dealers, bakers, fullers, decayed patricians, and thrusting industrialists dabbling in politics.'[15]

🎕
Development of
the 'crisis' theory

🎕
His view on the
fate of the elite
after AD 62

In all his publications, from the time he first argued his case in *L'Ultima fase edilizia di Pompeii* in 1942 until his retirement, Maiuri's language revealed his distaste at what he believed had happened. The following extracts were written 16 years apart.

1942—Pompeii
BUT IT IS ALSO IN THIS PERIOD [I.E. POST-EARTHQUAKE] THAT WE
WITNESS THE TRANSFORMATION OF MANY UPPER-CLASS HOUSES INTO
OFFICINAE AND IN THE INTRUSION OF SHOPS. *CUPONAE* AND
THERMOPOLIA INTO THE INTERIOR AND ALONG THE FACADES OF
PATRICIAN RESIDENCES. THE SPLITTING UP OF A SINGLE. GRAND.
UPPER-CLASS HOUSE INTO SEVERAL MODEST BUILDINGS. THE CHANGE
AND PERVERSION OF TASTE IN TYPE AND STYLE OF THE DECORATION OF
THE ROOMS. SACRIFICING BEAUTIFUL AND NOBLE OLD PAINTINGS FOR
BANAL AND POOR REDECORATION. IN SHORT. THE INVASION OF THE
MERCANTILE CLASS OF THE STRUCTURE OF THE OLD ROMANO-CAMPANIAN
PATRICIAN CLASS OF THE CITY.[16]

🎕
In Pompeii

Herculaneum—1958
BUT AFTER UPPER-CLASS OCCUPATION LASTING POSSIBLY AS LATE AS THE
CLAUDIAN ERA. THE PROFOUND TRANSFORMATION WHICH THE

🎕
In Herculaneum

COMMERCIAL LIFE OF THE CITY HAD TO UNDERGO WITH THE NEW
ARRANGEMENT OF THE VIA DEL FORO, THE GRAVE CRISIS WHICH THE
NEW CURRENTS OF OVERSEAS COMMERCE AND EARTHQUAKE DAMAGE
PRODUCED IN THE CLASS OF THE OLD PATRICIAN FAMILIES OF
HERCULANEUM, AND FINALLY THE NEED TO WITHDRAW FROM THE NOISY
AND PLEBEIAN COMMERCIAL LIFE OF THE FORUM, WERE THE MULTIPLE
REASONS WHICH DETERMINED THE DECAY OF THIS HOUSE FROM AN
UPPER-CLASS RESIDENCE TO THE PRACTICAL USE OF A LODGING
WITH SHOPS.[17]

To Maiuri, Pompeii and Herculaneum—particularly in the last 17 years of
their existence—were in decline. He maintained that the Pompeian
Forum was still in shambles when Vesuvius erupted, and that this
reflected the depressed economic conditions in Pompeii after the earthquake of AD 62.

❦
Criticisms of
excavation,
documentation and
interpretation

His views remained the established orthodoxy until a number of scholars found it 'necessary to tackle some of his presuppositions head on'.[18]
Although unaware of it, tourists today are still under the influence of
Maiuri with his picture of Pompeian society expressed in most of the guide
books and popular works. Some of the criticisms levelled at Maiuri include
the following:

- Much of his excavation 1951–61 was rushed, with few of the excavated
  buildings restored or protected, and in the same period there was virtually
  no documentation, let alone publication.
- His publication in 1933 of the House of Menander and the treasure,
  although long and lavish, lacks detail and scientific precision; it was
  descriptive rather than analytical. In concentrating on descriptions of the
  paintings and discussions of the more spectacular finds, he was following
  the current political line.
- His interpretation of social and economic transformation after the earthquake was based, according to Wallace-Hadrill, on anecdotal rather than
  statistical evidence and on false assumptions about the elite, trade and use
  of property; about the mix of commercial and residential establishments;
  and about the link between luxury, decoration and status. According to J.
  Andreau (1973), his view of an invasion of industrialists 'is sheer fantasy'.[19]
  Wallace-Hadrill has shown that, although there may be some truth in
  Maiuri's account of the crisis after the earthquake, 'his model is simply too
  rigid'.[20]

❦
Awareness of
future needs

It is easy in hindsight to criticise some of Maiuri's methodology and
interpretations, but it should take nothing away from his tremendous contribution to our understanding of Pompeii and Herculaneum. Maiuri set the
agenda for future work at both sites. When, on his retirement, he commented
that 'what is left to do is a complex, laborious and arduous, slow and costly

work of preservation, protection and restoration', he was foreseeing the problems that the site would face in the next half century.[21]

DEVELOPMENTS IN THE SECOND HALF OF THE 20TH CENTURY

By the late 1950s and early 1960s it was obvious that Pompeii was in a bad way. An array of natural and human forces were causing the remains to fade, crumble and disappear (see Chapter 12). The size of the site, with its kilometres of streets, hundreds of roofless buildings and thousands of walls that had not been documented properly—if at all—and the possibility of another eruption, made scholars aware of the need to stop large-scale excavation. In the last 40 years there has been little new excavation inside the city walls of Pompeii. The main efforts have been concentrated outside the ancient town, especially in areas threatened by building development.

✵ Reduction in excavation

Archaeological activities since the 1970s have been motivated by:
• the urgent need to preserve what has already been uncovered by documentation, protection and conservation programs
• the awareness that by using a more selective sampling approach and carefully probing beneath areas already exposed, the answers to new questions about the town may be answered 'at the same time as leaving significant areas of the site for new generations to excavate'.[22]

✵ Need to conserve, document and ask new questions

These activities have only been possible with advancements made in scientific and archaeological techniques, and the contribution of specialists in other areas. Much of archaeology is now carried out in the laboratory, as smaller and smaller amounts of material reveal their secrets: tiny fragments of charcoal, traces of pollen, and substances found in containers. An Applied Research Laboratory, under the auspices of the Superintendency of Pompeii, was opened in 1994. It uses both Italian and foreign specialists in many disciplines. Some of its recent research includes collecting, identifying and classifying all the samples of white and coloured marbles found in the Vesuvian area, organic finds from the Vesuvian area, a study of contents of unguent jars, a study of the natural environment of the Sarno plain and a geomorphologic reconstruction of the Vesuvian area before the AD 79 eruption.

✵ Laboratory work and contribution of specialists

Figure 11.5 summarises the specialists in other areas who have contributed to an understanding of the ancient Vesuvian sites.

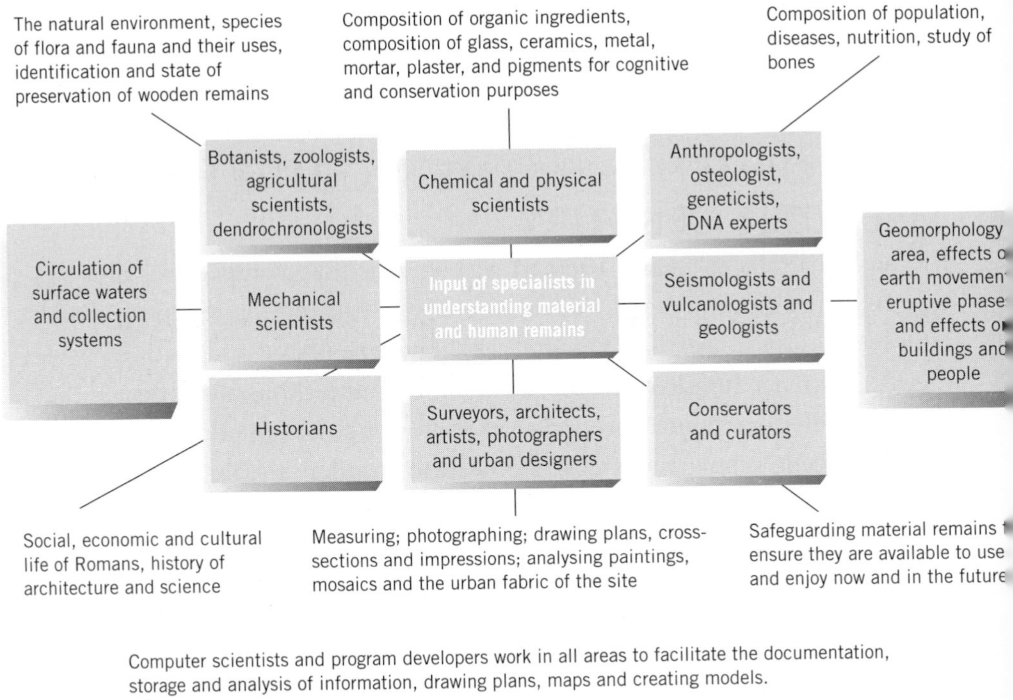

The natural environment, species of flora and fauna and their uses, identification and state of preservation of wooden remains

Composition of organic ingredients, composition of glass, ceramics, metal, mortar, plaster, and pigments for cognitive and conservation purposes

Composition of population, diseases, nutrition, study of bones

Botanists, zoologists, agricultural scientists, dendrochronologists

Chemical and physical scientists

Anthropologists, osteologist, geneticists, DNA experts

Circulation of surface waters and collection systems

Mechanical scientists

Input of specialists in understanding material and human remains

Seismologists and vulcanologists and geologists

Geomorphology area, effects of earth movement, eruptive phase and effects on buildings and people

Historians

Surveyors, architects, artists, photographers and urban designers

Conservators and curators

Social, economic and cultural life of Romans, history of architecture and science

Measuring; photographing; drawing plans, cross-sections and impressions; analysing paintings, mosaics and the urban fabric of the site

Safeguarding material remains to ensure they are available to use and enjoy now and in the future

Computer scientists and program developers work in all areas to facilitate the documentation, storage and analysis of information, drawing plans, maps and creating models.

Figure 11.5 Specialists who contribute to archaeology

DOCUMENTATION OF EXISTING FINDS

�֍ Urgent documentation programs

When the scale of the problems was realised in the late 1970s, three important documentation programs were implemented.

1 The Italian Central Institute for Cataloguing and Documentation undertook a complete documentation of 18,000 photographs of all painted walls and mosaic floors. Unfortunately, this represented less than 20 per cent of all that has been revealed on the sites since excavations first began, but fortunately it was completed just before the earthquake in 1981.

2 An independent Italian research institute set up a vast electronic database of all archival documents and archaeological remains, known as NEAPOLIS.

3 The first accurate map of the site was produced using improvements in photogrammetry (the process of making surveys and maps from photos).

✖ Computers, documentation and considerations for the future

Computers have played an invaluable part since the 1960s in recording, storing and comparing photographs, plans, maps and tens of thousands of finds. They provide instant, permanent access to virtually limitless amounts of information. However, according to Alexander Stille in his work *The Future of the Past: The Loss of Knowledge in the Age of Information*, 'one of the great ironies of the information age is that, while the late 20th century will undoubtedly have recorded more data than any other period in history, it will also almost certainly have lost more information than any other age . . . due to the problem of technological obsolescence—of fading words and images in odd-looking, out-of-date gizmos',[23] technology that depends on hardware and software that are no longer available. As technological change gathers momentum, so does the pace at which 'each new generation of equipment supplants the next', and there appears 'to be a direct relationship between the newness of technology and its fragility'. For example, 'digital technology—based on precise mathematically coding—either works perfectly or not at all'.[24] This will lead to questions in the future about how much and what kind of information to record and store.

LONG-TERM SITE INVESTIGATION AND DOCUMENTATION PROJECTS

From the late 1970s, through the 1980s and 1990s and into the 21st century, various Italian and international organisations have carried out long-term analysis and documentation programs in Pompeii.

'The Houses in Pompeii' project

In 1977, a 'Houses in Pompeii' project was set up by the German Archaeological Institute to investigate and salvage buildings 'at least on paper'[25] which had been excavated over the preceding centuries but which had not been recorded. From 1978 until 1986 this project involved an Australian and New Zealand team, whose task was to study two houses: the House of the Ancient Hunt and the House of the Coloured Capitals. Detailed information is available in K. Francis's 'The House of the Coloured Capitals' in *Australian Natural History*, vol. 19, no. 8, and in *Pompeii Revisited* (ed. J-P. Descoeudres).

❈ Australian participation in study of individual houses

'The Insula of Menander' project

Also in 1978, a British project (Ward-Perkins-Ling), began the first of a three-stage analysis and documentation of a whole city block: I. x.—The Insula of Menander. This insula included not only the grand House of Menander, but other significant houses, unnamed houses, and shop spaces. The project's aim was to redress the deficiencies in the earlier records of the insula conducted under Amedeo Maiuri between 1927 and 1933, which was 'hasty and bound to the year 79'[26] with little left in the way of documentation. Out of a total of 492 pages in Maiuri's original record of the house, only three pages were devoted to the identification of structural phases.

❈ A whole insula approach

❈ Deficiencies in Maiuri's original excavation and documentation

The project, whose overall aim was to draw general conclusions about the insula's social structure over time and in its final form in AD 79, included a large team of researchers: architects and draughts people to analyse the surviving structures; archaeologists to date the walls and floors; and experts in wall painting, mosaics and pottery to study loose finds and decoration. Stage I was to examine the architecture and structural history, Stage II to study the interior decoration and Stage III to examine the loose finds.

❈ Large and varied team

The project began with the production of 'an archive of drawings at 1:5 of the surviving wall paintings, and plans sections and elevations at 1:50 of

❈ Creating an archive

the visible architecture. These were to be supplemented by black and white, and colour photographs by drawings of selected pavements and certain architectural details at 1:10. In addition, there were pro-forma sheets providing a detailed record, room by room, of all architectural and decorative features.[27]

❈
Problems of
interpretation

Using the science of archaeology to meticulously analyse the physical evidence, the team investigated the site over seven seasons. However, the first stage of the project was not without its problems, particularly with regard to interpretation. Roger Ling outlined these difficulties as:

- the inability to excavate beneath existing walls and pavements
- reused building materials that made newer walls look like older ones
- early restorations and interventions (in the 1930s) that were rarely marked and therefore hard to identify.

❈
Changes in
insula identified

The first stage, published in *The Insula of the Menander at Pompeii: Volume I, The Structures* by Roger Ling in 1997, provided a detailed history of the insula showing that there had been frequent building changes, that the boundaries of properties also changed over time and that there appeared to be a late appearance of shops and the addition of upper storeys in the last years of the city. For example, the House of Menander expanded to include an adjacent house, and then around AD 60, an earlier part of the house was

❈
Refutation of
Maiuri's 'crisis'
theory

demolished to create more luxurious reception spaces, a stable yard and service quarters on two storeys. In the post-earthquake era much of the house was levelled for rebuilding. 'Counter to Amadeo Maiuri, Ling believes that rather than abandoning it after the earthquake of 62, the owner of the House of Menander was actively completing a large redecoration program at the time of the eruption.'[28] However, 'without digging up and dismantling existing structures, the construction history of the insula will continue to pose unanswered questions.'[29]

❈
Rejection of
earlier beliefs
about ownership

Ling also rejects the belief that the House of Menander belonged to Q. Poppaeus Sabinus, and this will pose further questions about the decoration of the house and particularly about the hoard of silver found by Maiuri in 1930. Hopefully Stages II and III of this project will reveal more about the lives of the inhabitants of the insula and the social life of the city.

❈
Time to ask
new questions

Although Amedeo Maiuri's 1933 lavish monograph of the House of Menander concentrated on the 'showy' features (decoration and hoard of silver), it was descriptive rather than analytical. Scholars today believe it is time, over 70 years later, to ask new questions in the light of recent archaeological thinking about Pompeii, and with the help now available from material sciences.

Figure 11.6 shows some of the questions that might be asked, or are being asked at the present time, about both the wall paintings and the silver found in the House of Menander.

Figure 11.6 New questions being asked

Future questions about the wall paintings suggested by J.R. Clarke, art historian from the University of Texas, in a review of Roger Ling's *The Insula of Menander,* Volume I	**Questions raised about the silver hoard by K.S. Painte, research associate of the Institute of Archaeology, Oxford University, in his *The Insula of Menander at Pompeii,* a supplement to Ling's book**
Who paid for the art? (patron) Who saw it? (viewer) Who made it? (artist/architect) Under what circumstances did the viewer see it? (reception and ritual) What other artistic forms does it resemble? (iconographic models)	Who was the owner of the silver and what was his status? Were he and his family from the top levels of society or were they further down the social scale? Was it an art collector's hoard, a dinner service or a deposit against a large loan? When was the plate (plus coins and jewels) put away in the cellar of the house? Did it have something to do with the earthquake? Was the silver used in the house? Was there such a thing as dinner service? Was it used for only the grandest banquets?
Clarke admits these questions are difficult to answer well.	Painte's conjecture at this point is that the silver was for no more than eight people and used for open-air dining.

'The Pompeian Forum' project

This ongoing project, which began in 1988, was collaborative, dependent on advanced technology—particularly computer science—and offered 'a bold challenge to traditional research methodologies and to widely published and generally accepted views about the Forum'.[30]

Use of computer science

Its team, led by John Dobbins (associate professor of classical art and archaeology at the University of Virginia) included classical archaeologists, a specialist in Roman architecture, an urban architectural historian, an urban designer and computer and AutoCAD specialists.

Wide range of experts

The project was initiated because:

Reasons for the project

- the existing architectural plans of the Forum were inaccurate and incomplete
- the architectural and decorative remains documented as late as 1983 were already deteriorating rapidly
- the Forum provided an opportunity to study the Pompeian response to the earthquake in AD 62 and to 'come face to face with civic aspirations, building techniques and urban design schemes of the third quarter of the 1st century AD'.[31]

The project's main objectives were to produce more accurate plans and elevations of the surviving remains, supplemented by large-format black-and-white photographs of archival quality, and computer models; to use the architectural analysis to stimulate discussions about Pompeian urbanism among scholars; and to use the data in the wider context to understand contemporary urban problems.

Objectives

The team brought structural engineering principles to bear on archaeological questions. Much of the documentation work was performed using what is called a 'total station', an electronic surveying device 'that interfaces with AutoCAD so that data an be transformed onsite into plans and models using a laptop computer equipped with AutoCAD'.[32] As with most modern archaeology, where much of the work is now done in the laboratory, the Pompeiian Forum team often worked in the Forum in the mornings surveying, and the afternoon back in a CAD work centre, building a computerised model.

By 1996, the team had concluded that the Pompeians did not see their urban centre as a series of separate structures, but as an urban ensemble. Also, the traditional view that the Forum was a 'builders' yard' (August Mau) in the years after the AD 62 earthquake, which reflected the depressed economic conditions in Pompeii in the last 17 years (Amedeo Maiuri), was disproved. In fact John Dobbins found evidence of a comprehensive and ambitious post-earthquake plan for the eastern side of the Forum, a design whose features were 'the unification and monumentalisation of the urban centre', achieved 'by blocking streets, linking facades, upgrading building materials and emphasising the more prominent NE and SE entrances'.[33]

FUTURE-ORIENTED ARCHAEOLOGY AT POMPEII

The Anglo-American Project (AAP) at Pompeii which has been investigating Region VI, Insula I since 1994, and its offshoot the Pompeii Trust, established in 2002, epitomise the future-oriented approach to archaeology and conservation. They are dedicated to the most meticulous techniques of excavation and documentation which will allow future archaeologists to ask new questions and challenge their story of the site, as well as to preserving the heritage of Pompeii for future generations.

The aim of the AAP is to carry out scientific archaeological exploration of the insula—one of the earliest to be exposed— through 'stratigraphic excavation where no ancient floors survive, with recording and analysis of the standing architecture' and with 'the fullest recovery of information from artefacts and ecofacts'.[34] The Pompeii Trust's aim is to 'conserve the buildings of the insula, complete the full academic publication of the research, and present the results to the more than two million visitors a year who come to Pompeii and to the wider public'.[35]

The work being carried out in VI-I follows what could be called a conservation and educational model of archaeology (see Chapter 12). As well as traditional excavation techniques (systematic removal, recording and interpretation of buried archaeological deposits), conservation-oriented techniques are carried out in situ to reduce deterioration of freshly excavated organic and inorganic materials when they are at their most vulnerable, and to ensure their safe transfer to facilities where they will be housed and stored.

Trench-side discussions with interested visitors are welcomed. These not only educate the public about the art, history and culture of Pompeii, as well as the urgent need to conserve the site, but can transform a mere visit into an archaeological experience. While encouraging tourists to the site is essential to the sustained future of Pompeii, it is also a major cause of destruction.

Field work in VI-I

At the time of the eruption, VI-I, located just inside the Herculaneum Gate, was a mixture of properties: the large House of the Vestals, the House of the Surgeon, workshops, four bars, an inn and upstairs apartments. For over a hundred years, the excavators at Pompeii chose to excavate only to the level of AD 79, and any interest in the pre-Roman history of Pompeii was sought from the standing structures rather than probing deeper. Despite a few stratigraphic samplings by Amedeo Maiuri in the 1930s and 40s, Pompeii 'remained a single-layer site',[36] generating a false picture of Pompeii's pre-Roman history. Due to work like that being done under the auspices of the AAP, the traditional picture of archaic Pompeii has been radically modified, and is much more complex than previously thought.

✶
Challenge to traditional view of archaic Pompeii

By 2000 the field team had:

- completed a thorough analysis and documentation of the standing structures of the northern part of the insula (House of the Vestals), revealing the effect of over two hundred years of exposure to the elements and human intervention

✶
AAP Results to 2000

- revealed a changing pattern of occupation over four centuries: they identified the first recognisable human intervention on the site; the earliest houses and the appearance of the first commercial structures; the expansion of the House of the Vestals; the first lavish displays of decoration; provision of water at the time of the Augustan aqueduct; the modification of commercial properties; the adjustments to water supply as a result of the damage done by the earthquake; and the addition of receptions rooms, a grand staircase and redecoration just prior to the eruption
- collected a wide range of ecofacts and artefacts from the various strata, including crucial information on diet and the economy: fish bones, egg shells, pottery, mammalian bone, plant microfossils and faecal deposits

Work is already advanced on the inns and bars of the insula, and in 2002 excavation began on the House of the Surgeon and the Shrine. The field work, estimated to be completed by 2006, is carried out during the summer season, while research is ongoing in the laboratories of Bradford University throughout the year. AAP runs a school each summer at the site for the next generation of archaeologists.

Other projects are continuing to delve below the level of AD 79. One, associated with the University of Perugia and Naples Oriental University, reported in 2003 that after three years of research in a series of houses in

✶
Discovery between 2000 and 2003 of 3rd-century BC town

Region VI, they found 'remains that reconstruct the entire history of the town, from traces of walls dating back to the sixth century BC to startling new evidence of a third century settlement . . . the town that is coming to light is slightly different. It was characterised by steps and narrow streets accessible only with donkeys, while rows of smaller houses lined larger streets.'[37]

THE FUTURE OF ARCHAEOLOGY

TODAY, ARCHAEOLOGY IS IN THE MIDST OF A SECOND METAMORPHOSIS. HAVING TRANSFORMED ITSELF INTERNALLY—INTO A SCIENCE—IT IS NOW BEING RESHAPED BY EXTERNAL SOCIAL, CULTURAL AND POLITICAL FORCES. BUT IT IS STILL A WORK IN PROGRESS.[38]

❀ Metamorphosis in archaeology

Archaeology is no longer cloistered in academia as it was 50 years ago when archaeologists worked as individuals with their own goals, seeking to distinguish themselves through the publication of their findings. With increasing specialisation, dependence on public funds and corporate research efforts, there are 'additional voices that have legitimate claims on what is being done to and with the archaeological record'.[39] Archaeologists have moved out into the world of business, in the form of resource management, and into the political arena, where they are involved in issues of public policy that have a bearing on the integrity of their profession and the future of the material remains which are 'a fragile, finite, and non-renewable resource'.[40] They must now be able to justify the need to excavate, see that conservation is built into any archaeological project from the initial assessment, and remember that they have a responsibility to the public. As archaeology has become politicised, there are few aspects of the profession that are not subject to questions of ethics and none more so than the excavation and treatment of human remains (see Chapter 12).

Not only has the role and responsibility of the archaeologist changed, but it is now accepted that the past can never really be known and there is no 'right' interpretation of the material remains. It depends on the political and cultural context of the time and on what questions are being asked. Recently there has been a shifting 'away from the old certainties of "fact" and "truth" towards multiple and varied interpretations'.[41] This will have a direct impact on what is expected of conservation and on how conservation develops.

Chapter review

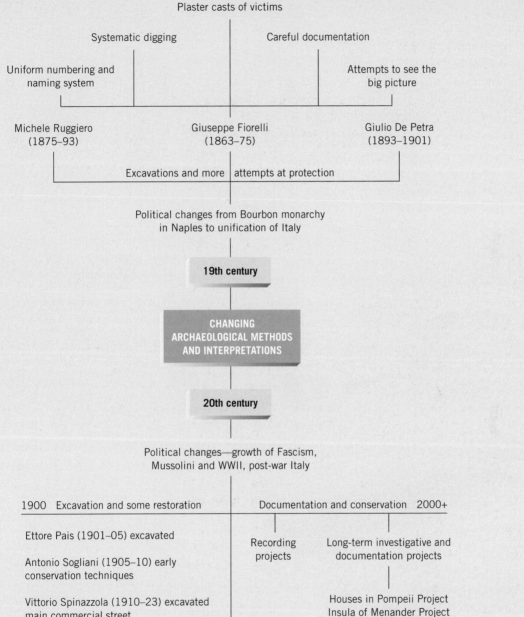

Plaster casts of victims

Systematic digging

Careful documentation

Uniform numbering and
naming system

Attempts to see the
big picture

Michele Ruggiero
(1875–93)

Giuseppe Fiorelli
(1863–75)

Giulio De Petra
(1893–1901)

Excavations and more | attempts at protection

Political changes from Bourbon monarchy
in Naples to unification of Italy

19th century

**CHANGING
ARCHAEOLOGICAL METHODS
AND INTERPRETATIONS**

20th century

Political changes—growth of Fascism,
Mussolini and WWII, post-war Italy

1900   Excavation and some restoration

Documentation and conservation   2000+

Ettore Pais (1901–05) excavated

Antonio Sogliani (1905–10) early
conservation techniques

Vittorio Spinazzola (1910–23) excavated
main commercial street

Amedeo Maiuri (1924–61) excavation on
a massive scale, some poorly documented,
some interpretations reflected the current
political and cultural context. His 'crisis'
theory challenged later.

Recording
projects

Long-term investigative and
documentation projects

Houses in Pompeii Project
Insula of Menander Project
Pompeian Forum Project
Anglo-American Project

Stratigraphic
investigation

Analysis of standing
structures

Use of computers
and scientific
developments

New interpretations and new
questions to be asked

Activities

1 Describe what is happening in the three sketches shown in Figure 11.7. Write a short paragraph for each one.

2 SINCE THE 1960S, COMPUTERS HAVE MADE THE ARCHAEOLOGIST'S JOB EASIER: A MAP OF THE TOWN, A MAP OF THE GEOLOGY OF THE AREA AND THE PLANS OF EVERY BUILDING AND STREET CAN BE DRAWN AND EXAMINED IN DETAIL ON A COMPUTER SCREEN. IF ONLY THE FOUNDATIONS OF A HOUSE HAVE BEEN FOUND, THE COMPUTER CAN BUILD UP AN IMAGE OF WHAT THE HOUSE MIGHT HAVE ONCE LOOKED LIKE. IT CAN STORE AND COMPARE DETAILED RECORDS OF THOUSANDS OF FINDS, DOWN TO THE TINIEST FRAGMENT OF POTTERY TO A COIN.

a How has the archaeologist's job been made easier by the use of computers?

b Provide several examples of the use of computers in recording projects in Pompeii since the 1970s.

c What is photogrammetry and how is it used in archaeology?

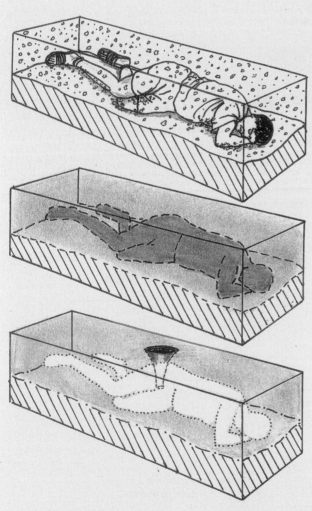

Figure 11.7

Activities

d How has the input of physical and chemical sciences contributed to a greater understanding of the finds?

e Choose two other specialist areas and explain how they have benefited the archaeologist in his or her understanding of the site of Pompeii.

f Although computers are used in all disciplines associated with archaeology, they may not prove to be 'the holy grail of infinite memory and of instant, permanent access to virtually limitless amounts of information'[42] they were once believed to be. Why?

g Suggest some problems that this may pose for the future of archaeology.

3 a Define the term 'stratigraphy'.

b What is meant by the statement that 'until the second half of the 20th century, Pompeii remained a one-layer site'?

c Name two projects that have tried to address the problem of the pre-eruption history of Pompeii.

d What are some of the problems faced by archaeologists in attempting to find more information on the history of particular houses and insulae?

e What was Amedeo Maiuri's 'crisis' theory?

f What new interpretations have archaeologists involved in late 20th-century projects been able to come up with to refute the 'crisis' theory?

4 What is meant by 'political and cultural context' with regard to interpretative archaeology? Provide an example of the 'shaping' of the past in terms of the present.

5 Comment on each of the following quotes in regard to the contribution made to archaeological excavation at Pompeii by Giuseppe Fiorelli, Vittorio Spinazzola and Amedeo Maiuri.

. . . FIORELLI ARGUABLY REMAINS THE INDIVIDUAL WHO HAD THE GREATEST IMPACT UPON THE WAY IN WHICH POMPEII HAS BEEN BOTH EXCAVATED AND PERCEIVED.

Alison E. Cooley,
Pompeii, *p. 96*

SPINAZZOLA WAS 'PROMPTED BY A CONCERN WITH THE REALITIES OF TOWN PLANNING RATHER THAN THE ILLUSORY SATISFACTION OF MAKING EXTRAORDINARY DISCOVERIES . . . HE REVEALED A POMPEII THAT HAD SCARCELY BEEN DREAMED OF.

R. Etienne, Pompeii:
The Day a City Died,
pp. 38–40

AMEDEO MAIURI'S 'MASSIVE PRESENCE LIES BEHIND THE EXCAVATION, PUBLICATION AND INTERPRETATION OF THE MAJORITY OF HOUSES.

Andrew Wallace-Hadrill,
Houses and Society
in Pompeii and
Herculaneum, *p. xvi*

---

6 Topic for extended response, class discussion or oral presentation: 'Pompeii is at once the most studied and least understood of sites. Universaly familiar, its excavation and scholarship prove a nightmare of omissions and disasters.'[43]

Destruction, conservation and ethical issues

THINGS TO CONSIDER

- Excavation inevitably leads to destruction
- The nature of the forces of archaeological destruction
- Differences between preservation, restoration and conservation
- The notion that not everything can be saved

- The recent collision of archaeology and ethics
- The re-evaluation of the treatment of human remains
- The question of ownership of cultural property

THE SECOND DEATH OF POMPEII AND HERCULANEUM

Changes that follow exposure

There is a well-known saying that 'to dig is to destroy' and this applies particularly to Pompeii. Once a site is excavated there is 'an abrupt change in the environment which causes a series of devastating changes in structures and objects'.[1] Most materials change, even when exposed to light, and many of the ancient building materials (e.g. mortar, which is low in lime) 'crumbles easily . . . and can be eroded by the wind . . . it encourages rising damp, which damages the painted murals'.[2]

Evidence of long-term neglect at Pompeii

For over 200 years, the remains of Pompeii have been subjected to a whole range of destructive forces, natural and human, some unavoidable, others preventable. Long-term neglect and failure to take adequate precautions when these material remains were at their most vulnerable has caused wall paintings and structures to fade, crumble and decay. In 1957, Karl Schefold carried out an inventory of all the existing wall decorations and discovered that almost a third had faded completely with none ever having been recorded. Twenty years later, J-P. Descoudres and Kay Francis of Sydney University found that of Schefold's original inventory of wall paintings, one out of every two that he had recognised as reconstructable was lost forever.

Early conservation disasters

Even the well-intentioned archaeologists of the past have contributed to the decay as a result of failed attempts at restoration and conservation. For

Figure 12.1 The destruction of wall paintings over time

Figure 12.2 Failed repairs to theatre tiers

Figure 12.3 Crowds of school children

Figure 12.4 Vandalism

example, the replacement of lintels over doors and windows by softwood instead of seasoned hardwood has resulted in rotting, mould and the infestation of termites. The rusting of iron armatures in reinforced concrete used for repair in the mid-20th century split open the concrete and caused the collapse of both restored and ancient structures. Frescoes have been damaged by the application of modern mortars (the release of salts), paraffin wax and even more recently, paraloids which prevented the plaster from breathing.

Vandalism and theft have taken their toll over the years. In 1977 someone cut 14 frescoes from the walls of the House of the Gladiators and, according to an Italian preservationist group, over the next 15 years, nearly 600 items were stolen from Pompeii. Authorities have even had to minimise the use of in situ copies of original artefacts. The following is an eyewitness account of vandalism of the worst kind.

'POMPEII, EASTER 1979: THERE IS A VAST CROWD OF TOURISTS. AMONG THE BUILDINGS STANDS A PRIVATE HOUSE, NOT OPEN TO THE PUBLIC, WHERE IN THE ATRIUM, OR INNER COURTYARD, THE STONE COLUMNS ARE STILL STANDING. IT IS IMPOSSIBLE TO KEEP AN EYE ON EVERYONE. SOME OF THE TOURISTS FIND THEIR WAY INTO THE COURTYARD AND, BY

WAY OF A GAME, START TO PUSH AGAINST THE COLUMNS. EVENTUALLY
THEY SUCCEED IN KNOCKING THEM DOWN.[3]

Catastrophes

Human and natural catastrophes, such as the allied bombing in 1943 and
the earthquakes that rocked the area in the early 1980s, added to the destruction, but far more damaging to Pompeii and Herculaneum are the relentless
'attacks' by weather, prolific plant growth, pollution and the millions of
tourists who now visit the sites every year.

Effects of sun, rain and pollution

Weeds and parasites

The strong sunlight and ozone, created in large quantities in the highly
polluted conditions of Campania, cause fading and bleaching of frescoes and
breakdown of organic materials. Other pollutants such as acid rain and air-
borne substances (gritty particles, carbon particles, oil droplets and bacterial
and mould spores) cause discolouration, abrasion and corrosion. The winter
rains penetrate inadequate roofing and run down exposed walls, and damp
rises from the floors. Wherever a small piece of mosaic lifts from a floor, the
damp encourages the growth of algae and lichens. Weeds and parasitic plants
grow over many of the ruins—even those most frequently visited—roots
buckle and loosen floors, and ivy clings tenaciously to inner and outer walls.
Attempts to remove it causes the walls to break away and crumble. Even
insects can weaken structures, and excreta from birds has a corrosive effect
on metal.

Vistors confined to smaller areas

By far the greatest negative impact on the sites are the millions of visitors
each year, especially as they are confined to smaller and smaller areas as streets
are barricaded off and houses, braced by scaffolding, are shut to the public;
only half of what could be seen in the 1950s and 1960s can be experienced
today. Most tourists are unaware of the impact they have on the fragile sites:
millions of feet trample the mosaics and street pavements, wearing them
down, and in some cases exposing lead pipes which eventually crack and

Figure 12.5 Graffiti

Figure 12.6 Rubbish left
by tourists

Figure 12.7 Damp showing through mosaics

break up; hot humid breath and camera flashes cause further deterioration to already faded wall paintings; rubbish is dumped, cigarette butts discarded carelessly; fragments of marble and pottery are collected as souvenirs, and of course there is the inevitable damaging graffiti.

In 1986, Henri de Saint-Blanquat declared that Pompeii was 'an archaeological disaster of the first order'.[4] The headline of a November 1997 Associated Press news article stated 'Chances to see Pompeii dwindling as time and decay take its toll.'[5] In the same article, Andrew Wallace-Hadrill was quoted as saying 'What happens in Pompeii is writ larger and more catastrophic than in most places.'[6] The present archaeological superintendent of Pompeii, Pietro Giovanni Guzzo, said, 'Pompeii's death is not in one blow. It is slow, but sure.'[7]

Despite the increased revenue from tourists and the admirable work done by Pietro Guzzo and the Soprintendza di Pompei during recent years to address some of the problems, the sheer size and complexity of Pompeii and the years of neglect make the job daunting. Added to this have been the activities of the local Campanian crime syndicate (strikes and arson) who want to cash in on the revenues generated by tourism and the contracts for conservation.

In 2001, Guzzo stated that it would take an estimated 300 million US dollars to bring the archaeological areas of Pompeii, Herculaneum, Stabiae, Oplontis and Boscoreale up 'to acceptable levels of conservation and readiness for tourism'.[8] Evidence of the scale of the problem is revealed in the photographs in this chapter, which were taken by the author in May 2004.

Pompeii and Herculaneum are two of the planet's most endangered cultural sites, but not everything can be saved for the future. Since conservation can only be carried out at considerable cost and compromise, a resource management plan must be put into effect which will balance the competing interests of tourism, the local economy, scholarly research and the obligation to hand down a unique cultural legacy to future generations.[9] There have been growing international efforts to ensure that this happens. The Pompeii Trust, the World Monuments Watch and the Kress Foundation are three organisations raising money and developing a master conservation plan for the future.

✘ Awareness of time running out

✘ Crime syndicates

✘ Choices for the future

Figure 12.8 Overgrown ruins on the edge of an unexcavated area

Figure 12.9 Ivy growing over walls

The objective of the Pompeii Trust, which was the first organisation in the world to specifically support conservation at Pompeii, is 'the preservation, restoration, improvement, enhancement and maintenance of all objects, artefacts, structures or antiquities of architectural, historical or archaeological interest relating to Pompeii and its neighbouring regions'.[10] However, this international input will require the making of a number of ethical decisions with regard to the:

* role, standards and integrity of the archaeologists and conservators
* degree and type of intervention at the sites
* interests of specific groups and the greatest public good.

PRESERVATION, RESTORATION AND CONSERVATION

There has been a tendency in the past to use these three terms interchangeably: 'preservation' with 'conservation' and 'conservation' with 'restoration'.

Preservation generally means total protection from harmful and damaging factors, such as the closure of streets, houses and rooms to protect against the effects of excessive tourism; the addition of roof coverings and glass or plastic for frescoes, graffiti and political slogans to protect against fading and vandalism; and the erection of permanent scaffolding to prevent the crumbling of walls.

Figure 12.10 Protection provided for a nymphaeum

Figure 12.11 Roof protection for painting on the facade of a house/shop

Figure 12.12 Scaffolding to support building while a protective roof is erected

Figure 12.13 No entry to many houses previously opened to the public

Restoration refers to 'any process which contributes to enhancing the visual or functional understanding of an object or building. It is intended to aid in the interpretation of objects.'[11] Many of the areas visited in Pompeii and Herculaneum today have been restored to help the public understand what they might have looked like in AD 79. However, restoration can be controversial; the result depends on the restorer's interpretation of the original and, if taken too far, could almost be close to faking.

Definition of restoration

Conservation is 'the action of safeguarding the objects and structures which comprise the material remains of the past to ensure those remains are available to use and enjoy today and in the future.'[12] It is a cautious task which involves assessing the object's materials, rate of deterioration, original context and use; the causes of its deterioration; and all the risks inherent in the use of various treatments, and then applying procedures that will remedy existing damage and/or prevent future changes. Conservation is a collaborative, multi-disciplinary process, involving archaeologists, finds researchers, material scientists and curators.

Definition of conservation

Because careless conservation and restoration can cause damage, distortion, or even destruction, they are now carried out according to ethical codes of practice outlined in numerous international documents. The following are some of the principles of conservation:

Issues for conservators to consider

- Responsibility for the object or structure should begin from the moment it is removed from its burial environment (on-site conservation) and continue through all the post-excavation stages.

Figure 12.14 Restored garden in the House of the Faun

Figure 12.15 Restored stairs in a house in Herculaneum

Figure 12.17 Sign indicating ongoing conservation work in Herculaneum

Fig 12.16 Restored exterior roof

- No treatment or technique should be used that will endanger the true nature of the object or impede further treatment and information retrieval in the future.
- Where possible, only the minimum amount of intervention should take place to secure a satisfactory result.
- Only those techniques which current research shows will alter the object the least and which can be reversed most easily and completely (principle of reversibility) should be used.
- All intervention should be detectable and clearly documented.

E. Pye, in *Caring for the Past: Issues in Conservation for Archaeology and Museums*, raises a number of issues that a conservator/restorer should consider:

- 'Some objects are intended to deteriorate.'[13]
- 'Change is an inevitable consequence of using the objects and structures that make up a cultural heritage.'[14]
- 'It is inappropriate as well as impossible to restore to a pristine state.'[15]

So, although future conservation at Pompeii and Herculaneum should aim at slowing down the forces of deterioration and change, the sites cannot be 'held in a state of museological stasis'.[16] In fact, according to Alexander Stille in *The Future of the Past: The Loss of Knowledge in the Age of Information*, what people are so concerned about preserving is not really the past, but actually the present 'which offers a highly distorted, fragmentary version of the past'.[17]

THE QUESTION OF REPLICAS, VIRTUAL RESTORATIONS AND RECONSTRUCTIONS

✼
Use of replicas and digital imaging

Replicas can be used to make objects and structures more understandable and also as an alternative to restoring the original. However, a replica may represent only one possible interpretation of the original and hinder future reinterpretation. Digital imaging can manipulate and enhance an image of the original object, providing the conservator with a number of alternative interpretations. It can also be used to test potential approaches to reconstruction and restoration. Both techniques satisfy the principles of minimal intervention in the original object.

In 2004, the programmers and technicians at Capware enhanced the drawings produced during the early years of excavation, reconstructing the houses and monuments of Pompeii, Herculaneum and the nearby cities destroyed by Vesuvius. 'The images show new and unprecedented perspectives of the ancient drawings, such as views that were never represented . . . and animated walks inside imaginary but feasible buildings'.[18]

Figure 12.18
A replica faun

ETHICAL ISSUES

Today there is virtually no aspect of archaeology that is not guided by ethical principles laid down in worldwide charters. Some issues, however, have become more politicised than others, such as the excavation, treatment and display of human remains, and questions about ownership and the sale of antiquities.

88
The politicising of
archaeology

EXCAVATION, TREATMENT AND DISPLAY OF HUMAN REMAINS

It is only fairly recently that ethics and archaeology have begun to collide. The issue of human remains arose predominantly through the concerns of indigenous peoples such as the American Indians, Australian Aborigines and other groups for whom it is taboo to disturb the dead, and has evoked impassioned debate. It is not only the pressure exerted by these particular groups that has brought about a re-evaluation of the treatment of human remains. 'Archaeologists' standards are products of their time and changing values mean that every generation of archaeologists inevitably regards its predecessors as crude and insensitive.'[19]

88
Reasons for
re-evaluation of
human remains

In the early days, excavators and treasure hunters showed little regard for human remains. At Pompeii, skeletal remains were often destroyed in the rush to discover precious finds, while others were taken away as souvenirs. The English writer George Bulwer-Lytton is supposed to have kept a Pompeian skull on his desk which gave him inspiration for the villain in his novel *The Last Days of Pompeii* (1843). Some of the early Pompeian water colourists record the deliberate positioning of skeletons in grisly tableaux to impress visitors to the site. The number of bones removed or smashed is not known. Some skeletons were piled carelessly in bath houses during the later excavations where the bones became disarticulated and separated, making it almost impossible to study a whole skeleton (see Chapter 4). Museum collections of human remains were for long periods left in dark dusty basements wrapped in newspaper.

88
Insensitivity and
neglect of early
excavators

Although today human remains are generally treated with respect, there are some scholars who believe that all excavation of human remains should be stopped and that it is unethical to display those that have already been excavated. At the other end of the continuum are scientists such as osteo-archaeologists who find this unacceptable to their profession, and there is a generally held belief that the public should have access to the stories human remains tell.

88
Either end of the
continuum

The study of human remains has always been an integral part of archaeology, and the following extracts from *Ethics and Archaeology* reveal the importance of scientific studies of human bones.

88
Importance of the
scientific study
of bones

HUMAN SKELETONS ARE INDISPENSABLE FOR ARCHAEOLOGICAL
RESEARCH. ANCIENT DIETS, DISEASE PATHOLOGIES, GENETIC PATTERNS

AND ENVIRONMENTAL ADAPTATIONS ARE BUT A FEW RESEARCH AREAS THAT OSTEO-ARCHAEOLOGICAL REMAINS CAN ILLUMINATE.[20]

ARCHAEOLOGISTS AND ANTHROPOLOGISTS HAVE LONG CONSIDERED ARCHAEOLOGICAL HUMAN REMAINS AN IMPORTANT SOURCE OF INFORMATION ABOUT BOTH BIOLOGICAL AND CULTURAL ASPECTS OF PRIOR HUMAN POPULATIONS. DATA DERIVED FROM HUMAN POPULATIONS OF ALL ETHNIC AND SOCIO-ECONOMIC GROUPS ARE CRITICAL TO OUR UNDERSTANDING OF MANY ASPECTS OF MODERN HUMAN BIOLOGY AS WELL AS TO THE FIELD OF FORENSICS.[21]

❈ **Concerns for sacred and cultural beliefs**

However, today the authority of science 'over the dead is not absolute',[22] and modern archaeologists, conservators and curators do not operate in a vacuum. They must pay due regard to the sacred, spiritual and metaphysical beliefs of those cultures with which they come in contact.

❈ **Ethical questions**

Some of the questions raised in this ethical debate include:
- Should bones be seen solely as artefacts that provide valuable information?
- Should our view of the human remains be a function of the age of the remains?
- Should archaeologists have the freedom to pursue knowledge and scientific enquiry without political pressures and legal constraints.
- Who should have custodianship over human remains?
- What is the most appropriate way to store and display human remains?

❈ **To excavate human remains or not**

It is generally agreed that human bones 'of great antiquity (pre-1000) with no demonstrations with the present can be exhumed for study and long-term curations as long as they are accorded respect',[23] and treated with the same professional approach as with other artefacts. Also, the interests of the scientists and their rights of enquiry do not necessarily override the wishes of living relatives, direct descendants or 'cultural' descendants. However, where the ethnic connections of human remains 'are lost in the mists of time . . . the presumption for custody favours the scientist rather than any cultural group.'[24] The question of custodianship of human remains seems to lie along a continuum, with direct descendants and cultural descendants at one end and museums as custodians of the general public at the other. However, there has been some concern in recent years that the accusations of 'cultural thievery' and demands for custodianship among some indigenous people may have more to do with establishing claims to land.

❈ **Questions of scientific testing of bones**

Often past treatments of bone have been carried out (e.g. substances for adhering bones) with no understanding of future ramifications. Even today, with the ability to conduct a wide range of sophisticated tests, people are questioning whether it is 'ethical to jeopardise the physical characteristics of bone for potential future analysis on elements that have not necessarily survived in the sample.'[25]

In some museums, the storage facilities for human remains have long been substandard. Storage should conform to sound conservation practices which protect the remains against physical deterioration: wrapped in acid-free paper, placed in protective containers with environmental controls, as well as being guarded against theft or malicious use. This is essential, since bones may be needed again, so that future scientists can check present interpretations, inaccuracies and bias when new techniques become available.

❀
Appropriate storage procedures

The display of human remains has always been controversial. Every effort must be made to avoid giving offence. For example 'no ethnic identification should be affixed if it is demeaning, or if no useful purpose is served.'[26] Also, the sensitivities of certain religious groups such as Jews and Muslims, who object to being in close proximity to human remains, should be taken into account, as should the interests of children. Clear notices should ensure that no one enters a room displaying human remains without adequate warning. While the aim of a museum is to 'provide a fascinating exhibition',[27] skeletal remains should only be displayed when furthering the 'public's understanding of the past and present activities of archaeologists'.[28] In the opinion of Richard I. Ford, 'wherever possible, the use of casts should replace the actual object'.[29]

❀
Considerations for display

There are a few people who would not agree that one of the most fascinating aspects of a visit to Pompeii today is the chance to see plaster casts of the victims displayed in a number of locations. For example, 13 figures can be seen in the Garden of the Fugitives, lying where they fell; two in the Stabian baths, two in the Villa of Mysteries and two in the Macellum. Others are displayed in houses that are only occasionally opened to the public, such as the house of the Cryptoporticus.

❀
Casts at Pompeii

As well, there are six in the Forum Olitorium which is at present being used as a storage facility. They were originally displayed in the Pompeian Museum, which was closed in 1975 after thieves looted it of jewellery and coins. These are certainly not displayed to the best advantage and hopefully will find a more appropriate 'home' in the future.

Although these casts reveal more than anything else the full horror of those fateful 18 hours in August AD 79, they are intended to help the general public understand Fiorelli's unique contribution to archaeology and the tragic deaths of the inhabitants of the city. Despite the evidence of the suffering experienced, which may cause some to reflect, and the fact that the casts contain the remains of bones, they do not offend, and provide a fascinating display. Others are safely and sensitively displayed behind glass in the Naples Museum, as are some of the intact skeletons from Herculaneum. However, coming face to face with these twisted agonised skeletons can create a greater response from the viewer than all the plaster casts together.

❀
Displays in Naples Museum

It is possible that in the future, during construction, road building or agricultural activities, more remains may be found in the countryside around

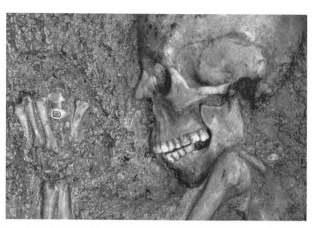

Figure 12.19 Temporary display of casts in the Granary   **Figure 12.20** Herculanean skeleton

Pompeii where many people fled and died in AD 79. Although there would be no particular religious or cultural reason for not excavating, archaeologists would have to come up with a convincing rationale for it and fulfil the ethical propositions involved in cultural resource management.

The question of the excavation, treatment and display of human remains will continue in the future as it is 'an evolving topic'.[30]

ETHICS, OWNERSHIP AND THE INTERNATIONAL TRAFFIC IN ANTIQUITIES

❈
Looting and the
black market

There has always been treasure seeking, souvenir hunting and looting of archaeological sites—none more so than at Pompeii and Herculaneum—as well as a lucrative antiquities market. Many of the ancient objects in museums around the world and in private collections have been acquired in this way. Artefacts sold as objets d'art fetch high prices, which is a further incentive to looters.

❈
Crime and
the internet

However, the booming international traffic in antiquities today is different in two ways from that of decades ago. Today it is 'big business and dangerous. Felons, narcotic dealers and other criminal elements participate in the antiquities black market',[31] and the advent of the internet, with its online auction houses, has made it easier to dispose of artefacts and harder to police, especially since many objects have been in private collections for generations. The growing demands from the market and the manufacture of forgeries are destroying archaeological heritage and distorting archaeological evidence.

❈
Conflict of interests
over ownership

'Although international laws provide limited protection for selected sites and materials . . . to be effective the laws require international co-operation and respect.'[32] Over the years there have been many conferences on cultural property, but there are often conflicts of interest between archaeologists, museums, auction houses and art dealers. In 1999, the Italian government requested the USA State Department's Cultural Property Advisory Committee to block the import of thousands of years worth of ancient artefacts. Both the Italian government and archaeologists believed it would help 'curb looting and theft of a treasured Italian heritage', but art dealers and museum curators insisted that 'such a restriction would limit US public access to Italy's great cultural past.'[33]

Most international laws claim the ultimate ownership by the state of all antiquities found within its borders and yet, as recently as November 2004, members of the Italian government shocked archaeologists by proposing to 'legalise the private ownership of archaeological treasures in Italy'.[34] Under this proposal, 'treasure hunters who declare their finds can keep and own them if they pay the state five percent of the object's estimated value.'[35] Scholars call the plan 'an incitement to theft' and 'a looters' charter'.[36] The professor of archaeology at Cambridge University said 'this legislation would be a slap in the face for those in administration who work for the conservation of its heritage.'[37]

Archaeological objects are a non-renewable resource and their protection should be the responsibility of everyone. However, once they have left the country of origin, proving that they have been stolen is one of the most difficult of legal issues, and if a country is to re-acquire them it has to pay, often at astronomical cost.

Recent government decisions in Italy

Chapter review

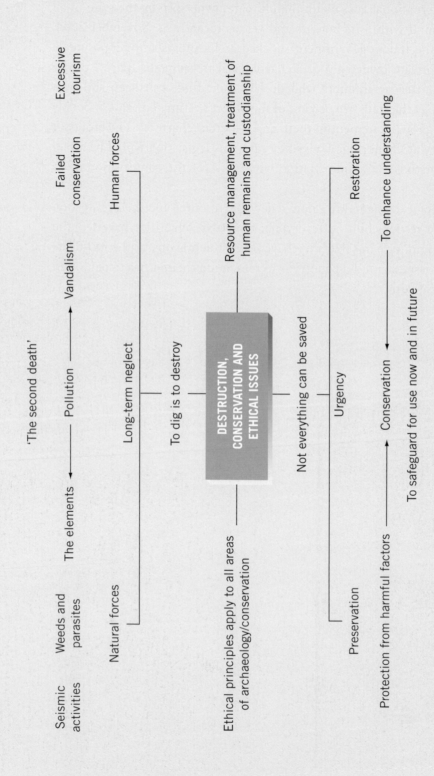

Seismic activities

Weeds and parasites

The elements

'The second death'

Pollution ———→ Vandalism

Human forces

Failed conservation

Excessive tourism

Natural forces

Long-term neglect

To dig is to destroy

Ethical principles apply to all areas of archaeology/conservation

DESTRUCTION, CONSERVATION AND ETHICAL ISSUES

Resource management, treatment of human remains and custodianship

Not everything can be saved

Urgency

Restoration

To enhance understanding

Preservation

Protection from harmful factors ———→ Conservation

To safeguard for use now and in future

Activities

1 Study the following extract and figures and answer the questions below.

IF HISTORY DOES NOT REPEAT ITSELF AND A FUTURE ERUPTION OF MOUNT. VESUVIUS DOES NOT ENGULF THE CITY WITH A BLANKET OF VOLCANIC ASH, THEN THE WELL-MEANING TOURIST WILL SURELY DESTROY IT BIT BY BIT. IT SEEMS LIKELY THAT IN TIME POMPEII WILL END UP LIKE THE CAVES OF LASCAUX WITH ITS PREHISTORIC PAINTINGS BEING RECREATED IN AN ARTIFICIAL SETTING AWAY FROM THE SITE ITSELF, WHERE GAGGLES OF TOURISTS CAN BE HERDED THROUGH AT SPEED. ALTHOUGH IT (POMPEII) IS TOO OFTEN PACKED WITH INDIFFERENT SCHOOL CHILDREN ARMED WITH CLIPBOARDS AND COACH PARTIES BUSSED FROM ROME WITH ACHING FEET AND DWINDLING INTEREST, POMPEII IS MUCH MORE THAN JUST ANOTHER ATTRACTION TO TICK OFF YOUR LIST. THE PARADOX IS THAT WHILE WE NEED VISITORS, AND MORE ESPECIALLY THEIR MONEY, TO FINANCE CONSERVATION AND RESEARCH PROJECTS AT POMPEII, IT IS THE VISITORS WHO ARE SPEEDING UP THE DECAY.

www.oxbowbooks.com/feature.cfm/FeatureID

a How does the author describe the typical tourist?

b What is the paradox described in this extract?

c Why are tourists 'speeding up the decay' at Pompeii?

d What kind of future for Pompeii does the author envisage?

e What is meant by 'Pompeii is much more than just another attraction to tick off your list'?

f What does Figure 12.23 tell you about the situation in Pompeii? Comment on the appropriateness of it.

Figure 12.21 A high-school excursion

Figure 12.22 Rubbish left by tourists

Figure 12.23 A card shop in the House of the Faun

Activities

2 Write a paragraph describing the significance of Figures 12.24 and 12.25.

have played a part in the 'second death' of Pompeii and Herculaneum.

e Explain what is meant by the statement that preservation, restoration and conservation 'offers a highly distorted, fragmentary version of the past'.[39]

Figure 12.24 Attempt to support the fragile face of a house

Figure 12.26 Francios Mazois' watercolour (1812) showing a 'prepared' discovery of a skeleton

Figure 12.25 Attempt to support the interior of a house

3 Even if all tourism were banned from Pompeii and Herculaneum tomorrow, there would continue to be massive problems. Draw a detailed diagram illustrating all the natural and human forces which

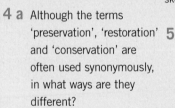

4 a Although the terms 'preservation', 'restoration' and 'conservation' are often used synonymously, in what ways are they different?

b To which of these terms does the following quote apply: 'Most of the wall paintings, the colonnaded houses, the statues and mosaics are now off limits.'[38]

c Give four specific examples of 'restoration' in Pompeii and Herculaneum.

d Give three important principles that modern-day conservators should follow, and explain why.

5 a What does Figure 12.26 reveal about the early treatment of human remains at Pompeii?

b Why has the display of human remains on the site of Pompeii not become a major issue, even though the question of treatment of skeletal remains has evoked impassioned debate in other parts of the world?

c What are the ethical responsibilities of museum curators and scientists with regard to human remains?

6 Discussion topic: Who owns the past?

Glossary

aedicule shrine made of two columns supporting a pediment placed against a wall

aedile town magistrate who looked after day-to-day administration

alae plural of the Latin 'ala' meaning 'wing'; small open rooms accessible from the atrium

ambulationes covered walkways

amphitheatre oval-shaped arena used primarily for gladiatorial games and spectacles

amphorae two-handled clay vessels for liquids, especially wine and oil

antiquities objects remaining from or belonging to ancient times

apochae receipts issued by a creditor for payment of a debt

apodyterium changing room at the baths; used as a waiting room for slaves and attendants

arcae bolted chests

armaria cupboard

artefacts objects made by man found on a site

as low-denomination red copper coin for everyday use

asellinae Oscan farces

atrium central hall of a Roman house with impluvium in the middle

Augustales group of freedmen who celebrated the cult of the emperor

aureus gold coin used for major purchases e.g. purchase of land or slaves

autoCAD computer program for building up models e.g. of buildings

bacchantes initiates in the cult of Bacchus

balnearis vestus female bathing garment

Basilica colonnaded hall on the Forum used for business and justice (law courts)

belvedere structure designed to afford a good view

bestiarii gladiators who fought wild animals

Boscoreale ancient town located on the slopes of Vesuvius, to the north of Pompeii

calcei outdoor shoes

caldarium room in the bathhouse containing the hot bath

Campania fertile plain in southern Italy

candida white toga

Capitolium temple to the Capitolium Triad (Jupiter, Juno and Minerva)

cardo (sing.) **cardini** (pl.) street which crossed a town along the north–south axis

cartibulum a table placed near the impluvium

castellum acquae huge cistern near the Vesuviun Gate for collecting water from the aqueduct

caupona tavern; inn

cavea seating section (auditorium) of a theatre or amphitheatre

cella vinaria room for the fermentation of grapes

cellarius household slave who controlled the food supply

cena dinner

cenaculum upper room or apartment

cistern underground water storage

civitas Latin for 'city'; name given to the excavation site before it was identified as Pompeii

claustrum bronze lock

clerestory upper part of a nave perforated with windows

clientes persons of subordinate rank (dependants) having dealings with a member of the elite

collegia associations

Comitium multi-purpose roofless building (Forum) used for public meetings and where people assembled for voting

compluvium central opening in the roof over the domestic atrium that allowed in air, light and water which was collected in the impluvium

conservation action of safeguarding the material remains of the past to ensure their use and enjoyment today and in the future

cryptoporticus subterranean covered portico

cubiculum small room which served various functions but most commonly described as a bedroom

culina kitchen of a Roman house

Curia meeting place of the city council on the Forum

dealbator someone who prepared (whitewashed) the walls prior to writing political slogans

decumanus main road on east-to-west axis

decurion member of the municipal council, often former magistrates

denarius silver coin used for major purpose e.g. purchase of land or slaves

dolium (sing.) **dolia** (pl.) large earthenware jar, globular in form with a wide mouth

dominus master or owner, especially of a house or domus

domus house; household

duovir/duumvir one of two equal magistrates elected annually to preside over the decurion with law-giving powers

Dionysus Greek god adapted to Bacchus, god of wine

dispensator slave who controlled his master's funds

dupondius zinc coin used in everyday business

ecofacts remains of organisms e.g. pollen, insects

edicta munerum program that announced public shows

editores munerum sponsors of games

emblema central picture in a mosaic floor

Epicureanism system of philosophy that followed the teachings of the Greek Epicurus, that the highest good in life is pleasure

epigraphy study of inscriptions

epitaph commemorative inscription on a tomb or mortuary monument

ethics the principles or rules of conduct recognised in respect to human behaviour

Etruscan advanced civilisation in Italy before the Roman era

eulogy writing in praise of someone of something

Eumachia high priestess of the imperial cult, after whom the Eumachia building is named

exedra room or alcove open on one side, often located off the peristyle

familia family; the Roman familia includes all persons under the control of the paterfamilias including slaves

farce light humorous play in which the plot depends on situation rather than character

fastigium top of a pediment

fauces the entrance passage leading from the street into the interior of a house or building

fercula main dinner course

fistulae pipes of various sizes

flames specialised priests

foedus treaty

foricae public latrines

forum the public square of a Roman city which acted both as a marketplace and centre for business and justice

frescoes wall paintings on plaster

frigidarium room in a bathhouse for cooling off

fullers those who washed and dyed cloth

fullonica laundry

galerus protective bronze plate worn on the left shoulder of a retiarus

garum fish sauce

genius spirit present in every person, thing and place

gustatio first part of the evening meal; appetisers

Hellenic pertaining to Greek culture before the time of Alexander the Great

Hellenistic pertaining to the culture in which Greek characteristics were modified by foreign elements after the time of Alexander the Great

Herculaneum small resort and fishing town on the Bay of Naples, north-west of Pompeii

hinterland inland area supplying goods to a port or receiving goods from a port

horreum storeroom

hortus (sing.) **horti** (pl.) produce garden and a service yard, around which were arranged the kitchen garden and stables

horti pompeiani suburban market gardens of Pompeii

hypocaustum small narrow spaces under the floor through which hot air circulated

imagines maiorem masks of the ancestors

impluvium rainwater basin in centre of the atrium, directly under compluvium

ingenuus/ingenua freeborn citizen (male and female)

insula (sing.) **insulae** (pl.) city block isolated by four streets; the buildings that comprised an insula were sometimes under a single ownership

Isis Egyptian goddess whose cult was adopted by the Romans

jentaculum breakfast

laconicum second, sauna-like, hot room in the bathhouse equipped with a brazier for creating a dry heat

lanista agent who trained and supplied gladiators for a show

lanterinarius one who held the lantern while wall writings were done at night

lapilli rounded tephra ejected from a volcano during eruption

lararium household shrine dedicated to the lares

lares deities worshipped as protectors of houses or particular localities

lares familiares household gods

lares compitales gods of the crossroads

lava tenera volcanic stone

libertinus freed slave or person of servile background

libertus/ liberta freed slave (male and female)

ludi (pl.) public games or festivals

Ludi Iuventus Youth Games

lupanar brothel

lustratio purification ceremony

Macellum central provision market of the Pompeian Forum

manica armband worn by a gladiator

(pl.) **manumission** granting of freedom to slaves

megalography pictorial genre featuring monumental figures

mensa low table used in front of the couches in a dining room

mensa ponderaria measuring table

mensa secundae desserts

Mercury god of commerce

ministri food servers

mofeta term used by early excavators to describe the noxious and lethal carbon monoxide trapped within the pyroclastic debris left by the eruption

mosaics picture or decoration made from tiny pieces of stone, glass etc.

murmillo type of gladiator

Neapolis (Naples) major city on the Bay of Naples; originally a Greek colony

necropolis cemetery

negotium business

neo-classicism late 18th and early 19th century revival of art and architecture deriving from classical models

notarius slave secretary or clerk

nutrices wet nurses

nymphaeum room or grotto dedicated to the nymphs, usually with a fountain

Odeon small theatre in Pompeii used for concerts, lectures and poetry recitals

oecus richly decorated reception room

officina workshop

officina langifricare workshop where raw wool was degreased

officina olearia oil mill

officina textoria weaver's workshop

officina tinctoria dyer's workshop

olitorium granary

ordo decurionum members of the city council

Oscan one of the local languages of Campania

ostiarius doorkeeper

otium any leisure activity

palaestra sports ground (from the Greek for 'wrestling school') with a large open courtyard dedicated to competitive athletics and training

palla cloak worn by women

pars rustica quarters for slaves and workers on a country estate

patera broad, flat dish or saucer used for offerings

pedagogue educated slave in charge of boys' education

pediment triangular gable crowned with a projecting cornice

pedisequae personal attendants

pergula upper floor; mezzanine level

peristyle inner courtyard surrounded by a colonnade

phreatomagmatic refers to a volcanic explosion created by heating of underground water

pila bladder ball

pinacothecae picture galleries

piscina swimming pool

pistrina bakery

plebs common people

plinian phase first phase of the eruption of Vesuvius which coincided with Pliny the Younger's description

podium raised base of a temple

pompa procession

pontarii gladiators who fought on a platform

prandium lunch

preservation protection from harmful and damaging factors

Priapus rustic god of fertility depicted with a huge penis

programmata electoral manifestos painted on walls

proscenium stage of a theatre

pumice light, porous stone discharged from a volcano

pyroclastic flow hot avalanche of pumice, ash and gases

pyroclastic surge cloud of volcanic ash and gases

quadran low-denomination red copper coin for everyday use

quadriporticus colonnaded space used as a foyer for theatres; later used as gladiatorial barracks

quattuoviri board of four

quinquennalis magistrate elected every five years to carry out the census and control public morality

regio an urban district or region

replica copy or reproduction

restoration process which contributes to enhancing the visual or functional understanding of an object or building

retiarius type of gladiator who fought with a net

Romantic pertaining to a style of literature and art of the 18th and 19th centuries characterised by freedom of treatment and imagination

salutatio morning ceremony at which clients attended on their patron

Samnites tough mountain tribes who conquered Campania

scissor slave who cut the food for guests at a banquet

scriptore professional scribe who painted public notices on walls

seismic pertaining to an earthquake

sestertius commonly used bronze coin

sistrum metallic rattle used in the cult of Isis

socii allies

sparsiones perfumed showers to cool the spectators at the theatre or amphitheatre

Stabiae an ancient port city south of Pompeii

stola loose woollen garment tied at the waist; worn by women

strigil curved bronze or bone scraper used in the baths

suspensure brick pillars which supported a suspended floor

sylvae groves

synthesis fine white toga

taberna shop opening onto the street with large stalls

tablinum main reception area of the atrium usually richly decorated

Tabularium a civic building next to the Comitium in the Forum, used for storing official records

tepidarium warm room in a bathhouse equipped with a warm pool and used for the application of oil and massage

thermae warm springs; warm baths

thermopolium bar serving warm snacks and drinks

thracian type of gladiator

thyrsus long staff entwined with ivy and vine leaves carried by Dionysus/Bacchus and his followers

torcula wine press

torcularia room for pressing grapes

travertine white limestone used in building

triclinium 'three couch room' or dining room

tufa stone formed from compacted volcanic ash

tunica interior vest-like garment worn by women

velarium canopy suspended over the seats at an amphitheatre or theatre

venationes hunting or the combat of wild beasts in the amphitheatre

venatores fighters of wild beasts

Venus patron goddess of Pompeii

vestibulum entrance lobby

villa otium villa built purely for leisure

villa rustica country residence often connected to a vineyard or farm

viridaria garden

vulcanology study of volcanoes

Notes

Introduction

1 R. Etienne, *Pompeii: The Day a City Died*, Thames and Hudson p. 41
2 Ibid.

1 Brief historical overview

1 A.E. Cooley, *Pompeii*, p. 125
2 Plutarch, *The Fall of the Roman Republic: Sulla* 6, Penguin
3 Appian, *The Civil Wars*, I: 95–6
4 Tacitus, *Annals*, XIV, 17
5 Ibid. XV, 22.5
6 Seneca, *Naturales Quaestiones*, Book VI in *Seneca* Vol. VII trans. T.H. Corcoran, VI.1. 1
7 Ibid.
8 M. Grant, *Cities of Vesuvius*, p. 28

2 Early history of the excavations and representations of the sites over time

1 Statius, *Silvae* 4. 4. 78–86
2 J. Winklemann, 'A Critical Account of the Situation and Destruction of Herculaneum, Pompeii and Stabia', from 'Documents' in R. Etienne, *Pompeii: The Day a City Died*, p.147
3 A.E. Cooley, *Pompeii*, p. 69
4 C. Amery & B. Curran Jn., *The Lost World of Pompeii*, p. 33
5 Winklemann, p.147
6 Ibid.
7 R. Etienne, *Pompeii: The Day a City Died*, p.18
8 Winklemann, p.147
9 P.G. Guzzo, *Pompeii*, p. 7
10 Amery & Curran, *The Lost World of Pompeii*, p. 37
11 Cooley, p. 14
12 Duncan C. Tovey (ed.), *Thomas Gray and His Friends*, p. 252
13 R. Hamblyn, *Transports: Travel, Pleasure and Imaginative Geography 1600–1830* ed. Chard, Chlore & Langdon, London, Yale Uni Press, 1996
14 W. Leppmann, *Pompeii in Fact and Fiction*, p.155
15 J.W. Goethe, 'Italian Journey, 1786–8', in Etienne, p. 154
16 Ibid. pp. 154–5
17 Ibid. p. 156
18 Etienne, p. 27
19 F. Mazois, 'Letters to Mlle Duval', in Etienne, p. 27
20 Leppmann, p. 103
21 Etienne, p. 164
22 Charles Dickens, 'Pictures from Italy 1845', in Etienne, p. 165
23 Ibid.
24 Leppmann, p. 127
25 Etienne, p. 101
26 Possibly Lansing and Varone
27 Leppmann, p. 157
28 Ibid.
29 Mark Twain, 'The Innocents Abroad, 1875' in Etienne, pp. 166, 167

3 The physical environment and urban landscape

1 M. Grant, *Cities of Vesuvius*, p.15
2 Pliny, *Natural History*, Bk III, 40. 3.40 and 3.60
3 Ibid. pp. 40–41
4 A. Mau, *Pompeii, Its Life and Art*, trans. F Kelsey, p. XX
5 Strabo, V, *Geography*, 4 and 227
6 Pliny, Bk IV, 10
7 Seneca, *Naturales Quaestiones*, VI, I
8 Strabo, *Geography*, V, 4
9 Mau, p. XX
10 A. Wallace-Hadrill, *Houses and Society in Pompeii and Herculaneum*, p. 136

4 The range of sources and their reliability

1 A. Wallace-Hadrill, *Houses and Society in Pompeii and Herculaneum*, pp. 65–66
2 A.E. Cooley, *Pompeii*, p. 11
3 E. Pye, *Caring for the Past*, p. 9
4 Ibid. p. 11
5 Pye, p. 11
6 Wallace-Hadrill, p. 88
7 Ibid. p. 66
8 J-P. Descoudres et al., *Pompeii Revisited*, p. 89
9 Wallace-Hadrill, p.15
10 A. Maiuri, *Pompeii*, p. 18
11 Ibid.
12 Ibid. p. 19
13 C. Amery & B. Curran, *The Lost World of Pompeii*, p. 77
14 Corpus Inscriptionum Latinarum (CIL), IV 3529
15 Ibid. IV 3884
16 Ibid.
17 Ibid. 180
18 Ibid. 7863
19 Ibid. 1136
20 M. Grant, *Cities of Vesuvius*, p. 210
21 E. Lessing & A. Varone, *Pompeii*, p. 95
22 Grant, *Cities of Vesuvius*, p. 122
23 D. Hoyos, 'Inscriptions, Graffiti and Literacy at Pompeii' in Descoudres et al., p. 60
24 Amery & Curran, p. 60
25 Grant, *Cities of Vesuvius*, p. 133
26 Ibid. p. 196
27 CIL IV 1837
28 Grant, *Cities of Vesuvius*, p. 196
29 Ibid. p. 210
30 Ibid. p. 122
31 Ibid. p. 210
32 E. Lessing & A. Varone, *Pompeii*, p. 115
33 Ibid.
34 Wallace-Hadrill, p. XX
35 Cicero, *On Duty*, I, 138
36 Lessing & Varone, p. 131
37 Ibid. p. 142
38 www. artsa.uc.edu/classics/syl/pompeii.html
39 S.C. Bisel & J.F. Bisel, 'Health and nutrition at Herculaneum:

An examination of the skeletal remains' in W. F. Jashemski & F.M. Meyer, *The Natural History of Pompeii*, pp. 454–5

40 Ibid. p. 455

41 Ibid.

42 B.D. Shaw, 'The age of Roman girls at marriage' JRS 77 (1987)

43 Suetonius, *The Twelve Caesars: Augustus*, 79

44 E. Lazer, 'The people of Pompeii' in J-P. Descoudres (ed.) *Pompeii Revisited: The Life and Death of a Roman Town,* p. 144

45 H. Sigurdsson, 'Mount Vesuvius before the disaster', in W.F. Jashemski & F.M. Meyer, *The Natural History of Pompeii*, p. 41

46 Pliny the Younger, *Letters to Tacitus*, VI, 16

47 Ibid.

48 Ibid.

49 Ibid.

50 Ibid. VI, 20

51 W.F. Jashemski & F.M. Meyer, *The Natural History of Pompeii*, p. 2

52 Ibid.

53 Wallace-Hadrill, p. 136

5 Eruption and the last agonies of Pompeii and Herculaneum

1 A.E. Cooley, *Pompeii*, p. 37

2 H. Sigurdsson, 'Mount Vesuvius before the disaster' in W.F. Jashemski & F.M. Meyer *The Natural History of Pompeii*, p. 35

3 Seneca, *Naturales Quaestiones*, VI.1. 1–2,

4 Ibid.

5 Ibid.

6 Pliny, the Younger, *Letters to Tacitus*, Bk. VI, 20

7 M. Brion, *Pompeii and Herculaneum: the Glory and the Grief*, p. 21

8 H. Sigurdsson & S. Carey, 'The eruption of Vesuvius in AD 79' in Jashemski & Meyer, p. 45

9 H. Sigurdsson, *American Journal of Archaeology* 86: 39–51

10 Pliny, the Younger, *Letters to Tacitus*, Bk. VI, 16

11 Ibid.

12 Ibid.

13 Ibid.

14 Ibid.

15 Ibid. Bk. VI, 20

16 Ibid.

17 Ibid.

18 Ibid.

19 Dio Cassius, *Roman History*, LXIV. 22

20 Pliny, the Younger, *Letters to Tacitus*, Bk. VI, 16

21 Ibid.

22 Ibid.

23 Ibid.

24 Ibid.

25 Ibid.

26 Ibid.

27 Ibid. Bk. VI, 20

28 Ibid. Bk. VI, 1614

29 Ibid.

30 Ibid.

31 Ibid. Bk. VI, 20

32 Ibid.

33 Ibid.

34 E. Lazer, 'The people of Pompeii' in Descoudres et al., *Pompeii Revisited*, p.148

35 M. Brion, *Pompeii and Herculaneum: The Glory and the Grief*, p. 35

36 Dio Cassius, *Roman History*

6 Social structure, economy and politics

1 R. Etienne, *Pompeii: The Day a City Died*, p.75

2 J-P. Descoeudres et al., *Pompeii Revisited*, p. 25

3 A. Wallace-Hadrill, *Houses and Society in Pompeian and Herculaneum*, p. 61

4 Ibid. p. 145

5 Ibid. p. 185

6 E. Cantarella & L. Jacobelli, *A Day in Pompeii: Daily Life, Culture and Society*, p. 20

7 CIL IV 3.4 9839

8 J.J Deiss, *Herculaneum: Italy's Buried Treasure*, p. 118

9 Vitruvius, *De architectura*, VI 5:1

10 M. Brion, *Pompeii and Herculaneum: The Glory and the Grief*, p. 98

11 Cantarella & Jacobelli, p. 52

12 Pliny, *Natural History XIV*, pp. 33–34

13 L. Zarmatti, 'Women and Eros' in Descoeudres et al. *Pompeii Revisited*, p. 108

14 Pliny, *Natural History*, XIV, 70

15 Brion, p. 132

16 Pliny, *Natural History*, XV, 5–6

17 Ibid. XIII, 20

18 Ibid. XV,10

19 Ibid. XV, 5–7

20 Ibid. XV, 19

21 Ibid. XXI, 93–4

22 Ibid. XXI 93–4

23 M. Ponsich & M. Tarradell, 'Garum et Industries Antiques desal aisson dans la Mediterranee Occidentale', *Geoponica*, XX, 46, 1

24 C. Amery & B. Curran, *The Lost World of Pompeii*, p. 77

25 Deiss, p.10

26 Cantarella & Jacobelli, p. 39

27 Deiss, p. 99

28 CIL IV. IV

29 CIL IV. IV, 1837

30 M. Grant, *Eros in Pompeii*, p. 58

31 S.C. Bisel & J.F. Bisel 'Health and nutrition at Herculaneum: an examination of human skeletal remains' in W. F. Jashemski & F. G Meyer, *The Natural History of Pompeii* p. 455

32 Grant, *Cities of Vesuvius*, p. 205

33 Amery & Curran, p. 58

34 CIL IV. IV, 677

35 Ibid. 113

36 Ibid. 7164

37 Amery & Curran, p. 60

38 CIL IV. 180

39 Grant, *Cities of Vesuvius*, p. 205

40 Petronius, *Satyricon*

7 Houses, villas and domestic life

1 A. Wallace-Hadrill, *Houses and Society in Pompeian and Herculaneum*, p. 99

2 Ibid. p. 4

3 Ibid. p. 22

4 Vitruvius, *De architectura*, VI. 3.1

5 E. Cantarella & L. Jacobelli, *A Day in the Life of Pompeii*, p. 55

6 M. Grant, *Cities of Vesuvius*, p.124

7 Ibid. p. 117

8 Ibid. p. 122

9 Ibid. p. 121

10 Ibid. p. 121

11 G. Capasso, *Journey to Pompeii: Virtual Tours around the Lost Cities*, p. 13

12 A. Maiuri, *Ercolano*, 1932

13 Grant, *Cities of Vesuvius*, p. 134

14 Capasso, p.76

15 Vitruvius, *De architectura*, VI 5:1

16 E. Robinson, 'Roman Cuisine' in *Pompeii Revisited*, J-P. Descoeudres et al. p. 115

17 Grant, *Cities of Vesuvius*, p. 121

18 Pliny the Younger, *Letters*, IV. 19

19 D. Hoyos, 'Inscription, Graffiti and Literacy', in Descoeudres, p. 62

20 E. Robinson, 'Roman Cuisine' Descoeudres, p. 119

21 R. Kebric, *Roman People*, p. 168

22 Ibid.

23 U.E. Paoli, 'Vita romana' in Capasso, p. 35

24 Cicero, *De Domo Sua* 41, p. 109

25 P. Connor, 'Lararium-Household Religion' in J-P. Descoeudres et al., p. 93

26 Grant, *Cities of Vesuvius*, p. 122

27 Adapted from Robinson

8 Relaxation, entertainment and sport

1 C. Amery & B. Curran, *The Lost World of Pompeii*, p. 91

2 E. Cantarella & L. Jacobelli, *A Day in Pompeii*, p. 81

3 J.J. Deiss, *Herculaneum: Italy's Buried Treasure*, p. 119

4 Ibid.

5 M. Grant, *Cities of Vesuvius*, p. 210

6 Deiss, p. 110

7 Ibid. p. 122

8 Ibid.

9 Ibid.

10 Seneca, *Epistles* Vol IV, 1–65,

11 Juvenal, *Satires*, VII, 129 f.

12 Pliny the Elder, *Natural History*, IX, 68

13 L. Zarmati, 'A visit to the baths' in J-P. Descoeudres et al., '*Pompeii Revisited*, p. XX

14 Deiss, p. 111

15 Cantarella & Jacobelli, p. 108

16 Vitruvius, *De architectura*, V. 3. 6–8

17 Deiss, p. 130

18 G. Capasso, *Journey to Pompeii 'Herculaneum: Virtual Tours around the Lost Cities*, p. 30

19 Plautus?

20 Grant, *Cities of Vesuvius*, p. 74

21 Ibid.

22 J. R. Green, 'Bacchus and the theatre', in J-P. Descoeudres et al., p. 141

23 Deiss, p. 123

24 L. Jacobelli, *Gladiators at Pompeii*, p. 97

25 Ibid. p 53

26 Ibid. p. 44

27 Ibid. p. 19

28 Ibid. p. 48

29 Ibid. p. 26

30 Tacitus, *Annals*, 15.32–33

31 Juvenal, *Satires* 6. 82 –113

32 CIL IV 4342, 4397

33 Ibid. 4345

34 Ibid. 4353

35 'Appendix Vergiliana Copa' 35–51, trans. H.R. Fairclough

36 D. Hoyos, 'Inscriptions, graffiti and literacy at Pompeii' in J-P. Descoeudres et al., p. 60

37 L. Zarmati, 'Women and Eros' in J-P. Descoeudres et al., p. 110

38 'Appendix Vergiliana Copa' 1–8, trans. H.R. Fairclough

9 Religion and death

1 E. Cantarella & L. Jacobelli, *A Day in Pompeii*, p. 38

2 M. Grant, *Cities of Vesuvius*, p. 89

3 Lucretius, I, I ff. trans. B. Bunting

4 CIL, IV,1824

5 Grant, *Cities of Vesuvius*, p. 98

6 L. Zarmati, 'Women and Eros' in J-P. Descoeudres et al., p.110

7 Ibid.

8 Grant, *Cities of Vesuvius*, p. 98

9 Cantarella & Jacobelli, p.41

10 Livy, *Rome and the Mediterranean*, XXXIX: 8, 13

11 Ibid.

12 Grant, *Cities of Vesuvius*, p. 108

13 Cicero, *On the Nature of the Gods*, 2. 67–8

14 B. Rawson, 'Family Matters' in J-P. Descoeudres et al., p. 66

15 Cantarella & Jacobelli, p. 19

16 Petronius, *Satyricon*, 35

17 C. Amery & B. Curran, *The Lost World of Pompeii*, p. 66

18 R. Kebric, *Roman People*, p.169

11 Changing archaeological methods and interpretations

1 A.E. Cooley, *Pompeii*, p. 96

2 A. Mau, *Pompeii, Its Life and Art*, p. XX

3 J-P. Descoudres et al., *Pompeii Revisited*, p. 44

4 Cooley, p. 93

5 Descoudres, p. 64.

6 R. Etienne, *Pompeii: The Day a City Died*, p. 34

7 Ibid. pp. 38–39

8 Ibid. p. 40

9 Descoeudres, p. 47

10 A. Wallace-Hadrill, *Houses and Society in Pompeii and Herculaneum*, p. 182

11 Ibid. xvi.

12 Ibid,. p. 183

13 'Kenneth Painter on the Insula of Menander', http://www.oup.co.uk/academic/humanities/classical_studies/viewpoint/kenneth_painter

14 Wallace-Hadrill, p. 141

15 A. Maiuri, *Pompeii*, p.188

16 A. Maiuri, *L'Ultima fase edilizia di Pompeii*, 1942

17 A. Maiuri, *Herculaneum: The New Excavations*, 1958, p. 248

18 Wallace-Hadrill, p. xvi

19 Ibid. p.123

20 Ibid.

21 A. Maiuri, in M. Grant, *Cities of Vesuvius*, p. 218

22 Cooley, p. 15

23 A. Stille, *The Future of the Past: The Loss of Knowledge in the Age of Information*, p. 300

24 Ibid. p. 302
25 Descoeudres, p. 50
26 John R. Clarke, *Bryn Mawr Classical Review*, 20 January, 1998 http://ccat.sas.upenn.edu/bmcr
27 Roger Ling, *The Insula of Menander at Pompeii*, vol. 1, *The Structures*, p.1
28 Clarke, January, 1998
29 Ibid.
30 'Pompeii Forum Project', http://pompeii.virginia.edu/pfp-descrip.html
31 Ibid.
32 Ibid.
33 Ibid.
34 'The Anglo-American Project in Pompeii', http://www.bradford.ac.uk/acad/archsci/field_proj/anampomp/aapp_urban.html
35 'The Pompeii Trust', http://www.pompeiitrust.org/The_Trust.html
36 Cooley, p.113
37 http://dsc.discovery.com/news/briefs/20030929/pompeii.html
38 E. Pye, *Caring for the Past: Issues in Conservation for Archaeology and Museums*, p. 11
39 M. Raab, 'Ethics and values of research design', in E.L. Green (ed.) *Ethics and Archaeology*, pp. 82–3
40 Pye, p. 11
41 Ibid. p. 9
42 Stille, p. 301
43 Wallace-Hadrill, p. 65

12 Destruction, conservation and ethical issues

1 E. Pye, *Caring for the Past: Issues in Conservation for Archaeology and Museums*, p. 23
2 H. de Saint-Blanquat, in R. Etienne, *The Day a City Died*, pp. 202–3
3 Ibid. p. 198
4 Ibid. p. 198
5 C. Hughes, 'Chances to see Pompeii dwindling as time and decay take their toll' http://seattlepi.nsource.com/getaways/112797/pomp27
6 Ibid.
7 Ibid.
8 http://www.archaeology.org/online/news/mob.html
9 C. Amery & B. Curran, *The Lost World of Pompeii*, p. 9
10 http://www.pompeiitrust.org/The_trust.html
11 Pye, p. 9
12 Ibid.
13 Ibid. p. 96
14 Ibid. p. 98
15 Ibid. p. 144
16 Ibid. p. 98
17 A. Stille, *The Future of the Past: The Loss of Knowledge in the Age of Information*, p. 34
18 G. Capasso, *Journey to Pompeii: Virtual Tours around the Lost Cities*, p. 1
19 http://www.economist.com/science/displayStory.cfm/story
20 R. Ford, 'Ethics and the museum archaeologist' in E.L. Green (ed.), *Ethics and Archaeology*, p. 139
21 A. Cheek & B. Keel, 'Value Conflicts in osteo-archaeology' in Green p. 195
22 http://www.economist.com/science/displayStory.cfm/story
23 Ford in Green, p. 138
24 http://onlineethics.org/reseth/appe/vol1/bones
25 G. S. McGowan & C.J. LaRoche, ' The ethical dilemma facing conservation: care and treatment of human skeletal remains and mortuary objects', aicstanford.edu/jaic35-02-003/
26 Ford in Green, p. 138
27 http://www.museumoflondon.org.uk
28 Ibid.
29 Ford in Green, p. 138
30 McGowan & LaRoche
31 K.D. Vitelli, 'The international traffic in antiquities: archaeological ethics and archaeological responsibility', in E.L. Green (ed.), *Ethics and Archaeology*, p. 143
32 Ibid. pp. 154–5
33 J. Hooper, 'Archaeologists fear looters charter', hhtp://www.guardian.co.uk/international/story
34 Ibid.
35 Ibid.
36 Ibid.
37 Ibid.
38 Hughes
39 Stille, p. 34

Bibliography

Amery, C. & Curran, B., *The Lost World of Pompeii*, London, Francis Lincoln Ltd, 2002

Andrews, I.A., *Pompeii*, Cambridge University Press, Cambridge, Cambridge 1988

Appendix vergiliana Copa 1–8, trans. H.R. Fairclough, Loeb Classical Library, Harvard University Press, Cambridge, 2001

Appian, *The Civil Wars*

Berry, J., *Archaeological Superintendency of Pompeii: Unpeeling Pompeii*, Electra, Milan, 1998

Bisel, Sara, *The Secrets of Vesuvius*, Maddison Press, 1990

Brion, Marcel, *Pompeii and Herculaneum: the Glory and the Grief*, trans. J. Rosenberg Elek Books Ltd, London, 1960

Cantarella, E. & Jacobelli, L., *A Day in Pompeii: daily life, culture and society*, Electa Napoli, Italy, 2003

Capasso, Gateano, *Journey to Pompeii: Virtual tours around the lost cities*, Capware–Culture Technologies, Ottaviano, 2004

Connolly, P., *Pompeii*, Oxford University Press, Oxford, 1990

Cooley, Alison E., *Pompeii*, Gerald Duckworth, London, 2003

De Carolis, E., *Gods and Heroes in Pompeii*, L'Erma di Bretschneider, Rome, 2001

De Carolis, E., *Pompeii: Life in a Roman Town*, Elemond Electa, Milan, 1999

De Saint-Blanquat, H., 'The Second Death of Pompeii', *Science et Avenir*, no. 469, March 1986

Deiss, Joseph Jay, *The Town of Hercules: A Buried Treasure Trove*, J. Paul Getty Museum, Los Angeles, 1995

Deiss, Joseph Jay, *Herculaneum: Italy's Buried Treasure*, Thomas Y. Crowell, New York, 1966

Descoudres, Jean-Paul (ed.), *Pompeii Revisited: The Life and Death of a Roman Town*, Meditarch, University of Sydney, 1994

Dio Cassius, *Roman History Books 12–35 in Vol II* trans. Earnest Cary, Loeb Classical Library, Harvard University Press, Cambridge, 1914

Etienne, Robert, *Pompeii: The Day a City Died*, trans. Caroline Palmer, New Horizons, Thames & Hudson, London, 1992

Francis, K., 'The house of the coloured capitals', *Australian Natural History*, vol. 19, no.8

Gore, R., 'The dead do tell tales at Vesuvius', *National Geographic*, May 1984

Grant, Michael, *Cities of Vesuvius: Pompeii and Herculaneum*, Phoenix Press, London, 2001

Grant, Michael, *Eros in Pompeii: the Erotic Art Collection of the Museum of Naples*, Stewart, Tabori & Chang, New York, 1997

Green E.L. (ed.), *Ethics and Values in Archaeology*, Collier Macmillan, London, 1984

Guzzo, P.G., *Discovering Pompeii*, Electa, Milan, 1998

Guzzo, P.G. & Ambrosio, A., *Pompeii: Guide to the Site*, Electa Napoli, Naples, 2002

Jacobelli, L., *Gladiators at Pompeii*, L'Erma di Bretschneider, Rome, 2003

Jashemski, W.F. & Meyer, F.M., *The Natural History of Pompeii*, Cambridge University Press, Cambridge, 2002

Jashemski, W.F., *The Gardens of Pompeii, Herculaneum and the Villas Destroyed by Vesuvius*, Meliss Media, New York, 1979

Kebric, R., *Roman People*, Mayfield, Mountain View, 2001

Lawrence, R., *Roman Pompeii: Space and Society*, Routledge, New York, 1996

Leppman, Wolfgang l, *Pompeii in Fact and Fiction*, Elek Books Ltd., London, 1968

Lessing, E. & Varone, A., *Pompeii*, trans. Jean-Marie Clarke, Editions Pierre Terrail, Paris, 1996

Ling, R., *The Insula of Menander at Pompeii, Vol. 1, The Structures*, Oxford University Press, Oxford, 1997

Ling, R., *The Insula of Menander at Pompeii: The Silver Treasure*, Oxford University Press, Oxford, 2002

Livy, *The War with Hannibal*, trans. Aubrey de Selincourt, Penguin Classics, London, 1965

McGowan, G.S. & La Roche, C.J., ' The Ethical Dilemma facing Conservation: Care and Treatment of Human Skeletal Remains and Mortuary Objects', *Journal of the American Institute for Conservation*, 1996, Vol. 35, NO. 2, Article 3

Maiuri, Amadeo., *Pompeii*, Novara, 1960

Mau, August., *Pompeii, Its Life and Art*, trans. F.W. Kelsey, Macmillan, New York, 1907

Nappo, S., *Pompeii: Guide to a Lost City*, Weidenfeld & Nicolson, London, 1998

Perkins, J.W. & Claridge, A. *Pompeii AD 79: Catalogue of the Pompeian Exhibition 1980*, Sydney, 1980

Pirozzi, M.E.A., *Herculaneum: The Excavations, Local History and Surroundings*, Electa Napoli, Naples, 2000

Pliny the Elder, *Natural History*, trans. Eichholz, Jones, Rackham, Loeb Classical Library, W. Heinemann, London, 1962

Pliny the Elder, *Natural History: A Selection*, trans. John F. Healy, Penguin Classics, London, 1991

Pliny the Younger, *Letters*, trans. B. Radice, Penguin Classics, London, 1969

Pye, E., *Caring for the Past: Issues in Conservation for Archaeology and Museums*, James & James, London, 2001

Richardson, L., *Pompeii: An Architectural History*, Johns Hopkins University Press, Baltimore, 1988

Shaw, B.D. 'The Age of Roman Girls at Marriage' JRS 77 1987

Sigurdsson, H, Cashdollar, S. & Sparks, S.R.J., 'The Eruption of Vesuvius in AD 79' *American Journal of Archaeology*, 86:1 (1982), pp. 39–51

Slayman, A., 'The New Pompeii, and picking up the pieces', *Archaeology*, Nov–Dec 1997

Stille, Alexander, *The Future of the Past: The Loss of Knowledge in the Age of Information*, Picador, London, 2003

Tacitus, *The Annals of Imperial Rome*, trans. M. Grant, Penguin Classics, London, 1981

Varone, A., *Eroticism in Pompeii*, J. Paul Getty Museum, Los Angeles, 2001

Vitruvius, *Ten Books on Architecture*, trans, I. D. Rowland, Cambridge University Press, Cambridge, Cambridge,1999

Vitrivius, *De architectura: The Ten Books on Architecture*, trans. Morris Hicky Morgan, Dover Publications, New York, 1960

Wallace-Hadrill, A., *Houses and Society in Pompeii and Herculaneum*, Princeton University Press, New Jersey, 1994

Zanker, P., *Pompeii, Public and Private Life*, Cambridge University Press, Cambridge, Cambridge, 1998

Websites

www.archaeology.org/online

www.archaeology.co.uk/cwa/issues/cwa/pompeii/excavations

www.pompeii.virginia.edu/pfp-descrip

urban.arch.Virginia.EDU/struct/pompeii/volcanic

www.academicpress.com/companions/012643140x/msie/Contents/chapt80

www.bradford.ac.uk/acad/archsci/field-proj/anampomp

www.pompeiitrust.org/The_Trust

www.ukic.org.uk/gacp

www2. pompeisites.org/database/pompeii/pompeii2

www.cib.na.cnr.it/mann/museol/mann.html

www.onlineethics.org/rrseth/appe/vol1/bones

aic.stanford.edu/jaic/articles/jaic35-02-003

www.classics.cam.ac.uk/Everyone/Pompeii/Hwerculaneum

ccat.sas.upenn.edu/bmcr/1998/98.1.20

www.guardian.co.uk/international/story

washingtonpost.com/wp-srv/aponline/19991013/

seattlepi.nwsource.com/getaways/112797/pomp27

www.bbc.co.uk/history/ancient/romans/pompeii_rediscovery

www.economist.com/science/displayStory.cfm?story

www.museumoflondon.org.uk

www. ancienthistoryhelper.com.au/pompeii/general/refer.htm

www.sfsu.edu/~avitv/avcatalog/26077.htm

sights.seindal.dk/sight/1073_National_Arch_Museum

www.rdg.ac.uk/archaeology/

volcano.und.nodak.edu/vwdvcs/vol_images/img_vesuvius.html

www.aarome.org

www.bsr.ac.uk

www.perseus.tufts.edu

www.oxbowbooks.com/feature.cfm/FeatureID

Index

All buildings are located in Pompeii unless otherwise noted. Page numbers in *italics* refer to illustrations.